DANTON
AND
THE FRENCH REVOLUTION

DANTON
From a portrait said to have been painted by David

DANTON
AND THE
FRENCH REVOLUTION

BY CHARLES F. WARWICK
AUTHOR OF MIRABEAU AND THE FRENCH REVOLUTION

WILDSIDE PRESS

*Copyright, 1908
By George W. Jacobs & Co.*

Published April, 1908

All Rights Reserved

PREFACE

When "Mirabeau and the French Revolution" was published, I stated that it would be followed in turn by the Lives of Danton and Robespierre, that it was my purpose to trace briefly the causes of the Revolution and group its principal events around these men who were the manifestation of the Revolution in its three distinctive periods. Although each book will be separate and complete in itself, the three volumes will form a series covering the entire period of the Revolution.

CHARLES F. WARWICK.

Philadelphia, February, 1908.

CONTENTS

CHAPTER I
Mirabeau and Danton.............................. 17

CHAPTER II
Danton's Birth—Arcis sur Aube—Political, Religious and Social Conditions in France................... 22

CHAPTER III
Home Influences of Danton—School Days—The Coronation of Louis XVI............................ 35

CHAPTER IV
Danton Chooses Law as His Profession—Comes to the Bar—Marries—Avocat aux Conseils du Roi—His Studies—Camille Desmoulins................. 45

CHAPTER V
Conditions Immediately Prior to the Revolution—Revéillon Affair—Louis XVI—His Ministers—His Habits—His Character........................... 53

CHAPTER VI
Advisers of the King—The Queen—The Finances—Revolutions Begin at the Top..................... 70

CHAPTER VII
Danton in the Early Days of the Revolution—The Affair of Soulés—Marat—The Incident of Marat—Early Events of the Revolution........................ 77

CONTENTS

CHAPTER VIII
Death of Mirabeau—Louis Attempts to go to St. Cloud—Danton Intervenes—The Flight of the Royal Family to Varennes............................. 102

CHAPTER IX
Paris After the Flight of the King—La Fayette in Peril—La Fayette Denounced by Danton at the Jacobins 127

CHAPTER X
Return of the King to Paris..................... 137

CHAPTER XI
Danton Favors a Republic—Danton Urges Deposition of the King—Republican Society Proclaims Republic—The Assembly Decrees the Inviolability of the King—The Club of the Cordeliers Issues Public Address—Fusillade of the Champ de Mars.. 149

CHAPTER XII
Convocation of the New Assembly—King's Return to Popularity—Reactions in His Favor—His Advisers—His Deception—Marie Antoinette—Return of Danton From Exile........................... 165

CHAPTER XIII
The Feuillants—The Club of the Cordeliers Where Danton Ruled—The Girondins—Madame Roland —War Issues—Danton After Some Hesitation Favors the War—Vetoes—Dumouriez—Danton and Dumouriez 176

CHAPTER XIV
Death of Leopold—Assassination of Gustavus III, King of Sweden—Francis II Makes Proclamation —Danton Hurls Defiance—War Declared April 21, 1792—Defeat of the French Troops—Death of Gen-

CONTENTS

PAGE

eral Dillon—Deputies From Marseilles Present Petition to the Assembly—Day of the Black Breeches—Pétion 193

CHAPTER XV
La Fayette Comes to Paris—La Fayette—Danton and La Fayette...................................... 209

CHAPTER XVI
The Marseillais—The Marseillaise Hymn—Lamourette Kiss—The Day of Federation...................... 220

CHAPTER XVII
Enlistment—Proclamation of the Duke of Brunswick—Marseillais enters Paris—Brush With the Filles St. Thomas 226

CHAPTER XVIII
The Tenth of August.............................. 238

CHAPTER XIX
Danton's Activity—Longwy Capitulates—Domiciliary Visits 256

CHAPTER XX
The September Massacres.......................... 264

CHAPTER XXI
Paris During the Revolution—Manners—Customs—Conditions—The Guillotine....................... 277

CHAPTER XXII
Was Danton Responsible for the September Massacres?—La Fayette Abandons His Command—Dumouriez Named His Successor—Cannonade of Valmy—Danton's Energy—Duke de Chartres—Dumouriez in Paris.............................. 295

CONTENTS

CHAPTER XXIII
Girondins and Jacobins—Louvet's Accusation of Robespierre 307

CHAPTER XXIV
Victory of Jemappes—Girondins Propose Opening of the Scheldt—Edmund Burke—England Joins Coalition—Danton Visits Belgium—Death of Danton's Wife 315

CHAPTER XXV
Finding of the Iron Chest—Louis Summoned to the Bar 326

CHAPTER XXVI
Trial of Louis XVI 334

CHAPTER XXVII
Execution of Louis XVI 343

CHAPTER XXVIII
Danton Opposes Factional Strife—The Treason of Dumouriez—Lasource Attacks Danton—The Reply of Danton 353

CHAPTER XXIX
Danton—Marat's Arrest and Triumph—Girondins—Charlotte Corday—Assassination of Marat—Execution of Charlotte Corday—Marriage of Danton—Trial and Execution of Marie Antoinette 362

CHAPTER XXX
Trial and Execution of Girondins—Execution of Madame Roland, Philippe, d'Orleans, Barnave, Bailly—Dethronement of Religion—Danton Favors Reaction 385

CONTENTS

CHAPTER XXXI
PAGE

Trial of the Dantonists............................. 400

CHAPTER XXXII

Execution of the Dantonists....................... 418

CHAPTER XXXIII

Danton—His Appearance—His Style of Dress—His Character—His Religious Belief—Was He Venal?—Politician—Statesman—Orator—His Short Political Career—Results of the French Revolution—— 423

LIST OF ILLUSTRATIONS

	PAGE
DANTON. The original portrait in the possession of the family is said to have been painted by David .... *Frontispiece*	
HOUSE OF THE DANTON FAMILY AT ARCIS SUR AUBE	24
DANTON'S MOTHER	36
CAMILLE DESMOULINS.............................	50
LOUIS XVI. From an engraving by Bervic after the original portrait painted by Callet...................	60
MARIE ANTOINETTE. From an engraving in the collection of William J. Latta, Esq., of Philadelphia, by whom it was kindly loaned for this work............	72
MARAT. From an engraving in the collection of William J. Latta, Esq., of Philadelphia.....................	80
MADAME ROLAND. From an engraving in the collection of William J. Latta, Esq., of Philadelphia.......	180
PRINCESS DE LAMBALLE	274
DR. GUILLOTIN. From an engraving in the collection of William J. Latta, Esq., of Philadelphia...........	288
CHARLOTTE CORDAY. From an engraving in the collection of William J. Latta, Esq., of Philadelphia. After a portrait painted by David	374
FAC-SIMILE OF A LETTER WRITTEN BY DANTON. The original is in the possession of William J. Latta, Esq., of Philadelphia, by whom it was kindly loaned for this work...	438

DANTON

AND

THE FRENCH REVOLUTION

CHAPTER I

MIRABEAU AND DANTON

The death of Mirabeau marked the end of the first period of the French Revolution.

He had struggled hard against heavy odds to effect a reaction to restore order and to save the monarchy, but he failed because he could not secure the confidence and the support of those whose cause he had espoused. When he passed away the proud empire of the Bourbons was doomed. The bells that tolled his death rang, at the same time, the knell of the monarchy.

Even those who intimately knew him, and were in his confidence, did not comprehend how great was the work he had undertaken and with what marked ability he had carried it forward, not until some time after his death did they realize the fact that there was no one in France who could take up the task where he had laid it down.

He had directed the Revolution. To him it had a purpose, which purpose was the correction of abuses, the restriction within constitutional limi-

DANTON

tations of the absolute, the arbitrary power of the king, but not his deposition nor the destruction of the throne.

It surely must be admitted by all who have studied the Revolution, that the death of Mirabeau perceptibly gave it a new phase. He had been its manifestation. He had aided in the accomplishment of all its purposes; its results, in a great measure, were due to his genius and his energy, but he had watched closely the trend of events and with a vision that was far-reaching, almost prophetic, he saw the impending calamities that were menacing not only the monarchy, but also the welfare, the integrity, the future interests of all France. He therefore strongly favored a reaction, and bent every effort towards staying the torrent whose flood-gates he had helped to open.

When Mirabeau passed out of the Revolution, Danton stepped in. The great tribune was dead, and there strode forth a man with almost superhuman power, who was to tear down and destroy that system which Mirabeau would fain have saved. Danton gave to the Revolution a fresh impulse, his courage and his audacity aroused the spirit of the radicals. From now until the execution of the king he was the master. "He rode in the whirlwind and directed the storm."

At the time of Mirabeau's death France had lost every feature of a monarchy, save that a king still occupied the throne. The Revolution had leveled the walls of the Bastile, had given a declaration of rights and the form of a consti-

THE FRENCH REVOLUTION

tution to France, had equalized taxation, had removed the burdens of feudalism, had abolished privileges and exemptions, had destroyed titles and distinctions, had introduced a system of economy in the public administration, had scattered the nobles, had confiscated the lands of the Church, had proscribed the non-juring priests, had brought the king as a captive from Versailles to Paris, and had put him and his queen in the humiliating position of being held as hostages for the good behavior of the emigrants. There was nothing left for the Revolution to accomplish but the deposition of the king and the establishment of a republic. It was to these tasks that Danton devoted himself in earnest.

Had Mirabeau lived, a combat between him and Danton would most likely have taken place. These two Titans, it is reasonable to believe, had they not united their interests, would have grappled in a death struggle for the mastery, and no one can say with certainty what the outcome would have been.

But on the other hand, they might have formed a combination that would have resulted in the establishment of a constitutional monarchy, for at this period of the Revolution, that is in the early part of 1791, Danton was not so violent in his views as he subsequently became. Mirabeau and Danton, although they differed radically in their political principles, were reasonable, practical, politic, and patriotic, and it is not impossible to believe that they might have united their efforts in a common purpose to stay the

DANTON

Revolution and to make secure the reforms that had already been achieved.

Danton had been loyal to the monarchy, he was naturally of that conservative class that adheres to existing conditions, and fears radical reforms and sudden violent changes. "He was," says Michelet, "of the middle class, the heart of the nation." "He was certainly," declares Gronlund, "from the crown of his head to the sole of his foot a middle class man, but he was more than that, he was a middle class man with a heart for the masses." He opposed, of course, the system that created exemptions and privileges to be monopolized and enjoyed only by the chosen few. He had no sympathy with the old *régime* and as a man of spirit and independence he chafed and fretted under the unjust class distinctions that prevailed, but on the other hand he naturally favored law and order and dreaded that violence that suddenly and forcibly wrenches from their ancient foundations those customs, usages, and laws that have long obtained. His education, his social and professional position raised him far above the proletariat, and he had nothing in common with them except a desire to ameliorate their unhappy condition, but this amelioration he hoped to see effected gradually and without a shock or a violent convulsion.

In the early stages of the Revolution he no more wished the destruction of the monarchy than Mirabeau. To use his own language, "I am more monarchist than you, M. de La Fayette." He was a reformer, a revolutionist of a

THE FRENCH REVOLUTION

positive type, to be sure, but he believed that a king was as necessary to government in France as in England. He looked askance at M. de Mirabeau; he "had always from a long way off understood his brother in silk and with the sword," but really they were revolutionists of the same class, and the splendid talents of one united with the force and the superb audacity of the other might have avoided "The Terror."

With Mirabeau out of the contest the court could find no substitute to take his place. The French monarchy without the guidance of wisdom blindly groped its way through darkness to despair and finally plunged headlong to destruction. Achilles was dead and there was no friend nor adviser of the king who had diplomacy enough to secure the aid and the loyalty of Danton, the only man who could have stepped into the shoes and could have worn the mantle of the great tribune. Barnave, Duport and the Lameths, finding the Revolution getting beyond their control, undertook to divert and direct its course by attempting to apply the policies and to carry out the plans of Mirabeau, but they were in no way equal to the task.

CHAPTER II

DANTON'S BIRTH—ARCIS SUR AUBE—POLITICAL, RELIGIOUS AND SOCIAL CONDITIONS IN FRANCE

George Jacques Danton was born on the 26th day of October, 1759, at Arcis sur Aube, in the Champagne Pouilleuse, about seventeen miles north of Troyes and about one hundred miles from Paris. "His family, pure, honest, of property, industrious, ancient in name, honorable in manners . . . possessed a rural domain in the environs of that small town."
Arcis sur Aube was settled at a very early period and is mentioned in the register called "Antonini Itinerarium," which gave the stations and the distances along the various roads of the Roman empire and which was based probably upon the surveys made by direction of Julius Cæsar and continued by Augustus. It had no specially attractive feature except that an old picturesque castle situated upon a high bluff overlooked the town and was of historical interest, in that it was at one time the residence of Brunehaut, and at a later period was occupied by the celebrated Diana of Poitiers who had the honor of serving in turn Francis I and Henry II, father and son, as mistress.
It was the principal market town and the chief

THE FRENCH REVOLUTION

commercial centre in that immediate locality, it possessed a fairly prosperous population and enjoyed the advantage of being close enough to the capital of the kingdom to keep in touch with the news and the events of the day. A beautiful church, of the sixteenth century, gave the place some architectural renown.

In this country town Danton passed his early years, and it was a good school for the training of a boy who subsequently was to make Paris his home. In this provincial community he had an opportunity to watch the process of disintegration as revealed in the social and political conditions that prevailed in the country or peasant districts, and to observe and note those gradual changes that are not so apparent in a populous or crowded city.

The date of his birth fell in a very interesting historical period, one of the most important in the history of the human race, an era when men and events were preparing for " the most impassioned effort ever made for the attainment of public freedom."

When Danton was born, Mirabeau had seen ten years of life; Robespierre was a baby in arms; Louis XVI was five, and Marie Antoinette four years old; Camille Desmoulins was to see the light of day in five months, and Napoleon in ten years. Louis XV was on the throne and had been reigning for forty-four years. He had sixteen years yet to rule and riot before being stricken by the fatal and loathsome disease that carried him off. Absolutism was in its full vigor,

DANTON

although perhaps not so assertive as it had been under the prior reign when Louis XIV had declared that he was the State. Feudalism was imbedded in the life, in the very flesh of the people; its burdens were as grinding and as oppressive as they ever had been.

King and noble were virtually not amenable to law, the privileged classes enjoying rights in contravention of every principle of human justice.

The glory and the splendor of Louis XIV, which in a measure had concealed the vices of his reign and had made some atonement for its tyranny, corruption, and extravagance, were but a memory, and in the shadow of the great Louis ruled a king who was without ambition, who shed no lustre, no personal renown upon his times, and whose luxury, sensuality, prodigality, and indifference to the public weal, were hastening the country to destruction and the monarchy to its ruin. The aggregate duration of the reigns of these two princes, Louis XIV and Louis XV, was one hundred and thirty-one years, something unparalleled in history. It was most unfortunate for France that lives so long were vouchsafed to rulers so unworthy and so profligate.

Only one-third of the landed property of the entire country was in the hands of the lay commonalty, all the rest belonged to the Church and the nobles. The taxes too were so unequally distributed that the largest of them, the Taille, yielding about 200,000,000 francs, fell almost wholly upon the peasantry, neither the Church nor the vast majority of the nobles paying one sou. The

House of the Danton Family at Arcis sur Aube
From an old print

THE FRENCH REVOLUTION

privileged classes consisting of the nobility and the upper clergy numbered about 190,000 persons out of a population of twenty-five millions, and these few received and enjoyed all the benefits of government.

Many of the nobility, because of some trivial service rendered to the king by their ancestors, were relieved entirely from taxation and besides this were extravagantly pensioned out of the public revenues. These drones actually consumed the substance of the poor. It was calculated that if an acre of land afforded seventy-five francs of gross produce, two-thirds went to the revenue, and after the landlord was paid the wretched farmer or cultivator received about one-half of the remaining third, or twelve and one-half francs.

The social and political conditions of the lower classes were in a most deplorable state. Language cannot fully describe the real wretchedness that prevailed among the peasantry. Men, women and children went barefooted and were scantily clad, even in the dead of winter. They lived on black-bread and "slept on the mud of the cold clay floor," their homes were as comfortless, and often as filthy, as pig-sties. Wages were so low, and in consequence labor was so hard, that men were worn to the bone in earning a mere pittance; children were poorly nurtured and compelled to toil in their earliest years; women were haggard in feature and grew old long before they reached middle life, being obliged to perform the most servile labor, often actually being used as beasts of burden. In some districts they were, like oxen, harnessed to the plough and driven to the cart.

Agriculture had made no advance from the tenth century, its implements were rude and primitive in pattern and construction. The plough differed not a whit from that used in the days of Virgil. The peasant was virtually a serf, he was attached to the soil, he belonged body and soul to the lord of the manor. Although burdened with duties, he had but few if any rights. Under the infamous, iniquitous system of feudalism that existed, he was required to perform, in return for the use of his small strip of land, all sorts of menial and humiliating services, from the swishing of the pond to the loaning of his bride, from the patching of the public roads to the ploughing of the lord's glebe. In an agricultural country, herds of deer and droves of wild boars were permitted to go at large as in a savage wilderness, only to provide amusement for the great. When the royal game destroyed the crops of the peasant he had no redress, and if he dared to kill a rabbit or a quail he ran the risk, if the gamekeeper caught him in the act, of paying forfeit with his life. If a fox crossed his land he might expect to see, at any moment, a pack of hounds followed by a hunting party of lords and ladies, who would ruthlessly dash across his recently ploughed field or trample down the growing vines in his vineyard. Yet this wretched creature meekly submitted to his lot, paid the bulk of taxation, and supported the glory of the empire. No

THE FRENCH REVOLUTION

wonder, when the time came and the devil was let loose in his heart, that he took vengeance with pike and torch!

"The men are dying as thick as flies," wrote Argenson in the middle of the eighteenth century, "and the living are eating grass," and this condition continued with intervals of slight improvement up to the date of the meeting of the States-General. The fields were bare, the highways were deserted, except by armies of tramps and vagrants, the inns were comfortless and without conveniences, there were few carriages or diligences traveling on the public roads, which roads were sadly out of repair. Famine was decimating the population. While the peasants were living on roots and the bark of trees, the aristocracy flaunted their wealth and extravagance in the faces of the poor. In the shadows of magnificent palaces and chateaux men literally starved to death.

Notwithstanding the financial distress of the country the king abated not a jot of his luxury. He owned more palaces than he could occupy and the expenses of the royal household amounted to 250,000,000 francs annually. There were 300 cooks in the kitchen and over 2,000 horses standing in the stables. Nobles and also churchmen indulged in extravagances and excesses to such a degree that their conduct provoked the bitter hatred of the people and destroyed respect for authority and government and even reverence for holy things.

A few years later than the period of which

DANTON

we are speaking, the Cardinal de Rohan, a prince of the Church, the grand almoner of France who made religion a mockery, declared that it was impossible for him to live on an annual income of less than one million and a half. He indulged in such licentiousness that his example was most demoralizing and yet he was not, by any means, the only churchman who disgraced his calling. The Church, although possessed of nearly half the land in the kingdom and endowed with an immense revenue from tithes alone, assigned a miserable pittance of 500 francs a year to the parochial or working clergy; all the rest was consumed in luxurious living by an idle and a dissolute hierarchy. The administration of the law was venal, was corrupt. The penal code in some of its features was inhuman, and the criminal courts were merciless in prosecuting and punishing those who were unable to temper the severity of the judges with gold. The penalties imposed for the slightest transgressions upon those who were not able to pay for exemptions were cruel and monstrous. The plaintiff obtained entrance to the court by bribery. Justice was a wanton to be won by favors. Arrests were arbitrarily made, and men were immured in dungeons without even the faintest form of trial. One prisoner was confined in the Bastile for thirty-five years, and at the time of his release there could be found no record of his commitment.

A man merely suspected of a political offense would be seized under a *lettre de cachet* and would suddenly disappear from his usual haunts

THE FRENCH REVOLUTION

as if swallowed up by the earth. There was no uniform system of law throughout the kingdom; what was a crime in one district was not so considered in another, and the whole system of judicature was in utter confusion.

The cold-blooded insolence of the aristocracy created a consuming hatred in the hearts of the people, a hatred that was deep-seated and vindictive and that passed like a heritage from one generation to another, until at last it cruelly avenged with blood the grinding wrongs and the galling tyranny of centuries. The sufferings of the poor did not call forth even the commiseration of the rich. The nobles looked upon the common people as hardly worthy of consideration. Madame de Staël at a later period, in speaking of Napoleon in this connection, said: "*Il regarde une créature humaine comme un fait ou un chose, et non comme un semblable.*" So the nobles of this period looked upon the common people as mere chattels, and they had no respect for their rights as fellow-men. In the reign of Louis XV the Count de Charolais amused himself by shooting men whom he had employed to work on the roof of his barn, and every time he picked a man off he laughed aloud as he saw his victim roll to the ground; his conduct was in the spirit of brutal wantonness. The matter was brought to the notice of the king who sent word to the count that if he repeated the offense, he would pardon anyone who killed him. But there was no arrest, nor prosecution of the count, the authorities allowed the matter to end here. What justice could the people expect from such a monarch and under such a system?

Most inhuman were the punishments inflicted upon those who assailed royalty. A man had written some satirical lines on the king's mistress. The agents of his majesty seized the culprit at the Hague and in violation of every principle of international law, carried him to France and cast him into a cell below the sea level of Mont St. Michel. Here he lived or rather existed for eight years, in a stone hole in which he could neither stand upright nor lie down at full length, the cell being less than five feet long, but four feet wide, and three feet high. The sunlight penetrated the cavern only one hour during the entire day. In this hole he was attacked by rats and it was said that he sustained life by eating them. But in time he was so weakened by confinement that he was unable to resist them and the hungry rodents at last began nibbling at his toes and soon he was devoured.

Damiens, who assaulted the king and merely scratched his royal person, underwent a punishment so brutal that the heart sickens in the recital of its details. It was not much of a wound that was inflicted, it was not "so deep as a well nor so wide as a church door," but it was enough to bring down on the head of the culprit all the vengeance of the State. It might have been better for the poor wretch had he accomplished his purpose, for he could not have been tortured worse had he killed the king outright.

The tyranny of a king is as much treason

THE FRENCH REVOLUTION

against the sovereignty of the people as the rebellion of the people is against the sovereignty of a king. It required a revolution to vitalize this thought and to bring tyrants and potentates to a sense of personal accountability.

Superstition, bigotry, and intolerance, were on every hand. Religious persecution was relentless. Protestants or those who harbored them were punished remorselessly. One woman was sentenced to three years of imprisonment and subjected to a heavy fine simply because she spoke a kindly word to a dying heretic. A man was sent to the galleys for having so far forgotten his loyalty to the Church as to attend a Protestant service. A boy was arrested for having mutilated a crucifix. There was no proof that he had committed the offense, but it was shown, in the course of the trial, that he had read a book of Voltaire's. This was sufficient to control the judgment of the court and the poor lad was tortured till his bones cracked and life was almost extinct. To complete the infamy, he was then decapitated and his head was set up on a post as a warning to the faithful not to stray from the paths of orthodoxy.

Such were the conditions that prevailed at the time Danton first saw the light of day, and they grew but little better as he advanced towards manhood. These were the events that were brewing the Revolution and they explain why in its character it was so vindictive and retributive.

Meanwhile society was undergoing a change and men were beginning to long and strive for

DANTON

better things. General education was developing the human mind and opening the avenues to knowledge. The printing press was at work, people were thinking, reading, discussing. The Revolution was made by books, some one has well said. Michelet declares that when Voltaire and Rousseau, the apostles of humanity, passed away the revolution in the intellectual world was accomplished.

Montesquieu's "Spirit of the Laws," appeared in 1748; its aphorisms, though trite to-day, were new and startling then, and aroused in the French heart a longing for a constitutional liberty under which the humblest citizen in the land would be as secure in the enjoyment of his rights as the king himself.

Helvetius, whose great work "De l'Esprit" was published in 1758, was a philosopher of the so-called sensuous school, a direct descendant of Epicurus. In his materialism he deprived man of all spirituality and brought him to the level of the brute. He taught that pleasure is the only good and self-interest the only consideration. In an age so corrupt his teachings exerted a great influence and were congenial to a people and a court that could tolerate a Pompadour and a Du-Barry.

At the time of Danton's birth, Voltaire was in the heyday of his power; and in the full vigor of his intellect he was satirizing the follies of the day and with his trenchant pen was attacking tyranny, injustice, superstition, bigotry, and intolerance. Never did a writer exert a greater

THE FRENCH REVOLUTION

influence upon his age. The vices of both Church and State were cowering beneath his merciless assaults. He was the philosopher of Iconoclasm and under his terrific blows the idols of the past were broken and shattered.

Rousseau at this time was dreaming of his Utopia and arousing a sentiment in the hearts of men for a common brotherhood. He was an egoist and a morbid sentimentalist who professed a love for mankind, yet abandoned his own children. Voltaire had no cant, but Rousseau was full of it. About this time he was writing his "Contrat Social," "which preluded the doctrines of the Revolution" and which was to aid in destroying the influence, the power, and the privileges of the old order. It contended that society was founded on convention and that all men under that original contract were equal before the law. The character of Danton was molded under the teachings of Voltaire, while Rousseau had no more devoted disciple, no one who was more a reflex of his sentiments than Robespierre.

Diderot with his co-laborers was compiling the Encyclopedia, that great storehouse of information, and imbuing the thought of the nation with his wild ideas and theories of democracy. "Until a king is dragged to Tyburn," he declared, "with no more pomp than the meanest criminal, the people will have no conception of liberty. The law is nothing unless it be a sword suspended over our heads without distinction and leveling all who elevate themselves above the horizontal plane in which it circles." "Had there been no

DANTON

Diderot," says Lord Lytton, " there would have been no Marat." The Encyclopedia was a monument of learning and the greatest thinkers of the day added their contributions to this remarkable work, writing upon the topics to which they had devoted their lives. No one can estimate the effect it produced on the public mind. It was of itself an inducement to revolution. It was the womb of sedition.

CHAPTER III

HOME INFLUENCES OF DANTON—SCHOOL DAYS—
THE CORONATION OF LOUIS XVI

The influences that surrounded Danton's early home life were refining. His father, whose Christian name was Jacques, was a lawyer by profession. He was *procureur* in the bailiwick of Arcis. It was his duty to present the cases and the accused to the local court, an office somewhat resembling that of prosecuting attorney in our day. The office was of no little importance and gave to the incumbent social quality and political distinction. His income was from ten thousand to ten thousand five hundred francs per year. An income that, if it did not furnish the luxuries of life, enabled him at least to live comfortably. He died in 1762 leaving two sons and two daughters. George Jacques at that time was two and a half years old.

Danton's mother's name was Marie Madeleine and her family was of the class of skilled artisans, her social rank being somewhat below that of her husband, who as we have seen was of the professional class. Madame Danton after the death of her husband had means sufficient, by the exercise of strict economy, to retain the family home-

DANTON

stead and to provide for the education of her children. About eight years after the death of M. Danton she married a cotton manufacturer named Jean Ricordain, who is said to have been a good husband to her and a kind father to her children.

George Jacques was a robust, rollicking lad; mettlesome, high-spirited, somewhat rebellious, but most affectionate and generous. " He was," says Lamartine, " of an open, communicative disposition and was beloved in spite of his ugliness and turbulence, for his ugliness was radiant with intellect and his turbulence was calmed and repented of at the least caress of his mother." The discipline of the town school was irksome to him and he chafed under its restraints and often when he should have been at his desk he was swimming in the Aube.

Some writers have drawn the picture of his childhood in the darkest shades, but really the most careful research fails to find any substantial facts in the history of his early years to corroborate their exaggerated statements. One author goes even so far as to say that while a toddler he had the spirit of the devil in his little heart and had already started on the way to hell. Another calls him a monster in his infancy, stating that he had a passion for gambling, was a truant from school and was " ducking from morning until night in the river and wrestling with the dogs and the pigs in the town gutters." These statements are made to form a groundwork for what his detractors call his subsequent

DANTON'S MOTHER
From an old print

THE FRENCH REVOLUTION

career of crime, and thus to show that the boy was father to the man.

No doubt he was like most active, healthy boys of his age, full of fun and frolic and with a spirit of adventure and insubordination; but that he was vicious or exceptionally bad is not and cannot be vouched for by any reliable authority. " He was," asserts Lamartine, " rebellious against discipline, idle at study, beloved by his masters and fellow pupils; his rapid comprehension kept him on an equality with the most assiduous. His instinct sufficed without reflection. He learned nothing; he acquired all. His companions called him Catiline; he accepted the name and sometimes played with them at getting up rebellions and riots which he excited or calmed by his harangues, as if he were rehearsing at school the characters of his after life."

When quite young Danton was attacked by that dreadful scourge, smallpox, a disease that in those days ravaged every community and that completely baffled the skill of the medical profession. It seems to have raged with special violence in France and the public authorities adopted no precautionary measures that prevented the spread of this most spiteful epidemic. Many of the most distinguished men of that period were scarred with its venomous touch.

Danton also had an encounter with a bull which resulted in giving him a hare lip. One story is that when he was a baby and while being suckled by a cow, a jealous bull interfered and gashed his face. Some years after, perhaps to avenge the

DANTON

former assault made upon him, he had a personal encounter with the same beast and came out of the contest with triumph, but with a crushed nose. The injuries to the bull are not recorded. Another story goes that he was badly tusked by a savage boar.

Though these scars and wounds greatly increased his ugliness they appear to have added strength to his countenance. "In spite of all these misfortunes there was a commanding quality and rugged charm about his face which generally commended it to those with whom he came in contact."

In the town school at Arcis he was taught the Latin elements and laid a good foundation for a subsequent classical education. After leaving this school he entered the lower seminary at Troyes, an institution under the direction of the Oratorians, a religious order that had the honor of training so many of the popular reformers who helped in the regeneration of France. Here Danton was grounded in Greek as well as in Latin and specially trained in the history and the philosophy of the ancients. This system of education had long obtained in France and naturally imbued in the hearts of the students a love for freedom, in accordance with Roman forms, and at the same time inspired an admiration for the principles of Roman democracy and the austere virtues of the old Roman citizen. There was no student in France under this course who was not impressed by the characteristics that had made the republic of Rome great.

THE FRENCH REVOLUTION

The entire literature of the country also was affected by this system that made a special and patient study of the ancient writers. The drama especially, with its unities, was essentially classic. Desmoulins, the greatest journalist of the Revolution, was peculiarly a Latinist and possessed a style as concise and as incisive as that of Tacitus.

The leading orators in the National Assembly formed their styles on Roman models and it was this very classicism that gave a peculiar and dignified charm to the oratory of that period. Their frequent quotations from the Latin authors show what a deep impression the literature of the ancients had made upon them. The oratory of Barnave, Vergniaud, and Isnard was especially Roman in style modeled on the majestic eloquence of the forum, while the carefully written speeches of Robespierre reveal, in almost every line, the traces of his classical education.

Hardly ever was there a speech made in the Assembly that the speaker did not indulge in classical allusions. The Capitol and the Tarpeian Rock were shaken from their foundations, while Cæsar and Brutus were mustered into service upon every occasion. Of course this constant reference, in the debates, to the Greeks and the Romans became at times monotonous and subjected the stilted, bombastic orators of the second class to frequent ridicule, but the real orators controlled by a refined and scholarly taste enriched and adorned their speeches by apt quotations.

DANTON

Even down to the days of the First Empire this classical spirit prevailed. The eagles of Napoleon were snatched from the standard bearers of the great Cæsar. France borrowed Justinian's code and upon it framed her own. In no other state of modern times, indeed, has the influence of Rome been felt to so marked a degree as in France and this is to be attributed, no doubt, to the curricula of her schools and colleges.

Danton was an exception to the rule. His oratory was rough-hewn and forceful but without polish; it was characteristic of the man rather than of any school or of any age. The same thing may be said of Mirabeau. These two men were original, not imitative, and it never occurred to them to form their oratory upon any particular style. Their genius was not trammeled nor circumscribed by any rules.

During Danton's last term at the seminary of Troyes in the summer of 1775, when he was sixteen years of age, the coronation of Louis XVI took place. He made up his mind that he would witness this celebration for he was anxious to see how a king was made. He was yet to learn how to unmake one. He borrowed money from his schoolfellows sufficient to last him for the journey and without asking permission from his teachers, he set out afoot and trudged across the country, a distance of seventy miles, to the ancient, historic cathedral town of Rheims. A stout, hearty lad accustomed to exercise and the sports of the campus had little regard for the distance. To him, light-hearted

THE FRENCH REVOLUTION

and gay, released from his studies, the journey was a delightful vacation and the truant was as merry as a lark.

Rheims, about eighty miles northeast from Paris, is an ancient town, rich in historic associations. It was renowned as the place where the kings of France were crowned. The cathedral of Notre Dame, in which the coronations occurred, is most impressive in its architectural lines. Its façade has been pronounced by those competent to judge as one of the most perfect masterpieces of the Middle Ages. The interior of the church is sombre and impressive in color, its

"Storied windows richly dight,
Casting a dim religious light,"

create an atmosphere of reverence and pious devotion. It is adorned with tapestries, marbles, and paintings of inestimable worth, and contains some of the most valuable art treasures of the centuries. A long line of kings from the earliest days had been anointed, and consecrated within the walls of this sacred edifice. Clovis, after his victory at Soissons, is said to have been baptized on the spot where the cathedral stands. The kings of the second and third dynasties were anointed here with the sacred oil which a dove had brought from heaven. This pleasing legend was by the faithful implicitly believed and the oil was consequently guarded with the most pious care. Here Joan of Arc, holding the standard of France,

DANTON

stood by the side of Charles VII when the diadem of his fathers was placed upon his brow.

Louis XVI was crowned with no less pomp than his ancestors, the ceremony being unusually magnificent. The time, the place, the splendor of the occasion must have appealed to the poetic temperament of the boy visitor from Troyes. The grandeur and the glory dazzled his imagination; the excited, exultant throngs aroused his enthusiasm.

Incense and music filled the air. Bishops, priests and nobles in their gorgeous robes and costumes gave resplendent beauty to the scene, but all this glory was monopolized by royalty, the nobility, and the hierarchy. The people had no place nor part in this magnificent pageant except as mere onlookers and *claquers*.

Danton as a spirited, an independent lad may have felt rebellion rising in his heart. What reason was there, he probably asked, for all this power to be centred in a king who came to the throne by the mere accident of birth and whose authority to rule was founded on conquest and usurpation, and strengthened by centuries of misrule and tyranny?

In imagination, had he looked back through the dim vista of ages, he could have seen a crowd of mighty kings marching in stately and solemn procession through the broad aisles and under the groined arches of this grand old cathedral, to be crowned, sceptred, and anointed. But what had they done for the uplifting of the human

THE FRENCH REVOLUTION

race? What had they accomplished in the matter of the education, enlightenment and betterment of their people? In many instances they as tyrants had misruled the state, had imposed burdens on the poor, and had granted privileges to the rich. They had debased the peasant and had exalted the noble; they had squandered the public revenues in personal extravagance; they had waged wars for the acquisition of territory to which they could lay no just claim, or for the gratification of mere selfish ambition.

What had Danton, a child of the people, in common with such a system? What meaning was there to him in all this "boast of heraldry" and "pomp of power?" How could such a ceremony as he witnessed arouse his ardor and enthusiasm except in so far as the future promised better things? In this connection it was said that Louis XVI was more virtuous, more amiable and less selfish and ambitious than the majority of his ancestors had been, and that his reign would be a benefaction. No doubt, however, carried away by the enthusiasm of the scene and the event, Danton's voice helped to swell the cry of "long live the king," that king whose life in the course of time he was to shorten.

It is possible that Louis, while going to the church or returning therefrom, may have seen in the crowd the ugly scarred face of that lusty country lad who in seventeen years was to overturn the throne and to vote the king's death. Their eyes may have met, but little could they read the history of the future; it was fortunate for them both that it was a sealed book.

Upon Danton's return to school he was given a slight punishment for his truancy. He was soon forgiven, however, and he not only amused his companions but also interested his teachers by giving descriptions of the scenes he had witnessed. The feature of the ceremony which seemed to have impressed him the most was the liberating in the church, after the king had taken the oath, of a great number of birds. " Pretty liberty that," he said, " to flutter between four walls without a crumb to eat or a straw for a nest!"

CHAPTER IV

DANTON CHOOSES LAW AS HIS PROFESSION—COMES TO THE BAR—MARRIES—AVOCAT AUX CONSEILS DU ROI—HIS STUDIES—CAMILLE DESMOULINS

Danton left the Seminary of Troyes in 1775 when he was sixteen years of age. From this time until 1780 but little is known of his life or occupations. He had an uncle in the priesthood living at Barberey who intended to have him enter the Church, but he strongly objected to this plan and after a family consultation on the matter, as was usual in those days, it was decided that he should adopt the law as his profession. The Church lost a jolly priest and a robust defender.

In his twenty-first year, in 1780, he was apprenticed to a solicitor in Paris named Vinot. Under this preceptor, he served as a clerk for four years, and became familiar with the practice of the courts.

In 1785 he came to the bar; he was registered at Rheims but immediately returned to Paris where he began his professional career. At this time he was described as being robust, eloquent, and very industrious; he loved a joke, had a hearty contagious laugh, was a good companion, and enjoyed the pleasures of the table. He

DANTON

swore stoutly, but his oaths were used for emphasis rather than in sheer vulgar profanity. Riouffe, referring to him at a later period, says every sentence he spoke in the *Conciergerie* was interlarded with oaths and obscene expressions; yet the same writer records sentences that were noble and lofty in thought and absolutely free from such disfigurement.

He was not an idealist nor a dreamer; he was practical in every sense of the word, and sought substantial results. He consequently made rapid progress in his profession. One of his first cases after coming to the bar was a suit arising out of a contention between a shepherd and his lord. The young advocate won the cause as counsel for the shepherd by a strong argument and an eloquent appeal.

In manner Danton was independent and somewhat arrogant towards those whom he did not respect. In conversation with one of his old teachers he is said to have denounced the servile, obsequious conduct of the lawyers who paid court to the solicitors and the judges. "As for me," he said, "barbarian that I am, I confess I cannot put up with all these servilities of civilization. By temperament I am unable to indulge in such sycophancy, I am stifled by such an atmosphere. My lungs need a purer air to breathe." At this time his step-father, M. Ricordain, became involved financially and Danton in the generosity of his nature gave all he had to relieve the family from its embarrassment.

After practicing in the lower courts for two

THE FRENCH REVOLUTION

years he became one of the "*Avocats aux Conseils du Roi,*" who were seventy-three in number and permitted to practice in the Court of Chancery. To attain this grade, recognized as the highest in the profession, a rigid examination was required, after a specified term of practice as attorney at the bar. It also required the payment of a considerable sum of money. It was in the nature of a purchasable office and brought distinction and opportunity. Just before his admission to practice in the Court of Chancery he married Antoinette Gabrielle Charpentier, the daughter of the proprietor of the Café de l'École, a students' restaurant in the district of the Cordeliers. The marriage was a union of love. The bride's parents gave her a dowry or dot of 20,000 francs. It was with this money that his wife brought him, together with what he had saved and inherited, that he bought the office of "*Avocat aux Conseils du Roi,*" for seventy-eight thousand livres.

He had risen rapidly in his profession and his income is said to have been about 25,000 francs per annum, no mean income in those days for a lawyer of only two years' standing at the bar. He was now brought into communication with government officials, the leading solicitors and many representatives of the nobility and the upper classes. It is said that at this period of his life he changed his name to D'Anton, an affectation, if this be true, that seems inconsistent with his natural independence. Among his clients were DeBarentin, the minister of justice,

DANTON

and DeBrienne, the comptroller-general. The former offered him the office of Secretary of Seals, which offer he twice refused, declaring that he could not accept the post under prevailing conditions for the period was one that required not modest but radical reforms, for now he added: " We are at the dawn of a revolution."

Several of his written opinions given in important cases show a considerable knowledge of the law for a man of his years and experience, and reveal as well a remarkable power of close logical analysis. Had he devoted himself exclusively to his profession there is every reason to believe, judging from what he had accomplished in so short a time, that he would have made a great lawyer and would have ranked among the first advocates of France. But the law is a jealous mistress and she demands the undivided attention and devotion of her suitor, and the all-important questions of politics were soon to divert and occupy his mind.

Danton had not confined himself to the study of the law alone, for his reading took in a much wider range. When Madame Roland called him illiterate she was either ignorant of the facts, or prejudiced in her judgment.

He had acquired a knowledge of the English and Italian tongues and if he did not speak them fluently he read them with ease. He was a fair Greek and a good Latin scholar. Upon the occasion of his admission to practice in the Court of Chancery he was required to deliver a Latin oration, the subject of which was " The Moral

THE FRENCH REVOLUTION

and the Political Situation of the Country, in their Relations with the Administration of Justice." He acquitted himself with credit and his paper elicited the warm commendation of the judges.

He had studied carefully the Encyclopedia, that vast storehouse of general information,—a liberal education in itself. He had read Adam Smith's "Wealth of Nations" in the original and was familiar with Shakespeare and Boccaccio in their own tongues. His library consisted of about two hundred volumes, valued at 2,500 francs. In his collection were to be found the works of Shakespeare, Addison, Pope, Dr. Johnson, Venuti, Guicciardini, Boccaccio, Ariosto and Metastasio, besides the standard French classics. Strange to say the works of Dante and Milton were not found in his collection. It is said by some authors, however, that he was familiar with the writings of these two great masters. Their sublimity of style and thought must necessarily have appealed to the fervid imagination of such a man as Danton.

In view of his education and his subsequent study and reading, to call him illiterate is to do him a grave injustice.

We have brought his life down to 1787, two years before the meeting of the States-General. He was now twenty-eight years of age, in the full vigor of a healthy manhood, and has been described as a Hercules " needing a well turned down collar in which to move his bull neck, his bodily figure stately as well as massive, and more careful in his dress than has been generally thought. His voice is powerful and his gestures are bold. He is hot-tempered—easily moved to anger, terrible to an adversary, but easy also to conciliate."

He was living happily with his wife whom he loved constantly and devotedly. His practice was growing and he had for clients some of the richest and most influential men in Paris. His income was sufficient for his family wants and enabled him besides to invite occasionally a few choice friends to his table, for he was of a most sociable disposition and loved to chat and linger, far into the night, over a bottle of good wine. Madame Roland in speaking of Danton said that he was, at this time, " a wretched advocate more burdened with debts than with cases, whose wife said she could not have kept house without the help of a guinea a week from her father." This is evidently not true, for he was in receipt of a very comfortable income and far removed from the stress of want. He enjoyed a fair share of the good things of life. His intimate friends were Pétion, Brune and Camille Desmoulins. For the last named he had a deep affection which was never broken, and only ended when they went to their death on the scaffold hand in hand. " Thou poor Camille, say of thee what they may, it were but falsehood to pretend one did not almost love thee, thou headlong lightly-sparkling man." He has been well described as "the flower that grew on Danton."

B. Camille Desmoulins was born in Picardy in

CAMILLE DESMOULINS
From an old print

THE FRENCH REVOLUTION

1760. His father was the lieutenant-general of the bailiwick of Guise. He received a liberal education and by training was a lawyer, but at the beginning of the Revolution adopted journalism as his profession and rose at once to distinction. "As a writer," says Carlyle, "there is nothing French that we have heard of superior or equal to him for these fifty years." He was swarthy in complexion and not very prepossessing in appearance, but he was of an ardent and enthusiastic nature, as tender and affectionate in heart as a child, and of a most emotional temperament. His love for his wife was one of the romances of the Revolution. Lucile's nature was sweet and lovable and her "gentle figure moves through the blood-red pool of misery of the Reign of Terror as the pale ghost of Francesca da Rimini through the darkness of Dante's Inferno." When Camille was arrested she haunted the prison and begged to share his fate. Ten days after his execution she went to the scaffold and exhibited far more courage and firmness than her husband. Her gospel of life was expressed in her simple verse:

> "*Ma science et mon système,*
> *Et mes projets et mes désirs.*
> *Mes plus grands faits, mes doux plaisirs,*
> *Tout se reduit à ce mot: J'aime!*"

Camille early espoused the popular cause and not only reached prominence but rose almost immediately to leadership; he "has a place of his

DANTON

own in the history of the Revolution; there are not many notabler persons in it than he."

In July, 1789, in the garden of the Palais Royal, with a brace of pistols in his hands, he harangued the people, summoned them to arms, and urged the attack upon the Bastile. It was from this time that he called himself " the first apostle of Liberty." He afterwards assumed the appellation *" Procureur-Général de la Lanterne "*—Attorney-General of the Lamp-post. One of his favorite assertions was: " Society is divided into two classes—gentlemen and *sansculottes,* and to make the Revolution a success or to establish the Republic, it is necessary to take the purses of the one and to put arms into the hands of the other." What St. Just was to Robespierre, Camille was to Danton.

It is to his eternal honor that he suffered death because he favored and advocated a policy of clemency and belonged to the faction of mercy.

CHAPTER V

CONDITIONS IMMEDIATELY PRIOR TO THE REVOLUTION—RÉVEILLON AFFAIR—LOUIS XVI—HIS MINISTERS—HIS HABITS—HIS CHARACTER

At this time, 1787, the political condition of France was most unsettled. A spirit of discontent was present everywhere, among all classes of people. The finances were in a frightful welter. The ministers as a rule were incapable and apparently had no real conception of the dangers that menaced the future.

Louis XV and his harlots had disappeared long ago, but they had left behind them a train of misfortunes that threatened the destruction of the State and a burden of debt that had well-nigh bankrupted the treasury. He had squandered upon his pimps and favorites 500,000,000 francs, which amount was not even named in the public accounts, and he bequeathed to his heir a debt of 4,000,000,000 livres. After the death of this dissolute and voluptuous prince reforms were promised and attempted, but the extravagance continued and there was no material reduction in the deficit. The Notables had been summoned twice, but having accomplished nothing in the way of relief there was a general demand for the convocation of the States-General.

DANTON

A succession of fatalities greatly augmented the troubles.

During the spring and summer of 1788, a severe drought prevailed, which seriously damaged the crops, and in addition to this disaster just on the eve of harvest a hail storm devastated the region around Paris from Normandy to Champagne, a distance of sixty leagues. Winter closed in earlier than usual and was of great severity, being the coldest season since 1709, the thermometer reaching 18¾° below zero. In December the Seine was frozen over from Paris to Havre. The suffering of the poor was dreadful, food and fuel were scarce and dear. In the spring of 1789 there was a general famine and the people were clamoring for bread. So small was the supply of grain that the government was compelled to order the cutting of 250,000 bushels of rye before the harvest season to feed the troops.

The bread sold by the bakers was dark in color and musty or earthy in taste, and not only this, it was so scarce in quantity that the portion sold to each customer had to be limited.

The people in the slums began to break into the bread and meat shops and to help themselves. Thus even before the Revolution the mob was trained in the tactics of riot and revolt. It was rumored in the sections of Paris that Reveillon, a manufacturer of wall paper in the faubourg St. Antoine had said that a working man with wife and children could live on fifteen sous a day. The story was false; he was self-made, had risen

THE FRENCH REVOLUTION

from the ranks of the people, was kindly, generous, and benevolent and even in dull times had kept his men employed. But the mob was in an ugly mood, would listen to no explanation, and in a blind fury destroyed not only the factory of Revéillon but also his residence. He was compelled to seek safety in the Bastile, that was so soon to fall, and from the windows of that gloomy fortress he witnessed the sacking of his home. The rioters found some wine in the cellar and their intoxication only increased their ferocity; they also discovered a number of bottles filled with a poisonous preparation used in the manufacture of the wall paper, and those who drank this liquid were soon writhing in the agonies of death. The whole section was in a tumult when the troops arrived and a fierce conflict took place before the mob was dispersed.

The slums were seething with riot, crowds of hungry men and women paraded through the streets, and Paris made ready for the Revolution. Ladies and gentlemen returning from the races were compelled to alight from their carriages and pay obeisance to the rabble. The destruction of Revéillon's factory was the prelude to the Revolution.

Now that the Revolution is advancing, and having witnessed the first act in the drama, it will be useful for us to see what manner of man the king is who stands facing the tempest, for much will depend upon the pilot if the ship is to weather the storm.

Louis XVI had not come up to the expectations of the people. At the time of his coronation the future was full of promise, but all the hopes of the people had turned to bitter disappointments.

Madame Roland in her ecstasy wrote at the beginning of his reign: "The ministers are enlightened and well disposed, the young king is docile and eager for good, the queen amiable and beneficent, the court respectable, the people are obedient, the kingdom is full of resources. Oh, but we are going to be happy!" Even the shrewd and far-seeing Talleyrand came out of his cynical mood and, carried away by the general enthusiasm, predicted a glorious era; but "never did so bright a spring precede so stormy an autumn, so dismal a winter."

When Louis XVI came to the throne his first minister was Maurepas, an old courtier, stiff, precise, and narrow, who was without talent and had no just comprehension of the spirit of the nation or the genius of the times. A quarrel between him and Marie Antoinette resulted in his dismissal. Thus early it is seen that the queen exerted her sinister influence in public matters over her royal spouse.

Turgot, the ablest minister of that period, was too austere in his methods to suit the nobility, who were loath to abate any of the abuses that were sapping the strength, the vitality of the nation, and so they began to conspire for his overthrow. Besides this opposition, he soon fell under the displeasure of the king and the queen, because he was brave enough to insist upon ap-

THE FRENCH REVOLUTION

plying healing but drastic remedies to the corrupt and diseased body politic. His peremptory dismissal dispelled the last hope of reform and the conservative patriotic men of the nation stood aghast as they looked out into the future.

Maleshérbes, a lawyer of prominence, a statesman of ability, and a man of the loftiest character, was called to the cabinet. He boldly adopted the policy of Turgot and in consequence was soon requested to surrender his portfolio.

Necker tried his hand at unraveling the tangle, but accomplished nothing, because he received no support from the court. Fleury and D'Ormesson tested their skill at administering the finances but both fell by the way.

Calonne, surnamed the (necromancer,) brilliant, sanguine, of ready invention, with the tricks and the qualities of a mountebank rather than the wisdom and the judgment of a statesman, borrowed in every direction as if there was to be no day of final settlement, increased thereby the annual deficit, and plunged the State further into bankruptcy. His policy was that of the spendthrift whose only solution for every financial crisis is to borrow. Since the retirement of Necker he had added 1,646,000,000 francs to the public debt. It was during his administration that sums so vast were squandered on Trianon, that St. Cloud was purchased for the queen, and that Louis was induced to buy, at an exorbitant figure, the palace of Rambouillet. The courtiers, like an army of beggars, flocked around this genial and generous minister who cast upon them showers of gold. Gifts, perquisites, pensions were lavished on every hand. He paid the debts of royal prodigals and honored the most unreasonable demands. His career ended in disgrace and he went into exile amidst the execrations of the very profligates who had been the recipients of his bounty and had joined with him in depleting the treasury.

Loménie de Brienne, Archbishop of Toulouse, who had long sought political preferment but whose ambition for the ministry was greater than his capacity to fill it, bungled and stumbled along until the Revolution overtook him. Before his retirement he secured an additional Archbishopric and a Cardinal's hat. At his request Necker was re-called, who upon assuming charge of the office found in the treasury chest only 250,000 francs. Minister after minister had been summoned to the side of Louis, but they did not materially decrease the expenditures nor increase the revenues, and the country staggering under its load of debt was fast approaching a crisis.

Louis XVI was without practical and political wisdom. He was utterly incapable as a ruler; in every way inefficient. He was a king only in name. He had no policy of administration, no definite purpose of reform. His cruel execution has created a sympathy for him in the hearts of men and his submissive spirit and dignified demeanor in the face of death have induced some of his admirers to place his name high on the roll of martyrs. The truth is that he had few of

THE FRENCH REVOLUTION

the qualities that command respect. He lost his crown without ever making a bold effort to save it. He was worthy neither the devotion of his friends nor the confidence of his people. He inspired neither enthusiasm nor loyalty.

When a boy he was a butt for the indecent raillery of Louis XV, the old voluptuary often expressing for him a supreme contempt. The courtiers tittered at the remarks and the criticisms of the king, fearing, of course to laugh aloud lest their conduct should be remembered by the young prince, if he should ever come to the throne. They need not have exercised any prudence for he so lacked spirit that he neither resented the remarks of the king nor would he have remembered the insults of the courtiers.

He was designated "*un imbecile,*" "*un bête,*" "a mass of insensible flesh," "the big fat pig." Madame DuBarry called him "that fat ill-mannered boy."

In person he was short, being five feet, five inches in height. His face was fat and puffy, with a retreating forehead and a weak chin. His near-sighted eyes did not light up even in conversation. He was without strong emotions and seldom displayed any animation. Barère in his Memoirs says: "His physical structure was large and common looking, he had pale blue eyes without the slightest expression, and a loud laugh that savored of imbecility. His carriage was most awkward and his whole appearance was that of a badly brought up rustic."

He was untidy in his dress, he had but few

traits of gentle birth. He had not the bearing nor the dignity of a king. If he had not been born in a palace he would not have graced even a hovel.

The portrait painted by Callet and engraved by Bervic, showing him in his coronation robes, gives no accurate conception of his real personality. The artist idealized the king, but even then, the face is without force and dignity; it reveals no strength of character.

He was boorish in his manner and indulged in vulgar practical jokes and silly amusements.

When nineteen years of age he was seen chasing and tickling with a straw, a servant who was carrying through the halls of the palace an armful of clothes. He was cruel in disposition and is said to have amused himself by spitting and roasting live cats. This seems hardly credible, but Gouverneur Morris notes in his diary, that he conversed with Madame Flahaut upon this matter and told her that he could not believe such stories, but she said they were true and that the king was both brutal and nasty.

One day while strolling in the gardens of the Tuileries he was approached by a lady with a little spaniel. The dog ran up to the king but before its mistress could call it back, the king, who had a heavy walking stick, struck the dog with such force that he broke its back as well as the lady's heart. The dog howled and the lady screamed, but the king strutted off as if proud of his prowess and "laughing like any lout of a

Louis XVI
From an engraving by Bervic after the original portrait
painted by Callet

THE FRENCH REVOLUTION

peasant." "His laugh was loud and coarse," says Thiébault, "and more like that of a tipsy farmer than of a monarch." He was too clumsy to dance and took no part in the pleasures and amusements of the court. He was fond of the chase but when he was not hunting he was drawing maps and tinkering at door locks.

He was a glutton. "Do not overload your stomach," exclaimed Louis XV, fearing that his grandson would fall into convulsions at the table. "Why not," was the reply, "I always sleep best after a hearty meal." This was upon the occasion of his wedding feast. Instead of paying court and attention to his young bride, he was gorging himself with food, until the old king was afraid he was going to lose his successor to the throne.

After the feast he accompanied Marie Antoinette to her chamber, bade her good night without even kissing her and retired to his own room to sleep off the effects of the meal, which he had washed down with flagons of wine, for he was a doughty drinker as well as eater.

He kept a diary and on May 16th he wrote: "My wedding—a party in the gallery. Royal banquet at the theatre." The last entry in that month reads: "I have had the stomach ache." He evidently had not taken the advice of the king.

"He ate like a pig," writes Barère, "and drank like a fish; he scarcely ever left the table without being a little unsteady." Jefferson in a letter to Jay wrote: " The king hunts one half the day, is drunk the other. . . . The king goes for nothing."

He had not the qualities that go to make a jolly good king, fond of feast and revel. He took no delight in the real pleasures of the table. He was too reserved, stolid and stupid to enjoy the spirited conversation of merry companions. There was nothing for him " in the feast of reason and the flow of soul "; he had no sense of wit and humor. He could not recount a good story nor could he appreciate the telling of one. He ate and drank alone, choice fellowship added no zest to his appetite. After he gorged his food and gulped his wine, he dozed, he slept.

He seemed to be always hungry and under all conditions was ready to eat. No dangers nor crises could affect or moderate his appetite.

Baron Thiébault states in his Memoirs, that on the morning of the royal family's flight from Paris, Louis went into a roadside inn, and spent upwards of an hour lingering over his breakfast. Whether or not this be true it is hard to say, for it seems almost impossible to believe that under the circumstances, he would have taken such a risk, but there must have been a rumor to that effect, for Miss Miles in a letter to her father, the British agent, wrote, " If the king had not stopped to eat cutlets he would have escaped." When detained at Varennes where he had been intercepted in his attempted flight from France, he drank his wine with gusto, smacked

THE FRENCH REVOLUTION

his lips and declared it was the best bottle of Burgundy he had ever tasted.

After he returned to Paris from Varennes, when he reached the Tuileries, he sank into a chair and according to a statement made by Desmoulins exclaimed: "It's devilish hot," and seeing a valet at this moment passing through the room, he hailed him in a loud voice. "Ah! there you are and here I am, bring me a chicken."

After he had taken refuge in the Assembly on the 10th of August and while the mob was attacking the Tuileries, he sucked an orange. He ate his meals during his detention in the *loge* with so much relish that the deputies sneered and the queen was greatly humiliated by his conduct. While the Swiss were bravely fighting in defense of his palace, he was asking for food. "He eats while we die for him."

It is not, however, unusual for a king to be indifferent to the sacrifices made by his subjects and Louis does not stand alone in this particular. The story is told that Frederick the Great when some of his troops were breaking in battle dashed himself against the retreating column and drove them back into line. "Damn you," he cried, "do you want to live always?" Napoleon addressing his army on the eve of a conflict said, "Soldiers: I need your lives and you owe them to me."

Madame Campan relates, in her Memoirs, that on the morning of the 6th of October, 1789, when the mob of women stormed the palace at

DANTON

Versailles, two soldiers of the Body Guard, Miomandre de Sainte-Marie and Bernard du Repaire, at the peril of their lives, saved the queen from assassination. They were severely wounded at the time, and one day during their convalescence, while out for a stroll, they went into the gardens of the Palais Royal. They were immediately recognized and insulted, and at once withdrew to a place of safety. After this incident, advised by their friends to leave Paris, they made arrangements to quit the city. The queen hearing of their anticipated departure, sent for them to come to the palace. Graciously and with a heart full of generosity, she thanked and complimented them for their chivalry and gave them a present substantial in amount and sufficient to pay their expenses while away. The king was informed of the interview, came into the room, simply accosted the soldiers and then leaned his back against the mantel-piece. Not a syllable of commendation, no generous, kindly word passed his lips. He did not even take by the hand and cordially greet the men who had saved the life of his queen. After remaining a short time he left the room without even saying goodby. Madame Campan, to make some excuse for his conduct, says his eyes were suffused with tears. The queen because of his seeming indifference was deeply humiliated.

Louis was not a student nor did he keep himself well informed on current events and political conditions. He did not possess the first attribute of statesmanship.

THE FRENCH REVOLUTION

He was a king but without the qualities of a ruler. He had none of the graces that please and none of the arts that win the people. He was without force and decision and so vacillating, that his promise could not be depended upon over night. His brother defined the character of his mind " in the simile of the oiled billiard balls which no one could hold steadily together."

He was obstinate when he should have yielded, he was weak when he should have been strong and strong when he should have been weak. His opinion and judgment at the council table were not worth considering. He seldom, if ever, had any well-timed suggestions to offer.

In the language of St. Just he was *" brusque et faible, parcecu il pensait le bien, il croyait le faire . . . il voyait de sangfroid toute sa cour piller sa finance ou plutot ne voyait rien."*

Louis inherited the Revolution from his ancestors. He would have been a pliable, an easy-going ruler if his reign had fallen in peaceful times. He would willingly have left the government to others, better able to rule, and would have found amusement in the chase and in the construction of clumsy locks. For a revolution he was about the last man in all the kingdom fitted to cope with its violence. It must too be borne in mind that the French Revolution was the great, all powerful political event of modern times. So in every aspect of the case Louis was entirely out of place. " Of all the monarchs of the Capetian line he was the least able to stem, and yet the least likely to provoke a revolution."

DANTON

Such was the king who sat upon the throne of France when the nation was overwhelmed with debt and the monarchy threatened with destruction. At a time when a man of ability should have been at the head of the government, when the qualities of a statesman, of a politician, and of a diplomat were required to meet conditions, a weak, a vacillating, an impassive man without judgment, invention and purpose, was the ruler of the nation.

Dumont says: "We may reason *ad infinitum* upon the causes of the Revolution, but in my mind, there is only one dominant and efficient cause—the weakness of the king. Had a firm and decided prince been in the place of Louis XVI the Revolution would not have happened. . . . There is not a single period during the existence of the first Assembly, when the king could not have re-established his authority and framed a mixed constitution much stronger and more solid than the old parliamentary and nobiliary monarchy of France. His weakness, his indecision, his half measures and half councils, and more particularly his want of foresight, led to the catastrophe."

Unquestionably, even after the period of the first Assembly or States-General, had he acted with vigor, at several points of his reign, he could have saved his crown, and directed his empire out of the torrent of the Revolution into peaceful channels.

It was a long while before the nation became anti-monarchical. When the States-General met

THE FRENCH REVOLUTION

in 1789, no one in all France thought it would accomplish more than relieve the financial condition and perhaps enact a few measures of reform. The most sanguine reformer never thought that feudalism would be abolished and the king dethroned. Nothing seemed so remote. In fact the people at that time were in favor of the monarchy. "Even in February, 1791," Michelet declares, "Marat still remained a royalist."

But Louis allowed the Revolution to creep upon him by degrees and at no moment when he could have saved his throne, and could have won popular favor, did he act with that courage and decision which the contingencies required.

When, at the time of the meeting of the States-General, he ordered the delegates of the Third Estate to retire, and was defied by Mirabeau, he ought to have followed up his order by force and compelled obedience even at the point of the bayonet. If he was not prepared to enforce his command, he ought not to have given it. This was one of the decisive points in the Revolution, perhaps the turning point. The people had seen their representatives defy the royal authority, rebuke and dismiss the king's messenger, and send him back to his majesty with an impudent answer, and to crown all, they witnessed the complacent submission, the abject surrender of the king.

There was a time not very long before the period of which we are speaking, when Louis XIV swore that "he would have no more of these cringing assemblies," and this he declared to the parliament booted and whip in hand. But these days had gone by, and it is doubtful whether or not, at this time, even Louis the Great would have dared to enter the hall of the States-General in such a mood, but that he would have made every effort to enforce his orders and to save his throne goes without saying.

To be sure there was a vast difference between Louis XIV and Louis XVI. The former possessed all the arts of kingcraft and the audacious confidence of a Bourbon of the ancient *régime*. No king ever played his role with more consummate skill. His very word was law, his look awed into submission. While strolling or rather strutting through the gardens of the palace at Versailles, as was his daily custom, he would suddenly stop, and with head thrown back and chest thrown out, his right arm extended, leaning on a long staff, his eyes would sweep slowly over the crowd of courtiers in attendance, who bowing with looks cast to the ground, would not dare to meet the proud and searching gaze of his majesty, whom they worshiped almost as a god in human form. No king, even of the Bourbon line, ever received homage so obsequious nor was more absolute in power. It seems strange that so great a change could have been wrought in so short a time. Kings had grown somewhat out of public favor and no matter who the monarch might have been in 1789, a revolution of some sort was inevitable, but with

THE FRENCH REVOLUTION

a strong king it might have been effected without the " Reign of Terror."

The delegates of the Third Estate in the States-General of 1789 were not the timid deputies who cowered under the crack of the whip, nor the cringing flunkies who followed in the train of the Great Louis. They did not cast their eyes timidly to the ground under the haughty gaze of a king; they stood erect and wore their hats in his presence, in contravention of a rigid rule of ceremony that had been in vogue time out of mind. We cannot in our practical age comprehend to its full meaning the breach of that ancient and honored law of etiquette. It was revolutionary in itself to remain covered before the king, but times, men and customs had changed.

CHAPTER VI

ADVISERS OF THE KING—THE QUEEN—THE FINANCES—REVOLUTIONS BEGIN AT THE TOP

Louis XVI had not wisdom enough to accept the inevitable. He had the false pride of a weak man and knew not how nor when to surrender. Every concession he made to the public was wrung from him or given so reluctantly and in so graceless a manner that he aroused the resentment of the people instead of winning their gratitude.

He was most unfortunate in the selection of his advisers. The men directing public affairs were apprentices in state-craft, flatterers and time servers. A proud, an insolent aristocracy, a crowd of hungry, selfish courtiers, were swarming around the king, disconcerting him with their council, and still fattening on the public treasury. There was no thought in the minds of these silly and improvident people of reducing the expenditures; their only demand was to increase the revenues. If they scanned the political sky and saw the signs of an approaching storm, they calmed their fears by assuring themselves, that in the nature of things it could not last long.

Strange to say it took the king and the nobles

THE FRENCH REVOLUTION

a considerable length of time to appreciate the fact that the Revolution was more than a mere temporary disturbance. "Believe me, Madame," said Dumouriez in addressing the queen, " I abhor anarchy and crime as much as you do. This is not a transient, popular movement as you seem to think. It is an almost unanimous insurrection of a mighty nation against inveterate abuses."

The deluge predicted by Louis XV and Madame de Pompadour was rising rapidly but no one in the court circles was making preparations to pilot the ship of state into a port of safety. The monarchy was fast drifting toward the rocks and shoals.

The queen was looked upon as the evil genius of the king. It was claimed that she had advised him in all the mistakes he had made and that she was responsible for his attitude towards the public.

Her name had been mentioned in connection with several scandals and Dame Rumor had ceased whispering and was now talking aloud. All sorts of stories reflecting upon her character as queen, woman, wife and mother were put in circulation and spread broadcast. She was contemptuously called "*l'Austrienne.*" "Why do the people," she exclaimed, " hate me so. I am no foreigner, no stranger, but thoroughly French in purpose and sentiment. My children were born here. This is my home, all my interests are here, where else could I go?" But alas! her protestations were too late. By her frivolity, extravagance and apparent indifference to the sufferings of the poor, she had provoked the resentment of the entire community. A story was current that when she was told that the people were hungry and wanted bread, she innocently asked, " Why do they not eat cake? " Whether this was spoken ignorantly, facetiously or contemptuously, it is hard to say. But it was successfully used by her enemies to discredit her in the estimation of the people. She seldom appeared in public without being insulted.

The ministers of finance had juggled with the figures of their reports, but the truth would not down that the deficit was annually increasing. Calonne had borrowed and spent some 500,000,000 francs. The exchequer was exhausted and ingenious financiers could not suggest nor provide any new methods for raising money. The national credit was not sufficient to induce, at this time, under an inefficient administration, any more loans, and every means of taxation had been tried until the purses of the peasants were empty. " The deficit, now 100,000,000 livres per annum, threatened to devour the monarchy." Yet the income was not falling off but really augmenting.

At this period things were no worse than they had been but the trouble was that, although the revenues had grown in amount, the expenditures were increasing in a greater ratio than the revenues. The wealth of the country had not diminished. The burdens upon commerce and agriculture were relatively not heavier than

MARIE ANTOINETTE
From an engraving in the collection of
William J. Latta, Esq.

THE FRENCH REVOLUTION

in the past. In fact all agree that the country's material prosperity was advancing, but what was needed was a wise and an economical administration of public affairs. The extravagance of the court, the civil list, the pensions, the immense amount of interest on the loans, and the public debt together with the current expenses were far more than the revenues could meet, and the consequence was an annual deficiency.

As time wore on and the disasters multiplied, the court did make a spasmodic effort to practice economy but it was not sufficient to change materially the conditions.

A reference to the Red Book published in 1790, will give some idea of the immense sums of money that were squandered by royalty. The secret expenses of the court reached the highest mark in 1783, when the total was 145,000,000 livres. They were at the lowest point in 1787, when they amountd to 82,000,000 livres. Reign after reign, the facts in relation to these royal expenditures had been concealed from the public. The people had no voice; they were not consulted in the matter of the appropriation and spending of their money. The monarch had wasted these large sums annually without even the pretense of any accountability to the nation. But the people had improved intellectually, men were thinking, were inquiring, were complaining. They dared not express themselves under Louis XIV, they only whispered in the days of Louis XV, but now, with a weak king, they spoke aloud. Petitions for a redress of grievances had become public declarations and demands. In the past they had been lowly and even servile in tone, beseeching the king's favor, while the petitioners " with bated breath and whispering humbleness " would beg his majesty's pardon for having the boldness and assurance to complain. The peasant slave kept his eyes on the ground when he sought and asked relief, but now men had grown bolder and looked the king in the face when their demands were made.

Revolutions generally result from the attempts of the aristocracy or the government to effect slight reforms. Political revolutions begin at the top; their violence at last comes from below. "I perceive," said Danton, "that in revolutions the supreme power ultimately rests with the most abandoned." The French Revolution was not inaugurated by the peasantry and the rabble but by the upper and the middle classes; that is by the middle class assisted by a minority of the aristocracy, who understood the conditions, sympathized with the suffering poor, and were fair and just enough to urge reforms. Lawyers, doctors, journalists, students, merchants, manufacturers and artisans, men of the middle class who had been reading and thinking and who had been investigating and considering the causes that had produced and were producing the melancholy conditions that prevailed, made the French Revolution. The peasants and the proletariat could not read; they had made no progress; they knew nothing of the teachings and the doctrines of the great philosophers, who had pointed the way to

THE FRENCH REVOLUTION

revolution. They were steeped as deeply in ignorance as they had been in the past centuries.

The first impetus was given to the Revolution when the conservative nobles advocated reforms. It was then the middle class, that enjoyed no special privileges and exemptions, but felt the injustice of the system that had stopped the avenues of preferment to self-made, independent and ambitious men, rose in their strength to demand a change. "When therefore the French Revolution broke out, it was not," declares Buckle, "a mere rising of ignorant slaves against educated masters, but it was a rising of men in whom the despair caused by slavery was quickened by the resources of advancing knowledge."

The mobs in the early days of the Revolution were composed not only of the scuff and scum of the purlieus of Paris. Men of position were in the crowd that leveled the walls of the Bastile. Nobles who had no patience with the policy of the court and the tyranny of the State, marched with that mob in the attack upon that hated dungeon. Hérault de Séchelles, nobly born, of elegant manners, of education, a brilliant lawyer, related to the Polignacs, at one time a courtier and a favorite of the queen, was one of the first men over the drawbridge to demand the surrender of the garrison. The philosophers were the apostles of the Revolution, and their disciples in the upper and the middle classes, were the reformers who put their principles to a practical application. Their followers were not confined to one class but included the intelligent of all classes.

The *personnel* of the commonalty in the States-General proves the truth of the foregoing statement. Of the 584 deputies, 12 were classed as gentlemen, 2 were priests, 18 were mayors of towns, 162 were magistrates of bailiwicks, 212 were lawyers, 16 were doctors, and 162 were merchants, landowners and farmers. The deputies of the Third Estate had among their number some of the ablest men in France.

Several of these men were titled and they dared to denounce the old system and to urge the needed reforms. Lawyers of learning, of eloquence and of national reputation, donned the black garb of the Commons. Among the nobles, too, were many who favored the union of the three orders and who were liberal in their views; in fact after the royal *séance,* a number of them withdrew from the sessions of their order and joined the Third Estate. In the ranks of the clergy also were many who warmly sympathized with the popular cause.

The Revolution was made by the middle class and by a minority of the nobility and clergy. The real work was begun not by the rabble but by the best elements in the nation.

CHAPTER VII

DANTON IN THE EARLY DAYS OF THE REVOLUTION—THE AFFAIR OF SOULÉS—MARAT—THE INCIDENT OF MARAT—EARLY EVENTS OF THE REVOLUTION

The States-General met on May 5, 1789, at Versailles. Danton was not a delegate to that body, and during the early stages of the Revolution he did not appear prominently in the public eye. At the fall of the Bastile, it is said that he was present and took part in the attack, but there is no substantial proof of this. The royalists asserted that they saw him in the early riots.

On the 16th of July, two days after the fall of the Bastile, he was about to enter, at the head of a patrol, the court of the old fortress, when he was stopped by Soulés the new governor. Danton disregarded his orders, called his commission a rag and placed him under arrest for his interference. He took Soulés as his prisoner to the Town Hall and there after an investigation into the facts, the authorities censured Danton for his arbitrary act and reinstated Soulés. La Fayette was specially bitter in his denunciation of Danton's conduct and from this time they were sworn enemies.

Danton's reputation for a long while remained

DANTON

merely local, circumscribed by the boundary lines of his own district. He was, however, active in his section and was one of the first presidents of the Club of the Cordeliers, an organization that played a very prominent part in the events of the Revolution. In the beginning it was without question the most radical and revolutionary of all the political associations. The section of Paris known as the Cordeliers had nothing in common with the districts of St. Antoine and St. Marceau. It was a locality in which the courts were established and where judges, lawyers and students gathered. The cafés in this quarter were well conducted and the tables were surrounded by professional men of education, who argued intelligently upon events and conditions. It was a hot-bed of revolution. Although Danton, as we have already said, was not a deputy to the States-General, we may presume that he was watching closely the opening scenes in a revolution that he had predicted. He perhaps mingled with the throngs at the Palais Royal, he may even have addressed them. His friend Desmoulins was a frequent visitor to the gardens and, no doubt, Danton often accompanied him.

It is hard to find any trace of him during this period. He was not a journalist like Desmoulins nor even a pamphleteer, and consequently no articles came from his pen, touching the questions of the hour. He kept steadily plodding away at his practice and the part he took at this time in politics was only incidental. He did not

THE FRENCH REVOLUTION

make an appearance on the memorable days of the 5th and 6th of October. During this period, however, he was the recognized leader of his district. A brush he had with La Fayette brought him into great prominence, but in the end it was the means of sending him to the rear for a long space of time. It was called the incident or the affair of Marat, "*l'affaire de Marat.*"

Jean Paul Marat was one of the most remarkable creations of that most remarkable epoch, in many respects he was the worst product of the Revolution and he symbolized one phase of it. He was by birth a Swiss. His father, born in Sardinia, was a man of education and by profession a physician. His mother was a Swiss Protestant. The home influences that surrounded his youth were refining and educating. His capacious mind readily absorbed learning. He had a keen perception and his memory was marvelously retentive. He received a liberal education at the University of Bordeaux.

In his early manhood, possessed of a restless and an adventurous disposition, he started out into the world to make his way alone and to win the favors of Fortune. He traveled through foreign lands and acquired a facile use of many tongues. He was a linguist of no mean distinction.

He sought knowledge in every direction and in all the known branches of science. One of his publications provoked the criticism and raillery of Voltaire and brought him into public no-

DANTON

tice. Professor Charles, a man of considerable distinction in that day, ridiculed some of the medical views of Marat. The latter replied with a torrent of abuse and the controversy without reaching a satisfactory conclusion from a scientific point of view resulted at last in a duel. Neither combatant was injured.

Marat gained the friendship of Benjamin Franklin, the attention of the American philosopher having been drawn to one of his tracts on electricity.

He corresponded with learned men throughout Europe and was fairly well known in the scientific world. An honorary degree of M.D. was conferred upon him by the University of St. Andrew in Scotland and for ten years he resided in London and practiced as a physician in the fashionable locality of Soho Square.

About this time he wrote a work entitled "Chains of Slavery." It was originally written in English and published in England. It shows the bent of his mind in relation to matters political, even at this early period.

Upon his return to France he settled in Paris and was appointed by the Count of Artois physician to his body guards, and incidentally he looked after the health of the horses in the stables. It is from this fact that Carlyle calls him a horse-leech but in no sense of the word was he a horse doctor, nor is there the slightest reason for so intimating.

A nobleman, in the early days of the Revolution, with the purpose, no doubt, of reflecting

MARAT
From an engraving in the collection of
William J. Latta, Esq.

THE FRENCH REVOLUTION

upon the professional standing of Marat, and holding him up to public ridicule, declared that the doctor having been called in to prescribe, gave him a dose of horse physic and almost succeeded in taking his life. This story too may have given the rumor strength, but the truth is that Marat really was a physician of no mean standing.

His private practice brought him into immediate contact with the aristocracy. He acquired quite a reputation as a successful practitioner, made money, dressed well, was considered a man of fashion and was frequently referred to as "the friend of the great ladies." "He was, withal," says Barras, "a good easy man in society wherein he shone by his acquirements."

At this time he must have conceived a mortal hatred for the nobility and the privileged classes. He no doubt had been stung by their insolence and his proud, conceited and independent spirit had smarted under the social restrictions that were drawn, which restrictions he, perhaps, had rudely been taught to respect when, with his characteristic impudence, he attempted to cross the line of social demarcation.

He must have brooded over his wrongs, imaginary or otherwise, for when the Revolution came, he plunged into its vortex with all the ardor and malignity of his nature. At the opening of the Revolution he was a man of some means and of comparative leisure; had withdrawn almost entirely from the active practice of medicine and was absorbed in the study of science.

His publications were numerous but somehow

DANTON

failed to attract the attention which his vanity and conceit thought they deserved. They were of vast scope, from a work on optics and an essay on gleets, to a discourse on the immortality of the soul. Imbued with the teachings of the philosophers, urged by a consuming ambition and possessed by a deadly hatred for the aristocracy, the Revolution opened up to him a vista in which his imagination reveled. He would now find a theatre for his genius and an opportunity to avenge his hate.

Nervous, irritable, suspicious, eager for notoriety, this rabid fanatic assailed the old order and all those that gave it allegiance or support.

As the Revolution grew in intensity, so did he, in fact he was one of the leaders that outstripped it. As time wore on he became wild, unreasonable, intolerant with a consuming thirst for blood in his desire to exterminate the aristocrats, and not only the aristocrats but all those that differed with him in their views. His enmity was as bitter and as relentless against the Girondins and partisan foes, as against the royalists. "In truth," says Lamartine, "as his power increased he became so impressed with his own importance that he threatened everyone, even his former friends."

After losing his small fortune, he made his living by his pen. He became a journalist and his paper, called "The Friend of the People," preached the gospel of revolt, murder and pillage. "He had the clumsy tumblings of the brute in his thought, and its gnashing of teeth

THE FRENCH REVOLUTION

in his style. His journal smelt of blood in every line."

Nobody was safe from his scurrilous attacks. Mirabeau, Necker, Bailly, La Fayette, Dumouriez, men in the highest positions, were most bitterly assailed. He demanded among other things that eight hundred traitorous deputies, with Mirabeau at their head, should be sent to the gibbet. Mirabeau, when his attention was called to this article, merely shrugged his shoulders and laughingly said with his usual *sang froid*, " Why, the man must be drunk." In the Assembly he openly declared there would be no tranquillity in the State until two hundred and eighty-six traitors were brought to the scaffold. He himself had compiled the list of the proscribed. In the columns of his paper he made an exact calculation, showing how 260,000 men could be put to death in one day. He is called by a distinguished French historian " the apostle of assassination *en masse.*"

During the September massacres he proposed to Danton to set the prisons on fire and thus devour the aristocrats and " suspects " in the flames, a quicker method, and therein, perhaps, more humane, than slaughtering the victims one by one at the wicket.

It was from no sentiment of humanity, however, that he was induced to make that suggestion, he wanted wholesale butchery that none might escape. " Daggers! daggers! friend Marat! but torches, torches likewise. Blood must be mingled with ashes," says Lamartine,

DANTON

He advised the institution of a brotherhood of spies and informers. He wanted the authorities to set up a receptacle like the Iron Mouth of Venice, in which could be deposited the complaints of patriots; a post box and mail service furnished by the government for the exclusive use, without even the payment of postage, of that contemptible creature, the anonymous letter writer; an easy and a convenient method provided by the State for the inculpation of the innocent; a means to satisfy, to avenge the envy, hatred and fear of ignoble minds. The coward, without revealing his identity, could thus imperil the life and liberty of his rival.

Such a system would have created in every mind a feeling of dread and suspicion and would have warmed into life a brood of infamous spies and informers. But anything that furnished victims met with the approval of Marat. He had a ferocious heart and was most vindictive in temper. He was the fury of the Revolution, " the outcast of assassination."

" Give me," he cried, " two hundred Neapolitans, the knife in their right hand, in their left a muff to serve for a shield, and with these I will traverse France and complete the Revolution."

" His imagination thirsts for torments, he would have flaming stakes, conflagrations and atrocious mutilations." As time ran on, his rage became uncontrolable. " Brand them," he shrieked, " with a hot iron, cut off their thumbs, slit their tongues." His convulsions were hysterical. His incoherent vaporings were but the

THE FRENCH REVOLUTION

mutterings of a disordered mind. His appetite for gore was canine, not human.

"It was blood," says Sir Walter Scott, "that was Marat's constant demand, not in drops from the breast of an individual, not in puny streams from the slaughter of families, but blood in the profusion of an ocean." While Danton one day was standing in the hall of the convention talking with a friend, Marat came along, drew him aside and whispered in his ear. Danton upon returning to his friend said: "The brute! he craves more blood."

In his projected Constitution he wrote: "When a man is in want of everything, he has a right to take from another the superfluity in which he is wallowing, nay more, he has a right to take from him his necessary things; and rather than starve, has a right to cut his throat and devour his palpitating flesh."

"His political exhortations began and ended like the howl of a bloodhound for murder." When he entered the Assembly, he was shunned by everybody, even by the members of his own party. After speaking in the tribune, upon one occasion, a deputy moved that it should be purified before any one else should enter it.

Dr. Moore wrote in his diary, "Marat has carried his calumnies to such a length that he is apparently detested by everybody. When he enters the Assembly and seats himself, those near him generally rise and change their seats. I saw him, at one time, address himself to Louvet; and in doing so he attempted to lay his hand on

DANTON

Louvet's shoulder, who instantly started back with looks of aversion, exclaiming, 'Do not touch me.'"

One day when several accusations had been made against him, he cried out, " Men! if these be crimes, you know what to do," and at the same time he swept his hand suggestively across his throat. Upon another occasion he made a statement that momentarily aroused the anger of the deputies, but " such a declaration," said Dr. Moore, " issuing from a little, dirty mortal, whose murky visage scarce overlooked the tribune, turned the indignation of the Assembly into mirth and many of the members burst into laughter."

Nothing could abash or disconcert him, even when he was shunned by everybody and when the murmurs against him in the Assembly were loudest he strutted about among the deputies apparently unconcerned.

He lived in a dilapidated house in the Rue des Cordeliers. His library consisted of about fifty volumes of philosophical works, and these were arranged on a wooden shelf nailed to the wall. Montesquieu and Raynal were his favorite authors. The New Testament was always on his table, generally lying open as if frequently consulted. When some one referred to this fact he replied, " The Revolution is the Gospel," and bowing reverentially he added, " Jesus Christ is our Master, no one so loved the poor as he and so cast maledictions on the heads of the rich and powerful."

In manner and speech Marat was rough and

THE FRENCH REVOLUTION

insulting. There was one, however, whom he always addressed in a tone of tenderness—his housekeeper, a woman named Albertine. Perhaps she was the only creature in all the world he loved and she, in turn, looked upon him as an inspired prophet and a benefactor of the human race.

His customary attire was dirty and forlorn. He wore a dark vest or waistcoat, shabby, patched and mended; his shirt sleeves were turned up to his elbows, his trousers were cotton velvet, usually stained with ink. With his blue cotton stockings he wore shoes tied with pack thread. A dirty shirt was open at the breast, and his hair, cropped short at the temples and falling over his shoulders, was tied behind in a leathern thong; surmounting all was a large broad-brimmed hat. Sometimes he wore, wrapped around his head, a colored handkerchief.

He was almost a dwarf in stature, being less than five feet in height. His head was much too large for his body, and the ever-present insolent leer upon his features made his face most repulsive.

"He was," says Lamartine, "thin and bony, his body appeared as if consumed by an internal fire; gall and blood were marked upon his skin; his eyes, though prominent and full of insolence, appeared to shrink from the glare of full daylight; his mouth, deeply cleft as if to vent abuse, had the habitual sneer of disdain."

His effrontery and impudence were brazen. "No dangers can terrify him, no detection can

DANTON

disconcert him, his heart as well as his forehead seems to be of brass." Upon a certain occasion, although not bidden to the feast, he went to the house of the Rolands while a reception was in progress and, shuffling through the halls, reached the drawing-room, where he announced in a loud voice that he wanted to see Danton. Unclean, unkempt, covered with the dirt of the street, he seemed like a little imp in this goodly company of well-dressed folk; but the broad leer upon his face showed how much he enjoyed the discomfiture of the guests, especially that of some members of the Assembly, who, without offending the little tyrant, endeavored to avoid him.

At another time he interrupted a social function at Talma's, to interview Dumouriez upon some matters in relation to the army. Dumouriez, with a military air, drawing himself up to his full height, looked down disdainfully upon this little frog that seemed to have jumped into the parlor out of the gutter, and said: "Ah! and so you are called Marat. I have nothing to say to you." Then turning on his heel and walking aside, he left the saucy intruder to find his way out of the room, amidst the sneers and jeers of the guests. But the columns of Marat's journal next day fumed with rage and the general paid a heavy penalty for his insult. Marat publicly scolded La Fayette and almost every man of prominence. No person could escape his denunciation, no place or occasion was safe from his intrusion.

He knew the proprieties of life, for as we

THE FRENCH REVOLUTION

have seen, he had once enjoyed the amenities of society, but that was before he became an outlaw, before his envy like a cancer began eating into his heart and deadening his every sensibility. Danton at one time declared publicly, and this was when Marat had great influence with the mob, that he did not like this man. "I have had some experience with him and I find him boisterous, quarrelsome and unsociable."

Danton twice came to his assistance when he was in peril, but the great tribune was induced to act for reasons other than the personal safety of Marat and outside of any respect or regard he had for him.

One day Danton, while in conversation with him, became so disgusted with the doctor's filthy appearance, that he told him to "go home, wash and put on a clean shirt."

The lower he fell in social position and the more he was hunted and persecuted by the authorities, the greater grew his popularity with the mob. "None exercised," says Mignet, "a more fatal influence upon the period in which he lived, than Marat."

He was hunted from cellar to garret, and to avoid his pursuers he took refuge even in the vaults of the Church of the Cordeliers and in the public sewers.

His persecutions naturally endeared him to the people. His poverty, his want, his privations, his sufferings, aroused their sympathies. Danton was of course a rabid revolutionist, but he was a high liver, somewhat aristocratic in his tastes. Robespierre was loyal to the Revolution, but he was cold, proud and repelled all familiarity. Vergniaud was a dreamer who soared far above the heads of the multitude, and they could never get in touch with him. The people could stand aloof and admire these men, but they could draw close to and love Marat. He was of the rabble, the representative of the discontented poor. During the "Reign of Terror" he had the authority of a dictator, among the masses his word was law. "This modern Tiberius sent his orders to the multitude from the depth of his indigent Caprea," and exercised a power that was all but imperial.

Fanatical in his devotion to the Revolution, he could not be bought, driven, intimidated, seduced nor cajoled. Flattery fell upon his ears like water on a rock. Place, women, money could not tempt him; his estate when he died consisted of twenty cents in cash, and yet in his lifetime he could have sold the columns of his paper for any amount he might have asked.

He proved ever steadfast to the Revolution, he was its constant advance guard; while many of the men whom he had denounced, against whom he had railed and at whom he had pointed his canny finger in warning, either proved disloyal or fell one by one under public censure. Mirabeau's bust after his death was veiled. Necker, La Fayette and Dumouriez fled the country. No wonder the multitude looked upon Marat as one who spoke with the voice of a prophet.

THE FRENCH REVOLUTION

The most remarkable thing about the man was his indefatigability. He seemed never to tire, often he would write far into the night. Under the light of a tallow candle and while seated in a tub of cold water to allay a raging inward fever, he would toil until the morning dawned. He watched while others slept, but "his vigils," says Lamartine, "cost blood the next day."

We have drawn him in pretty dark colors, and it is but fair that he should be heard in his own defense. The following article appeared in his journal at a time when he thought it wise to soften the attacks that were being made upon him:

"I speak to-day of myself. I desire to appear in my true light, for the enemies of liberty unceasingly represent me as a madman, a cannibal, a tiger thirsting for blood. I was born with a sensitive heart, a fiery imagination, a frank and an impetuous character, a right mind, a heart that eagerly drank in all exalted passions, especially the love of glory.

"I was brought up in my father's house with the tenderest care and I arrived at manhood without having ever abandoned myself to the fury of my passions. At twenty-one years of age I was pure and had long given myself up to study and meditation. I owe to nature the stamp of my character, but it is to my mother that I owe its subsequent development. She planted in my heart the love of justice and humanity. When eight years old, I could not bear the sight of any

DANTON

ill treatment towards my fellow creatures, and the sight of cruelty and injustice aroused my anger as though it had been a personal outrage. In my early youth my body was feeble and I never knew the joy or the plays of childhood. My principal passion at that early day was love of glory, and I am now ambitious of the glory of immolating myself upon the altar of my country.

"Thoughtful from my youth, my choicest pleasures have been found in meditation. I have passed five and twenty years in retirement and in the perusal and consideration of the best authors on morals, philosophy and policy, in order to deduce the wisest conclusions.

"In eight volumes of metaphysics, twenty of physical sciences, I have been actuated by a sincere desire of being useful to humanity. The quacks of the Corps Scientifique,—D'Alembert, Condorcet, Laplace, Lalande, Monge, Lavoisier, wish to be alone, and I could not even pronounce the titles of my works. During five years I groaned beneath this cowardly oppression.

"When the Revolution convoked the States-General I soon saw whither things were tending, and I began to entertain the hope of beholding humanity and of mounting to my right place."

The article, although it delineates his character in the softest shades and adroitly appeals to the sympathies of the people, yet reveals in every line a consuming envy, an overweening ambition, an insatiable thirst for personal glory from his very youth. His envy even goes so far as to designate contemptuously a group of immortals

THE FRENCH REVOLUTION

as a "Corps Scientifique," under whose "cowardly oppression," he complains, he groaned for years, which oppression no doubt consisted in a neglect upon the part of some of them to recognize merit in his numerous scientific publications. He was simply envious of the recognition and distinction they had obtained in the learned world, which recognition and distinction, as an author, he could not secure and which he did not deserve. It is a difficult task to analyze the motives and to delineate the character of such a man. To some he was a monster, to others a sincere reformer. Many of his admirers eulogize him as a martyr to the cause of human liberty. No one can doubt his honesty, they exultantly declare. Honesty! What is honesty? The cannibal who spits and roasts the missionary is honest; it never occurs to him that he is committing a wrong when he offers up his victim as a sacrifice to his gods. With him the act is a religious ceremony. The Indian who tortures his prisoner, who scalps him and burns him at the stake is honest. The religious fanatic who cracks the bones of the heretic on the wheel or draws him asunder on the rack is honest. If this be honest, then it is well that "to be honest is to be one man out of ten thousand." But what has the world to say of such honesty? Are the perpetrators of the acts of cruelty, barbarity and inhumanity to be admired or defended because they claim to be honest?

There is one, and only one, excuse to be made for Marat, and that is that he was mentally irresponsible. If he were not a man insane, then he was a beast, a monster.

He did not elevate men by his teachings, he debased them. He incited them to pillage, to murder. He confounded liberty with license, ignored the underlying principles of human justice, and set at defiance every sentiment of humanity. He declared a faith in Christ, but he was in no sense a disciple. His gospel was not charity and mercy, but vengeance and death. He professed a belief in God and yet he was not controlled nor restrained by any laws, human or divine.

In his conduct he was actuated by the lowest motives of the human heart, envy, and a desire to avenge a personal hatred and what he considered a personal wrong. To encompass his ends he appealed to the lowest passions of men and aroused in their hearts envy, malice and all uncharitableness, till he made his followers as bloodthirsty as himself.

He was never so happy as when he added a new name to his proscription list. He gloated and rubbed his hands with glee when the gutters ran blood during the September massacres. He was bent on destruction and his purpose was to level the whole social mass, to bring it down to one level, a low level at that, to do away with all distinctions, not only in political life, which was the real purpose of the Revolution, but in social life as well.

There was nothing of the fool in Marat. " He was neither a mountebank nor a charlatan," says

THE FRENCH REVOLUTION

McCarthy. He did not "caper to amuse the pit," nor did he make false pretensions. He was a serious, a sincere fiend, controlled by a relentless hatred, by a consuming envy, and dominated by the spirit of a bloodthirsty fanaticism.

He was intoxicated with the strong wine of the Revolution, he was drunk with its dregs; his brain was turned, his mind was disturbed, disordered. "It is also fair to say," writes Belloc, "that he was nearly mad." "We are inclined to believe," says Sir Walter Scott, "that there was a touch of insanity in his unnatural ferocity, and the wild and squalid features of the wretch appear to have intimated a degree of alienation of mind."

In the early stages of the Revolution Dr. Bourdier, who used to read Marat's paper, would, when it got too sanguinary, seek out Marat and bleed him. The doctor really thought that Marat's mind was affected by the excitements of the period, and prescribed for what he called his mental malady.

But this creature grew in popular favor to such a degree, that after his death he was paid honors almost divine.

His obsequies were arranged by the painter David, who gave full scope to his artistic taste and made the funeral one of the most spectacular ever witnessed in France.

The artist endeavored to imitate the obsequies of Cæsar. The body was exposed upon a catafalque in the Church of the Cordeliers; the dagger of the assassin, the block of wood which

DANTON

Marat used as a desk, and the leaden inkstand were displayed in open view, so as to stir the emotions of the people. To make the funeral more impressive the *cortege* left the church in the evening and the place of sepulture was not reached until midnight. Under the glare of the torches and in the solemn step of the funeral march, the procession passed slowly on its way; the multitude in silence stood uncovered. Young girls dressed in white surrounded the funeral car and chanted hymns in honor of this demon of assassination.

In the Place du Carrousel, a monument in the form of a pyramid was erected to his memory, in which were placed his bust, his writing desk and his bath tub. Sentinels were placed at the entrance of the tomb to guard these sacred relics. A decree in the Assembly in November, 1793, ordered the removal of the remains of Mirabeau from the Pantheon and directed that those of Marat should occupy the space thus left vacant. Eventually, however, his bust was destroyed, and his body, taken from the tomb, was dragged by a howling mob through the mud of the streets of Paris.

We have thus fully drawn the character and the incidents in the life of Marat because he represented and embodied in himself the worst features and phases of the Revolution. He was the direct product of its dregs, its hate, its violence, its anarchism, its bloodthirstiness. He was its *ultra doctrinaire,* the apostle of its gospel of murder. He stood not alone, he was but one of a

THE FRENCH REVOLUTION

class, and to have a clear conception of the Revolution it is necessary to have a knowledge of this class. There is a vast difference between Danton and Marat, but after all they were both revolutionists, and in the matter of comparison it is but a question of degree. They were partisans in the same cause, only their dispositions and methods differed. Danton never countenanced the wild theories and exaggerations of Marat; one was a practical politician, the other an unreasonable fanatic.

In the summer of 1789, Marat used his paper to attack Necker, Bailly and La Fayette. He unreservedly charged them with the embezzlement of public funds and with conspiring to raise an army for the subjugation of France. Day after day he repeated these monstrous lies and the constant repetition, without any public denial, induced many people to believe the charges were true. They were of course without any foundation and found conception only in Marat's fevered and excited imagination.

The authorities, at last, decided that some action should be taken against this maligner of persons and arch disturber of the public peace. Accordingly in the latter part of September, 1789, Marat was summoned to the bar of the Commune to answer for these libels upon Bailly, the mayor of the city. Marat failing to appear, a warrant was issued for his arrest by the Court of the Châtelet on the 6th of October; but the officials because of the public excitement and tumult on that day, occasioned by the march of the women to Versailles, thought it prudent to defer action until the excitement should somewhat subside. When the officers started out to find the doctor he had fled to Montmartre. From this locality he continued to issue his journal, without in any wise tempering the bitterness of his attacks.

On the 12th of December, the officers renewed their search; the doctor was found and arrested. He was taken before a lower court, but as the matter had grown somewhat stale, the prosecution was not pressed and the prisoner was discharged without a hearing. At it he went again with all his might. His escape from justice was taken by him as a show of weakness upon the part of the authorities, and his venomous, slanderous attacks were only intensified.

The authorities again took the matter under consideration and decided to arrest him at all hazards. Armed with the old warrant of October 6, 1789, La Fayette on the 22d of January, 1790, in order to enforce service of the writ, marched with 3,000 soldiers of the National Guards, accompanied by two cannon, into the district where was located the printing establishment of the doctor. It was the section known as that of the Cordeliers, in which Danton resided. The marching of so large a body of troops to effect the arrest of one person, shows the progress the Revolution had made and also the weakness of the authorities in the matter of enforcing the process of the courts.

Such a force on such an errand aroused the greatest excitement throughout the locality, and

THE FRENCH REVOLUTION

of course created a rebellious sentiment. Hot words were bandied and Danton declared that if an attack were made, he would arouse the faubourg St. Antoine and "make the jaws of the National Guards grow white."

While the tumult continued Danton found an asylum for Marat in the house of Mademoiselle Fleury, an actress of the Théatre Français.

Danton, full of revolutionary ardor, and his temper aroused by the presence of armed troops, boldly undertook the defense of the doctor and raised a technical point in the proceedings, that caused the officers to hesitate before making an arrest. He contended that since the issuance of the old warrant, a number of changes had been made in the law, and that in consequence the charge as originally preferred could not be sustained. While the officers were perplexed by the point raised, and were advising together what should be done, the wily little doctor slipped away and hurried post haste to England.

When it became known that he had escaped, the printing office with its presses was destroyed.

Danton's defense of Marat identified him with the doctor, who at this time was under public condemnation. For a year and a half Danton, in consequence, wielded but little if any influence outside of his own district. After the escape of Marat, Danton himself was summoned to appear before the court of the Châtelet, and it required no little legal ingenuity to secure his discharge.

Although this affair put Danton in an unenviable position and kept him under a shadow for

DANTON

a long while, it was unjust to censure him, for he had no warm friendship for Marat, nor did he in any way approve of his conduct in so far as the management of his scandalous paper was concerned. "No two men could have been more different than the learned, irritable, visionary physician and the young, healthy, country lawyer." But Danton had become for the time being Marat's champion and he had to pay a heavy penalty for his interference. Yet, after all, his conduct was only that of a young, an impulsive lawyer, who believing that the process of the court was being used illegally, could not forego the chance of raising a technical law point. Empires might fall and dynasties pass away, but such an opportunity was too good to lose. Danton was now considered by the moderates and the conservatives as a dangerous demagogue, identified with the policy and the purposes of a fanatic and a madman. The people, without ascertaining his real intentions, looked upon him as a lawyer who had volunteered his services in behalf of an outlaw, and who had purposely interfered with the process of the courts.

Danton resolved, for he understood the public temper, to act with more prudence and circumspection in the future, and if possible recover his former standing. He was a man wise enough to take lessons from his mistakes and failures.

The Revolution advanced at a terrific pace. Event followed close on the heel of event. The Declaration of the Rights of Man, the revelry of the life guards, the first flight of the nobles, the

THE FRENCH REVOLUTION

march of the women to Versailles, the return of the king to Paris, the meeting of the National Assembly in the riding academy, the confiscation of Church property, the issuance of forced assignats, the removal of religious disabilities, the abolition of monastic vows, the suppression of religious orders, the execution of the Marquis de Favras, the abolition of *lettres de cachet,* the repeal of the salt tax, the publication of the Red Book, the institution of the jury, the abolition of all titles of nobility, the dismissal and banishment of Necker, the affair at Nancy, the funding of the public debt, and the " Day of the Daggers " were but a few of the successive steps in the march of the Revolution, and during all the period from January, 1790, to the spring of 1791, we see no sign of Danton, except that in the autumn of 1790 he was chosen commander of the battalion of the National Guard of his section. He was evidently waiting for an opportunity to render such service to the public as would restore him to popular favor and induce them to forget and forgive his past errors.

CHAPTER VIII

DEATH OF MIRABEAU—LOUIS ATTEMPTS TO GO TO ST. CLOUD—DANTON INTERVENES—THE FLIGHT OF THE ROYAL FAMILY TO VARENNES

In April, 1791, Mirabeau died. All Paris was plunged into gloom. The remains of the great statesman were carried to the tomb with a pomp that was truly magnificent and with a respect that was almost reverential.

His death was hailed with delight by Marat, who with fiendish glee gloated over what he called the glorious news. In his zeal he knew the purpose of Mirabeau and while doubting his sincerity, he appreciated his power. He could make La Fayette, Bailly and Necker wince and squirm under his vicious attacks, but against Mirabeau his shafts were hurled in vain.

Robespierre was pleased beyond expression, but he gave no outward sign in public of his satisfaction. We can almost hear, however, his quiet chuckle, like the death rattle in a throat, and see that stern, white face, " always systematically unmoved," relax into a smile.

No expression of joy escaped from Danton, there was no hate in his heart for the great tribune. He deplored the demise of so useful a man and considered it a public calamity.

THE FRENCH REVOLUTION

Louis XVI, in this instance, had sense enough to appreciate the loss he had sustained. Danton and the king, from two different points of view, measured the worth of Mirabeau. The former knew his power as a revolutionist and the latter valued him as a reactionist.

In the early spring of this year Danton was elected administrator of the department of Paris. Easter was approaching and Louis expressed a desire to spend that season in the quietude of St. Cloud away from the turmoil and the excitements of the capital. It was not so much the seclusion of this suburban retreat he sought as an opportunity to make arrangements to quit France. The people understood his purpose. The radical journals had been informing and warning them that it was the intention of the king, at the first opportunity, to abandon his throne and kingdom.

Danton at the Club of the Cordeliers thundered against the king's withdrawal from Paris. He openly charged him with deception, with violation of the laws, and declared that he had no regard for the oath he had taken to support them; that he did not deem it as binding on his royal conscience, and that he considered the "Declaration of Rights" as an assumption on the part of the people of the king's sovereignty. He boldly asserted that Louis sought the retirement to St. Cloud, not for the purpose of convalescence, as was alleged, nor for religious contemplation, but for an opportunity to conspire with the enemies of France.

La Fayette had advised with the king in relation to his Easter trip, and was fully in accord with the plan. He assured Louis that there would be no trouble, but unfortunately he had no true conception of the public temper. The position taken by La Fayette gave Danton an opportunity to win public favor, and at the same time to oppose and humiliate his old-time enemy. He had not forgotten the treatment he received at the time of the Soulés affair and the incident of Marat, and he was determined to do all in his power to exhibit the weakness of La Fayette; also to prove to him and the people how little was the personal influence he wielded, even with the National Guards. It was a chance that Danton long had sought. He had patiently bided his time. On the morning of April 18, 1791, the king, the queen and a small *entourage* came out into the courtyard of the Tuileries to take the carriages that were waiting to convey them to St. Cloud. A great many people had gathered to witness the departure and after the royal party were seated and the postillions were ready to start the horses at the crack of the whip, the crowd choked the way. It was useless to attempt to persuade that mob, for they announced in no uncertain terms that they were determined that the king should not leave Paris. The crowd was growing larger every minute, the people came hurrying from every quarter of the city, for the news had gone forth that the king was about to abandon his capital. Lawyers, doctors, merchants, clerks, artisans and laboring men were in that crowd and they were all of one mind—

THE FRENCH REVOLUTION

the king must stay at home. They claimed that if Louis had the right to rule over them, they had the right to insist upon his performing his duty. They believed he was about to desert them and at the first chance seek the protection of the enemies of France.

They had the further right, under the circumstances, they insisted, of designating the palace in which he should reside. It was their money that maintained it and provided his meat, drink and raiment. If they were his people, he was their king. Their relations were reciprocal.

Even if they did not love Louis they did not want to lose the king. If he had abandoned them, they would have had the fear that comes to children in the dark. They could not yet imagine the State without a royal head. They had been accustomed to a monarchy and there could be no monarchy without a monarch.

If the time should ever come when a change in the form of government would be desirable, the people then would decide what disposition should be made of him—they might even cut his head off—but that was another matter, that point had not yet been reached. For the present, the people were of one mind, the king must remain at home.

La Fayette appealed to the crowd which had now grown to a multitude, and begged them to desist, but his eloquence went for naught. He turned to the National Guards and called upon them to secure for the king the right of way; he threatened, he cajoled, he commanded, but the soldiers laughed at his threats, turned a deaf ear to his flattery, and refused to obey his orders. Danton boldly combated him at every point and kept alive the courage of the mob. The mayor was sent for, but his efforts were as unavailing as the general's. Even the queen's tears did not touch the sympathy of the crowd.

La Fayette galloped in hot haste to the Town Hall, but Danton was there before him and strenuously opposed his demands. The general hurried back to the king, but during his absence the crowd had become more insistent than ever, and were growing angry, some of the leaders going so far as even to insult the queen.

For two hours the royal party sat in their carriages, hoping to start, but at last, finding it impossible to overcome the obstinacy of the crowd, they alighted and entered the palace vexed and humiliated.

Danton played well his part as tribune of the people and completely discomfited La Fayette, his old-time enemy. The Easter season was spent in Paris. The king was now convinced that the only thing for him to do was to escape the kingdom. He was no longer ruler, he was a prisoner. The Tuileries was not a palace, it was a dungeon. Louis had read carefully the history of James II of England, and believed that prince had lost his crown because he had left his kingdom, and it required considerable persuasion to get him to agree to such an enterprise, an enterprise that meant the abandonment of his throne and of his capital. But now being convinced

THE FRENCH REVOLUTION

that not only was he deprived of his liberty, but that his life was in danger, he decided upon departure. Preparations were immediately made for the journey. It was enjoined that every precaution should be taken to keep the anticipated flight a secret. It would have been death to the undertaking if the public suspicion had been aroused. This time the king was not to go to St. Cloud, but, if possible, beyond the borders of France. He thought it better and safer to wear a crown outside the kingdom than within its limits. The time had come, he believed, when he could not save the throne without abandoning it. His intention was to flee from France and then invade it at the head of foreign armies, and, if possible, reclaim and recover his heritage by subduing his own subjects. There had been many plots arranged by his friends to effect his escape but they had all fallen by the way because of the king's indecision, but now after much consideration, he finally made up his mind to take the risk. Under the circumstances, from his point of view and in consideration of the subsequent events in the Revolution, it was about the wisest thing to do.

Correspondence was opened with General Bouillé and arrangements were made to give the king military protection after he reached a certain point in his journey. The plans were carefully arranged for a quiet departure. The details were left to the direction of Count Fersen, the devoted friend of Marie Antoinette. He was a Swede by birth, a finished courtier, an accomplished man of the world, a soldier of distinction and as gallant a knight as ever drew sword in a queen's defense or breathed a soft tale into a woman's ear. He had been one of the darlings of Trianon and the queen's most ardent admirer. Indeed it was believed that he had played the role of lover and his protestations had been listened to with favor by the queen. It was said that he had leaped half clad out of the window of the queen's bed-chamber early on the morning of the 6th of October when the mob attacked the palace at Versailles. The excitement at that time was so great and the royal family in so dangerous a situation, that it is hard to believe that a lover under such circumstances would have spent the night with his mistress. The story contradicts itself.

The queen herself was to blame for much of this idle gossip. Her conduct in the past had been inconsiderate, she had ignored many of the conventionalities of life and had often shown a defiant indifference to public opinion, especially during the periods of her sojourn at Trianon. It goes without saying, however, that Fersen was devoted to the queen and was willing to forfeit his life, if necessary, in her defense.

He was in Stockholm when the plan of escape was agreed upon and he hastily came to Paris at the request of the king. He was exactly the man for such an adventure as this on hand, and he entered upon it with all the zeal of his nature.

He took two friends into the secret, Mr. Quentin Crawford and a Mrs. Sullivan, and it was ar-

THE FRENCH REVOLUTION

ranged that they should contract for the immediate construction of a commodious traveling vehicle, known in those days as a Berline, large enough to accommodate six persons. "It was a solid, well-built carriage, painted black and green, with the perch and the wheels the customary yellow," and drawn by eight horses. General Bouillé, who was to take the king under his protection if he should reach the frontier, had urged him to use two light English coaches, but Louis persisted in packing the whole family into one conveyance.

The queen, of course, had to make every preparation for the trip and, womanlike, she could not travel without a specially prepared wardrobe. "No queen can stir without new clothes," and so maids and sempstresses were set to work to prepare the royal outfit. "Dame Campan whisks assiduous to this mantua maker and to that; and there is clipping of frocks and gowns, upper clothes and under, great and small; such a clipping and sewing as—might have been dispensed with . . . But the whims of women and queens must be humored." The queen acted as if she were about starting on a pleasure tour instead of attempting to flee for her life.

While these preparations were going on, gossip in the palace began to whisper, and curiosity and suspicion were needlessly, foolishly, aroused. News of what was being done reached the ears of La Fayette and a closer watch, temporarily, was kept upon the king. When La Fayette questioned him in relation to what he had heard,

DANTON

Louis emphatically declared that he had no intention of leaving France.

At last everything was in readiness for the journey. The wardrobe was completed, the trunks were packed, the Berline was built, and the attendants were chosen. Baroness de Korf, a Russian lady, secured the passport that was to give the right of way over the public roads and across the frontier. When it was applied for the Baroness represented herself as a German lady going to her home in Frankfort. It was signed by Montmorin, minister of foreign affairs, and read as follows:

"*De par le roi. Mandons de laisser passer Madame la Baronne de Korf se rendant a Frankfort avec ses deux enfants une femme de chambre, un valet de chambre et trois domestiques.*
"*Le Ministre des Affaires Etrangeres,*
"*Montmorin.*"

The party were to start on the night of the 19th of June, but unfortunately, the departure was postponed until the 20th. This was a disastrous mistake and ruined the project. The plan was that they should travel to Montmédy by the shortest route, and there be met by Bouillé, who would give them protection until they were safe in a strange land and under the folds of a foreign flag.

The night of the 20th of June, 1791, was clear and starlit. Camille Desmoulins in referring to it said: " The evening was most tran-

THE FRENCH REVOLUTION

quil. On going home from the Jacobin Club about eleven o'clock with Danton and several other companions, we met only a single patrol the whole distance. The streets seemed to me so deserted that I could not help remarking the fact."

Just before midnight while the inmates of the palace were asleep and the guards were dozing at their posts, the king, the queen and those who were with them in the secret were astir. The children were awakened and dressed, the dauphin was disguised in the apparel of a girl. He was enjoined to keep quiet, but whispering into the ear of his governess he asked: "Then is this a play?" Oh, yes, my little prince, it is somewhat of a comedy with the sequel of a dreadful tragedy.

Madame Tourzel, the governess, led the children quietly through the empty corridors of the palace. They passed out of a door that by previous arrangement had been left unfastened and unguarded, and came into an unfrequented courtyard. Here was Count Fersen disguised as a coachman sitting on the box of a hackney. After the governess and the children entered the conveyance, they were driven to the Petit Carrousel, the place of rendezvous agreed upon. At this point they were joined, at once, by the king and Madame Elizabeth. The queen was late in arriving, having lost her way in the darkness of the night while groping through streets with which she was not familiar. She seldom, if ever, had traveled afoot through Paris and to her the avenues were a labyrinth. It is said that La

DANTON

Fayette's carriage drove directly past her, the lights flashing in her face while she crouched in an archway. "She had even the whim to touch a spoke of it with her *badine* — little magic rod which the beautiful then wore."

At last they all met, took their seats in the carriage and began their flight. The hoofs of the horses as they clattered along awakened the echoes of the street. Surely the noise will disturb the sleepers, for the quiet of the night was never so broken. The king is galloping out of his capital!

Not a soul in all Paris knew or even suspected that he was escaping. Here and there a stray light from a window threw its dart into the night showing that all Paris was not asleep, but no citizen made an inquiry, no patrol gave an alarm, no sentry stopped the way or called a halt. The fugitives passed through the gates of the city into the open country. They found the Berline awaiting them just beyond the barriers. The hackney coach was overturned into a ditch and abandoned. Fersen gave the word and off they started for Bondy, the first relay station out of Paris, just seven miles distant from the capital. When they reached this village the horses were changed and a fresh start was made. Here Fersen left the party. He begged the king to be allowed to continue on the journey, but Louis was obdurate and the gallant count rode back to Paris sending his god-speed after the queen. He subsequently reached Brussels in safety. When Louis was decided it was always at the wrong

THE FRENCH REVOLUTION

time. Had Fersen been permitted to accompany the royal party, the mistakes that were made might have been avoided. He was brave, practical and sensible, a soldier and a man of the world, and he possessed the wit and the resources that would have been of use in a crisis. All the details of the preparations had been arranged by him and the plans were successful so long as he was in charge.

The enterprise now had no leader and it blundered along every step of the way. The attendants were loyal but stupid. The hours were speeding, there was no time to tarry and so the horses were driven under the lash.

It was a lovely summer night, one of the shortest of the year, and before the second inn was reached, the sun was already dappling the eastern sky and the day was beginning to dawn. The atmosphere had been warm and close, but the morning air, coming out of the shadows of night, was cool and refreshing; it rustled the leaves on the trees, awakened the songs of birds, and wafted in every direction the perfume of flowers and the sweet incense of growing crops. Old chanticleer in every barnyard rang out in clarion tones a welcome to the morn. All life was soon astir. The lowing cattle in the meadows turned their faces homewards and waited patiently at the stile. The milkmaid passed the coach on her way to bring in the cows. The ploughman drove his team afield and following him slowly came the drowsy farm boy, as yet only half awake, who, rubbing his eyes, stared with curious surprise at the great coach and its occupants. The sun was up and all nature was responding to the magic touch of day. Louis was exultant.

Come, lads! put spurs to your steeds and gallop apace! an extra coin for your trouble. The promised "tip" produced the desired effect and the great coach traveled along the road at an unusually rapid pace.

It had been some time since Louis had sniffed the country air and it acted upon him like a tonic, and as the miles were rolled off and the distance increased between him and his capital, his spirits rose correspondingly, and he felt the ecstasy of a new-born liberty. He began to chuckle over the success of the expedition and wondered what the sensations of La Fayette would be when he discovered that his prisoners had fled.

He insisted upon poking his fat face out of the window at every relay station, confident that he could not be recognized through his disguise.

Every minute passed and every mile traveled made the escape more certain, so on they sped as rapidly as so cumbersome a vehicle, "with its mountain of band boxes," could speed. The constant relays enabled them to travel at a good pace and to keep up a fair average.

The travelers on the highways and the peasants in the fields turned to watch the vehicle till it passed out of sight, then they pursued their way or resumed their toil and wondered why the rich folk were in so desperate a hurry. They ascertained the reason for the haste the next day.

At Montmirail a trace broke and considerable

time was lost, upwards of an hour, it is said, in making repairs, repairs that would have taken an experienced horseman or driver not more than twenty minutes at the most. This precious time was frittered away by bunglers when every moment counted in this race for life. Fersen's skill here would have been of incalculable service.

It is related that, at this point, Louis dismounted and walked up the hill "to enjoy the blessed sunshine" and that he was so slow in returning that he lengthened the delay.

All day the journey continued, town after town was passed without interference and the destination of the royal travelers was not far distant. There was now almost a day's journey between Louis and his enemies and every mile-stone that was passed lessened the distance between him and his friends. He was all but in touch with safety. The royal party would soon be under the protection of Bouillé and his army. Hope was in every heart, there apparently was no question now as to their happy deliverance. The afternoon was wearing late when they reached Châlons. The postmaster at this town recognized the king, but being a royalist he gave no sign. It is said he even assisted in hitching the horses, in order that there should be no delay in starting.

Wherever the party had stopped, their conduct and appearance had aroused suspicion. Their anxiety at every station to get away as quickly as possible; the speed at which the horses were driven; the presence of three body guards; the lavish manner in which the couriers spent money, and the fat face of Louis at the window set people to guessing and the party no sooner left a station than a general discussion ensued.

Following the Berline was a carriage occupied by two ladies, whom the queen had insisted upon taking along. This also started inquiry. The next day when the news was abroad of the arrest of the king, there was scarcely a person who had seen him in any town through which he had passed that did not say to his neighbor, "I told you so." What a great opportunity they all had missed. If any one of them had captured the king, his name would have been written in the pages of history for all time. There had been but a narrow line between any one of them and fame, but they had all made up their minds too late. They had failed to act when glory stared them in the face. Opportunities make renown but the opportunities have to be seized.

Troops under the orders of Bouillé had been posted along the road from Pont-Sommeville, the first town beyond Châlons. The soldiers had created great anxiety among the people, who curiously inquired the reason for the presence, in a peaceful community, of this armed force. "We are waiting for a treasure and are to guard it," was the answer.

The king was six hours late according to the schedule, and the excitement of the people was increasing to such a degree that the officers in command gradually withdrew the troops, fearing that the plans had miscarried.

THE FRENCH REVOLUTION

When Louis reached Pont-Sommeville, the first town where he expected to meet the troops, his heart failed him when he realized that the arrangements had not been carried out. In desperate resolve he urged the drivers to lose no time in reaching the next town and the horses were put to their top-speed. It was nine o'clock when the travelers drove up to the inn at Sainte-Menehould. The horses hot and thirsty, their heads drooping, their bodies covered with a white foam of sweat, gave evidence of the furious gait at which they had been driven. This of itself created a suspicion, for why should horses pulling so heavy a coach be compelled to travel at so hot a pace?

As usual Louis poked his head out of the window at the very moment when every precaution should have been taken and at once he was recognized by Drouet, postmaster of the town and a rabid republican. Drouet had served at one time as a dragoon at Versailles and he saw at once that the companion of Louis was the queen. Some say that the inn-keeper was paid for the hire and fodder of the horses in a new fifty-franc assignat, and Drouet comparing the portrait on the note with the face in the coach was convinced that the occupant was none other than the king. The doughty republican took in the situation at a glance. The report was soon put in circulation, the news spreading like wild-fire. The excited people ran from every direction towards the inn, and somebody to add to the general alarm, rang the town bell. But the royal party were allowed to proceed and they started for Clermont at full gallop.

Night was rapidly advancing and the fugitives plunged with desperation into the darkness. It was indeed now a race for life. Not a moment was to be lost for all depended upon outstripping the couriers who surely would carry the news to the next town, arouse the people and detain the coach.

Now axle, spoke, tongue and trace hold together, let not a bolt fly from its place. Urge the steeds, postillion, with whip and spur, but hold a steady hand on the reins, for if a horse stumble or a strap break, all may be lost. Tonight a king rides for his life.

At Sainte-Menehould, Captain D'Andoins, an officer in the army of Bouillé, yet neither brave nor sensible, was in command of a detachment of troopers, but when the royal party arrived, he was so intimidated by the attitude of the people, that he was afraid to act. The National Guards turned out and threatened him with arrest if he attempted to aid the king. After the departure of the coach the captain mustered up some courage and ordered his dragoons to mount and follow, but the people surrounded the barracks, closed the stables and fraternized with the soldiers, who being plied with liquor became not only intoxicated but insubordinate.

This was the first body of troops the king had seen, but under a hesitating, if not a cowardly officer, they were of no practical use. Only one dragoon, a quartermaster in rank, and Lagache

THE FRENCH REVOLUTION

by name, displayed any resolution and courage. Mounting his horse, holding the reins between his teeth, and taking a pistol in each hand, he put spurs to his charger and dashed through the crowd scattering the people right and left in every direction. He was fired at and wounded, but he never drew rein until he reached Clermont and gave information of what had transpired in Sainte-Menehould.

It may be interesting to know that Lagache afterwards won distinction in the campaigns of Napoleon, was medaled time and again for bravery on the field, was promoted to a generalship and ennobled under the empire. His name is chiseled into the enduring marble of the imperial "Arc de Triomphe" and his glory made immortal.

After the fugitives left Sainte-Menehould, Drouet mounted a horse and, familiar with every inch of the road, followed the royal coach with the speed of light. As he galloped, he spread the news on all sides. Little did he know that he was riding to fame and that he was making for himself a place in the world's history.

The king reached Clermont before the arrival of Drouet, who was following the royal party like a spectre, but had not yet overtaken them. No time was wasted in changing the relays and the coach started on its way at once. A flying horseman dashed past the Berline and looking in the window shouted, "You are known." "Is he friend or foe?" anxiously inquired the queen.

DANTON

The stars were shining but dimly and the darkness as the night advanced increased every moment. The very air was filled with terror, for the bells from the steeples in all the neighboring villages were ringing the tocsin, arousing the people and greatly adding to the tumult.

No soldiers were in sight but the king's party were getting every moment closer to the army of Bouillé and they knew that their only safety was in reaching his protection. The queen pressed the dauphin to her bosom and for once in his life the king was anxious and excited.

Before leaving Clermont the post boys were directed in a loud voice by the body guard to drive to Varennes, so that when Drouet arrived in the village, he received just the information he desired, for upon reaching the crossroads he might have taken the one leading to Verdun instead of that to Varennes. In fact the statement is from his own lips that it was his original intention to go to the former town if he had not been informed by the fugitives as to the route they were to take. Had he gone to Verdun the king, no doubt, would have escaped.

When Varennes was reached at 11:30 p. m., the relay of horses could not be found. The king and the queen in consequence alighted from the Berline and walked through the town to look for the post boys. Frightened, anxious and excited, they lost their presence of mind and became bewildered. If they had crossed the bridge of the river that divides the town they would have found the horses awaiting them.

THE FRENCH REVOLUTION

It was now approaching midnight and the village was sound asleep. There were no people abroad and so the king knocked at the doors of several houses, in some of them lights were burning. He inquired of the inmates if they knew anything about a relay of horses waiting for the arrival of a coach.

While he was seeking this information, Drouet dashed into the town at full gallop, the clatter of his horse's hoofs making such a din that windows were raised and night-capped folk asked the reason for the excitement. As the rider passed the royal coach he shouted to the post boys: " In the name of the nation, dare to go no further, you drive the king." He reached the town inn, the " Bras d'Or," leaped from his horse, rushed into the house, found the landlord who had not yet retired, took him aside, and whispered into his ear, " Comrade, are you a patriot? " " Yes," was the answer. " Then let me tell you that the king is escaping from the kingdom." And now see Boniface bustling as he never did for the jolliest toper. A company of young men had been dining at the inn and were about to break up their feast when Drouet told them the news and appealed to them as patriots to give the alarm, call out the people, muster the guards and prevent the escape of his majesty.

The mayor of the town was awakened, and his children, frightened almost to death, ran into the street and not knowing what else to do began shrieking the cry of fire. Drouet, who seems to have had a clear head amidst all the tumult and excitement, hurried with some companions to the bridge, which had not yet been crossed by the king's party, there overturned a wagon and thus most effectually blocked the way. The journey of the royal fugitives had suddenly come to an end.

The troops of Bouillé that had been posted in the town mingled with the crowd, were served with wine, and were soon won over to the people's cause. It was an easy matter to convince them, after the facts were explained, that they should take no hand in the affair. The commands of their superior officer were not heeded and, deciding at once upon his own safety, he rode away in hot haste to the camp of Bouillé to report the insubordination and disloyalty of the troops.

The royal carriages were stopped at the entrance to the bridge. They had traveled sixty-nine miles in twenty-two hours, a pretty fair showing when all things are considered. The mayor of the town, Sausse by name and a grocer by occupation, demanded to see the passport. The king positively declared that he was none other than M. Durand and so emphatic was he in his tone and manner that he raised a doubt in the mind of Sausse, who hesitated to act, fearing he might be held responsible if he should exceed his authority. He was at once assured, however, by Drouet that there could be no question as to the identity of Louis. The mayor then politely, with hat in hand, invited the king to accept his hospitality for the night. Louis insisted upon proceeding on his way and ordered the drivers to go on, but it was no use, the people would not yield. Louis appealed to them but in vain. Had Fersen been there he would have been a host in himself, a stern command backed by the courage of a determined man would have been worth a score of timid requests or kindly tempered appeals. "For five and thirty minutes by the king's watch the Berline is at a dead stand. Round hat arguing with churn boots, tired horses slobbering their meal and water."

Louis again insisted upon proceeding, but some armed men in the crowd pointed their guns at him, and he lost no time in surrendering. He and his family took refuge in the shop of the grocer and sat on boxes and barrels till the morning dawned. Worn out with the excitement and the anxieties of the day, the dauphin slept. Poor little fellow! his troubles were only beginning, he was yet to drink the cup of sorrow to its dregs. It makes the heart ache to read the story of his sad and wretched life.

The villagers and peasants standing around discussed openly the question of the king's identification. "Oh, we know who you are," some of the men exclaimed in addressing Louis. "Then if you do," said Marie Antoinette sharply, with her usual indiscretion, "speak to him with the respect which is his due."

For some time the king endeavored to conceal his identity, but at last finding there was no longer any use in attempting to deceive the people, he admitted the truth. He then changed his manner and pathetically appealed to the sympathies of the bystanders, declaring that it was not his intention to desert France but to take up his residence at Montmédy; that he had left Paris because his life there had been in constant peril. He begged most earnestly to be permitted to proceed, and solemnly asserted that he would not betray those who at this crisis of his life would trust him. The queen, too, personally appealed to Madame Sausse and although she softened the heart of the woman she could not weaken her resolution. "You are thinking of the king," said the woman, " and I am thinking of Monsieur Sausse; each for her own husband." Just before daybreak the royal party ascended the narrow corkscrew staircase that led to the upper floors of the mayor's house. Under the windows the crowd shouted, " Back to Paris!" Louis was hungry, and called for bread and cheese and a bottle of Burgundy. What a contrast between him and his queen. Lamartine in speaking of her says: "Rage, terror, despair, waged so terrible a conflict in her mind that her hair which had been auburn on the previous evening was in the morning white as snow."

About this time officers of the royal troops began to arrive and they imparted courage to the king. Choiseul and Goguelat forced their way through the crowd, reached his side and bravely offered their services, declaring they were ready to draw their swords, to rally the troops and cut their way out. They told him that if he would mount a horse he could, with a sabre, carve his road to liberty. "If I were alone I would do what you suggest," said Louis, "but you must bear in mind that by such a course I would endanger the lives of the queen, my sister and my children." The king has been criticised for his timidity at this time, but few men under the circumstances would have taken such a risk, and he would have been a poltroon had he attempted to escape by the desertion of his family.

A brave officer named Deslon, five leagues distant from Varennes, heard of the king's plight. With sixty hussars he covered the distance in two hours and presenting himself to the king asked for orders. "I have none to give," said the disconsolate Louis. "If you can reach Bouillé, tell him I am a prisoner. I suspect that he cannot do anything for me, but I ask him to do what he can." Deslon, heavy-hearted, rode away.

Bouillé also started for Varennes, but meeting Deslon on the road was informed of the condition of affairs and at once retraced his steps. It was all over with him as it was with the king. The project that meant so much for both of them had failed; the plans had miscarried. Louis intended to make Bouillé a marshal of France, and had brought with him a baton for the purpose of conferring the honor upon his friend and rescuer, but they never met. Louis was taken back to his capital and Bouillé, humiliated by the failure, discarded and condemned by the emigrants, withdrew from public view and in a foreign land and among strangers ate the bitter bread of disappointment. He was censured for a failure for which he was not in any way responsible.

CHAPTER IX

PARIS AFTER THE FLIGHT OF THE KING—LA FAYETTE IN PERIL—LA FAYETTE DENOUNCED BY DANTON AT THE JACOBINS

Early in the morning of the 21st, Paris was startled by the news that the king had fled.

Baron Thiébault in his Memoirs writes: "When I awoke before eight o'clock, the streets of Paris were resounding only with the cries of the usual street venders, and with the noise of a few heavy vehicles. Presently a murmur was heard like the roar of a wave driven by a tempest. I leapt from my bed and had scarcely opened my window when I heard the cry repeated from mouth to mouth: 'The king is gone! The king is gone!'"

"In the name of God who is responsible for this misfortune?" cried the people.

The streets were soon thronged with excited multitudes and, to add to the tumult, every steeple began to peal forth an alarm and the roll of drums mustering the troops resounded in every quarter of the city. Danton hurried to the Club of the Cordeliers to quiet the fears of his followers and to urge that the time had now come to arouse a public sentiment against the further continuance of the monarchy. The Palais Royal rang with rumors, immense crowds gathered there and all was confusion, bewilderment. While the people were discussing in alarm the consequences of the king's flight, a man dressed in a threadbare great coat leaped upon a table and said: "Citizens: Listen to a tale which shall not be a long one and draw from it a moral. A certain Neapolitan once upon a time, while taking his evening walk, was startled by the astounding intelligence that the pope was dead. He had hardly recovered from his surprise when he was informed that the King of Naples was no more. 'Surely,' he exclaimed, 'the sun of heaven must vanish at such a combination of fatalities.' But alas! it did not end here for immediately the news was announced that the Archbishop of Palermo had just expired. Overcome by these disasters he hurried home, sought his bed, but could not sleep. In the morning he was startled by a rumbling noise which he recognized at once to be the motion of the wooden instrument which makes macaroni. 'Aha!' he cried, starting up, 'the pope is dead—the King of Naples is dead—the Bishop of Palermo is dead—yet my neighbor, the baker, still makes macaroni.' Come, my fellow citizens, mourn not, fear not, the lives of these great men are not so indispensable after all!" The man in the great coat jumped down and disappeared. The meaning of his sermon was understood, a broad smile spread over the faces of his audience and the people took fresh courage.

The crowd swarmed around the Tuileries and every moment their anger increased. The rabble

THE FRENCH REVOLUTION

from the slums gathered, pikes in hand, and threatened destruction to the palace. It was invaded, the doors of the royal apartments were forced. A fruit woman sat in the queen's bed and offered her plums and cherries for sale, declaring that the time had come when the poor should take their ease. The palace belonged to the people, the lawful tenants had abandoned the premises, without notice to the owners, and the latter were simply claiming and enjoying their own.

The women with a keen curiosity looked into the closets and tried on the garments of the queen. One of her caps was placed on the head of a young girl, but she snatched it off, threw it on the ground, and indignantly trampled it under foot, declaring she would not have her forehead sullied by such a head-dress.

The mob would let no one disturb the toys and the books of the little dauphin and they remained in his nursery just as he left them. There is always a chord of sympathy running through the hearts of the people; it has only to be touched aright to make it respond.

The walls of the Tuileries were placarded with offers of a small reward to be paid to any one who would bring back the unclean animals that had escaped.

Louis by his departure had abandoned his friends to the savagery of the mob. Especially did he jeopard the life of his minister, Montmorin, who only a short while before, June 1st, had addressed a letter to the Assembly, in which he had affirmed " on his responsibility, on his life, and on his honor," that the king had never thought of leaving France. He also imperiled the safety of both Bailly and La Fayette, who were his custodians and who had given every assurance to the people, upon the word of the king himself, that he had no intention of quitting the capital. Bailly and Montmorin, of course, came in for a share of the public abuse, but it was upon La Fayette chiefly that the suspicion of the people fell. They openly insulted him in the streets and charged him with connivance in having been a part of the plan. " You are false to us," they cried, " you are a traitor to the Revolution." He appealed to their generosity, declared his ignorance of the purpose of the king, and denounced his conduct as infamous. Danton lost no opportunity to increase the suspicion of the people and to discredit the general's loyalty. La Fayette displayed considerable tact in soothing the public temper, for he smilingly said when the complaints were loudest, " My friends, you forget that you all derive a personal benefit from the king's flight. His income is no longer to be paid out of the public revenues, and by the suppression of the civil list you save twenty sous each." The crowd quickly saw the point and applauded. It was strange he was not torn to pieces, for the people were exasperated beyond measure. He had time and again laughed at their fears and had denied every rumor in relation to the king's leaving the kingdom. He had placed implicit confidence in the royal word and was grossly deceived. La Fayette was an honest man and as such was prone to place too much dependence on the assertions and declarations of those whose interest it was to deceive him and to break the promises they made.

There really was no ground to suspect La Fayette, for no one in the kingdom had less of the confidence of the king and the queen. He was about the last man to whom they would have imparted the secret, or on whom they would have placed any reliance; but an excited people were looking for a scapegoat and they were not in the mood to weigh facts.

La Fayette rose to the full stature of a man during these perils; his serenity, his courage were admirable. He mingled with the crowds and saved one of his officers, the Duc d'Aumont, from the hands of the mob that had threatened his massacre. "He cast himself with calm audacity amidst the people to grasp again, at the peril of his life, the confidence that he had lost." Although covered with reproaches and charged with perfidy, he showed no wavering, no weakness in his conduct and "thus recovered by courage the dominion which he would have lost had he hesitated." He had the audacity of honesty and the composure that reflects the clear conscience.

"He is gone," cried Fréron, "this imbecile king, this perjured monarch. She is gone, this wretched queen who to the lasciviousness of Messalina unites the insatiable thirst for blood that devoured Medea. Evil genius of France, the

DANTON

soul of this conspiracy." Of course the columns of "The Friend of the People" teemed with abuse. Marat clamored for the death of Bailly and La Fayette; all the scoundrels of the staff, all the traitors in the Assembly. The Austrian woman, he said, seduced La Fayette in the night. Louis, disguised in a priest's robe, fled with the dauphin and now laughs at the folly of the Parisians and ere long will swim in their blood. "People," he cried exultantly, "behold the loyalty, the honor, the religion of kings. Remember, if you will, the story of Henry III and the Duke of Guise. At the same table they broke bread and pledged their friendship; at the same altar they received the holy sacrament and made their vows of eternal loyalty, but no sooner had they quitted the sanctuary, than the king distributed poniards to his followers, sent for the duke to come to his cabinet and there calmly witnessed his cruel murder. Trust then to the oaths of princes!"

La Fayette, in a measure having calmed the fears and the suspicions of the people, hurried to the Assembly and, mounting the tribune, demanded to be heard. He impressed the deputies with the truth of his words. He solemnly affirmed that he had taken every precaution against such an occurrence; that he knew nothing of the plot and never for a moment imagined that the king, after his positive declarations, could be so base as to deceive those whose confidence he had sought and whose doubts he had allayed.

The general also thought it prudent on the

side of personal safety to attend the meeting of the Jacobins. There was nothing better than to beard the lion in his den. When he entered the hall of the Jacobins, Danton was speaking and, leaving the line of discussion, the orator turned suddenly on La Fayette and assailed him most bitterly. " You have deceived us, you swore the king should not leave us. Either you have betrayed your country or you are stupid enough to have stood sponsor for a person whose confidence you did not have, and for whom you could not answer. How was it that the very same men who were on guard when the king tried to go to St. Cloud on the 18th of April, were on guard last night when the king fled? In the most favorable view that can be taken of the case, you are incompetent to command. I will leave the tribune, for I have said enough."

Danton was enraged to such a degree against La Fayette, whom he charged with negligence, incompetency or treason, that he imperiled the general's personal safety.

While the conservatives and the reactionists were endeavoring to soothe the public temper, Danton was inflaming it by his impassioned harangues. He had a most bitter dislike for La Fayette because of old scores, but he also had no exalted opinion of his capability. He considered him weak, unstable, vain, and inordinately ambitious to secure popularity, and further, at this point, he doubted his loyalty. La Fayette took the abuse complacently without making any reply, trusting that time would prove his innocence, but his composure only irritated and increased the anger of Danton.

Camille Desmoulins in describing the events of this day said that while on his way to the Jacobins he met La Fayette on the Quai Voltaire. "Convinced of the necessity of rallying round a chief, I yielded to the impulse that drew me towards the white horse. 'Monsieur,' said I, in the midst of the crowd, ' for more than a year I have constantly spoken ill of you. This is the moment to convict me of falsehood. Prove that I am a calumniator, render me execrable, cover me with infamy and save the State.' La Fayette answered warmly while pressing my hand, ' All goes well! The conduct of the king is infamous.'"

Camille then hurried to the Club of the Jacobins. When he entered the hall, Robespierre was in the tribune delivering one of his characteristic speeches. Cæsar, Antony, Lepidus, Brutus and Cassius were mustered into service; conspiracies were unveiled; patriots were in imminent danger of assassination; foreign legions were advancing towards the gates of the capital. The orator, carried away by his emotions, was willing to sacrifice himself upon his country's altar. "I know," he cried, "the fate that awaits me and I shall look at death as a mercy if it prevents me witnessing my country's misfortunes." Men sprang to their feet and cheered the orator to the echo. "We will die with you," exclaimed Camille, with his accustomed enthusiasm, and extending his arms towards the speaker. "Con-

THE FRENCH REVOLUTION

trolled by his impulses," says Lamartine, "he passed from the embrace of La Fayette into that of Robespierre, like a courtesan."

After the flight of the king, the Assembly directed his arrest and passed a decree of suspension. He had voluntarily abandoned the kingdom; therefore, it was asked: why should he longer reign? The throne was empty; why not establish a free government? was the cry. Now was developed and nurtured for the first time in the heart of all France, a longing for a republic. Louis himself had scattered and sown the seed. When the king abandoned the throne, Danton thought it was high time to destroy it. From this point he favored the absolute deposition of the king.

To avoid the perils incident to a vacancy, it was argued by many that Louis had been abducted. But this matter was immediately put at rest when his proclamation was read to the Convention.

It was, under the circumstances, a most foolish document to leave behind. It would have been wiser had Louis sent it to the Assembly after reaching the vantage ground of safety. It announced that he had been detained under duress, that he had been a prisoner in his own palace, and this being the case, he renounced his acceptance of those decrees of the Assembly, which he had approved under constraint.

The paper went on further to state that he had not been treated with the consideration to which as king he had been entitled; that his allowance was not sufficient to meet his expenses and to enable him to maintain properly the dignity of his sacred office. "Want of due furniture in Tuileries palace; want of due cash in civil list; general want of cash, of furniture, of order; anarchy everywhere."

The reading of the manifesto of the king in the Assembly was interrupted time and again by murmurs of indignation and shouts of laughter; especially was it derided when it related that "your attachment to your king was reckoned among your virtues; this attachment is now changed into hatred, and homage into insult. From M. Necker down to the lowest of the rabble everyone has been king except the king himself. You have threatened to deprive me even of my empty title and to shut the queen up in a convent. My aunts were arrested when they wished, from religious motives, to journey to Rome, and my conscience has been time and again outraged. When I desired to go to St. Cloud, my horses were unharnessed and I was forcibly driven back into my palace."

The Assembly, to show its utter contempt, took no action on the paper, but immediately proceeded with the order of the day.

CHAPTER X

RETURN OF THE KING TO PARIS

On the evening of the 22nd, news of the capture of the king reached the capital. At this time Louis was on his way to Paris, having left Varennes on the morning of that day.

Barnave, Pétion, and Latour Marbourg were named as Commissioners by the Convention and were directed to start out at once to meet the king and escort him in the name of the nation to the capital.

They repaired hastily to Eperney and met the procession just outside of the town. The commissioners straightway assumed control and all orders emanated from them.

On the night of the 23rd the king put up at the tavern in Dormans. A howling mob under the windows made the night hideous and with their shouts kept the royal travelers awake until daylight. Before leaving this town, Madame Tourzel, who had been riding with the king and the queen, was requested to take her seat in a second carriage with Latour Marbourg. Barnave and Pétion rode with the royal family. Barnave occupied the back seat with the king and the queen, while Pétion rode in front seated between Madame Elizabeth and Madame Royale.

DANTON

The dauphin was held alternately by his mother, his sister and his aunt.

Latour Marbourg was a man of some distinction; the personal friend of La Fayette and a royalist who was devoted to the king. He purposely rode with Madame Tourzel that his colleagues might be brought into close contact with the royal family, hoping that their sympathies would be aroused by the sad spectacle of fallen greatness. His plan worked well in so far as Barnave was concerned, but it went awry as to Pétion. Barnave was a barrister and was chosen as a deputy to the States-General from Grenoble. He was a man of superior talents and one of the most finished orators in the Assembly. He so moved the admiration of Mirabeau in the early sessions of that body, that the great tribune said of him: "It is a young tree which, however, will mount high, if it be let to grow." The queen was surprised to find him so polite in deportment, so thoughtful in his attentions, and of so superior an intelligence. So strongly did he impress her that she afterwards emphatically declared: "If ever power is again in our hands his pardon is already written on our hearts." He in turn was affected by her graceful dignity and his sympathies were stirred by her distress and humiliation. From this time he was devoted to the interests of the royal family.

Pétion, on the other hand, was stern and rude in manner and conduct, and openly in conversation insulted the king. While eating his luncheon, he threw chicken bones out of the window

THE FRENCH REVOLUTION

past the faces of the ladies who were under his protection. In his Memoirs he was indecent enough to write that Madame Elizabeth, as pure and as pious a woman as ever lived, cast her eyes upon him with affection, and he believed that if they had been alone, she would have fallen into his arms and declared her love.

At some places the royal party were received with honor and respect, but at most of the towns they were jeered and insulted by the populace. It was a long and weary ride, for Varennes is about seventy miles from Paris. The weather was hot, the roads were dusty, the crowds were dense and their temper was ugly.

No king ever made so sad, so humiliating a journey through his state. Twice before Louis had been escorted by the mob to his capital. Once when he came to Paris from Versailles after the fall of the Bastile, and again when he was carried a prisoner on the 6th of October, 1789, to the palace of the Tuileries; but those processions were of little moment as compared with this one. They were revolutionary but not antimonarchic. This time, he had been caught disguised as a valet, while attempting to sneak out of his kingdom; apprehended like a criminal, he was being taken back to his palace, but which from this time forth would be virtually a prison.

Louis took this degradation as he took everything else, amiably, complacently; but language fails to describe, even faintly, the queen's agony of soul, the indignation she felt, but which she had to conceal, the shame, the despair, the humiliation of her proud heart. "It was a Calvary of sixty leagues every step of which was a torture."

The people that crowded the roadside jeered and insulted the royal procession, but few kind words of welcome greeted the ears of the king. The constant cry was "Long live the nation."

An old royalist, M. de Dampierre, approached the carriage to pay respect to his sovereign. He was seized at once and murdered in cold blood; the wheels of the king's coach almost passing over his bleeding form.

A priest forced his way through the crowd and respectfully saluted the king; he was thrown down by the mob and it was with the greatest difficulty that the commissioners could save him from their brutality. "Tigers," cried Barnave, "have you ceased to be French? From a nation of brave men are you changed into a nation of cut-throats?"

In the afternoon or the early evening of the 25th of June, the procession entered Paris. "On Monday night royalty went; on Saturday evening it returns." The streets were crowded, windows and housetops were filled, the trees were loaded with people, every inch of available space along the route of the procession was occupied.

All the spectators kept their hats on, with the exception of a deputy named Guilhermy who remained bare-headed in spite of curses and threats. He was roughly jostled by the crowd but he threw his hat far over the heads of the people,

THE FRENCH REVOLUTION

and after this display of heroism he remained unmolested.

The order was explicit and imperative that the royal party should be received in silence. Posters bore the inscription: "Whoever applauds the king will be flogged, whoever insults him will be hanged." Paris was hushed, ominously hushed, the quiet only occasionally broken by the cry: "Long live the nation." The National Guards received the king with arms reversed but he was accorded no military honors.

It was a sorry entry of a monarch into his capital. The days had been when the city would have echoed with the cheers of a rejoicing populace in giving him welcome, but now there was none in all that vast concourse of people, to pay him the slightest respect. Drouet was the hero of the hour; he had galloped into fame in a night. He rode in the procession and his appearance aroused the greatest enthusiasm. The warmth of his reception only made the coolness shown the king more marked by the contrast. Drouet must have been a man of remarkable decision. It is not everyone that would have possessed his presence of mind and would have acted so decisively, under the circumstances, as he did.

The country postmaster, however, had risen so high and so rapidly, that the sudden elevation made him dizzy. He received so much laudation and attained so great a prominence that his head became somewhat turned and he annoyed his friends and the Assembly, to which body he was afterwards returned as a delegate, by his constant reference to the affair. He had only one theme and he never tired of repeating it until it grew

> "As tedious as a twice-told tale
> Vexing the dull ear of a drowsy man."

The palace of the Tuileries was, at last, reached. When the gardens were entered the mob made an attack upon the three *gardes du corps,* and they no doubt would have been murdered had they not been rescued by the commissioners. The royal family quickly sought the seclusion of their rooms. The first thought of the queen was to send a message to Count Fersen informing him that they were safe. Is it a wonder that she was thinking of some one other than her royal spouse, some one loyal and courageous upon whom she could depend, for how was it possible for any woman of spirit to have respect for such a man as Louis? His indifference, his complacency, produced in the proud and impulsive heart of his wife a feeling of disgust. She is almost to be excused for seeking the admiration and regard of other men. Her temptations were the result of her husband's weakness and inattention.

Louis was no sooner in the palace, than he was troubled by his appetite, and as usual called for chicken. He does not induce our sympathies even when he is in dire distress.

When La Fayette presented himself to the queen at the palace and politely placed himself under her orders, she insolently threw him her keys exclaiming sneeringly. "You are our jailer. I give you the custody of my goods." "Oh! your majesty," said the general in his gentlest tones, and bowing with the greatest courtesy, "you well know I shall assume no such duty."

The return of the king did not change the opinion of Danton, that it was time to lay the foundations for a republic and that the king's desertion of his throne and of his people was an abdication of his power.

Every precaution was taken to prevent another attempt to escape, and the guard was in consequence doubled. Sentinels were placed at every door, all the approaches to the palace were guarded. Every movement of the king was watched, his steps were dogged, and so humiliated was he by this system of espionage, that he did not speak to any one for several days. All the liberty the king had left to him was to stroll in the garden of the Tuileries in the early morning before the park was open to the public.

The queen too was seldom out of sight of the guards. Indeed she complained that her privacy was invaded even while she was dressing. At night when she slept the door of her bed-room was open.

Matters in a short time quieted down, a reaction set in and the moderates made a determined effort to restore the king to popular favor. The people were happy in the fact that they had him once more in their midst. They did not know how much they needed him until they lost

DANTON

him. They had been thrown into great confusion and excitement at the time of his escape, but they were soon to be convinced that they had gone to a great deal of trouble to recover that which they did not want, and after wrangling over the matter for a couple of years, they ended the discussion by chopping off his head.

The king prepared a report to be submitted to the Assembly and in this important work he was materially aided by Barnave. In his message Louis declared that it had never been his intention to leave the kingdom, that he had effected no concert with foreigners, with his relatives nor with the emigrants. He also stated that he had chosen Montmédy as the place to which he was to retire, because being near the borders, it would have given him a better opportunity to protect France from foreign invasion. The journey, he said, convinced him that the people favored the Constitution, and this fact he could never have ascertained had he remained in Paris. He also left his capital to show to the world that he was free to go and come as he pleased. Was there ever such a tissue of misstatements, of falsehoods? He had no more idea of going to Montmédy to remain, than of going to heaven. How could any one believe he left Paris simply to convince the world that he was free to go and come as he pleased, in view of the methods of departure he had adopted? He had donned the garb of a menial, he had assumed a false name, his very passport was a counterfeit, a lie on its face. He had crept

THE FRENCH REVOLUTION

stealthily out of his palace in the dead of night. He had arranged with Bouillé to be protected by his troops and he had told M. Valory that it was his intention to take refuge in the monastery at Orval, a town in the territory of the Austrians.

The truth was he tried to sneak out of his kingdom. There may have been every justification in the world for his conduct, and if he had boldly admitted the facts and had forcibly given his reasons, he might have strengthened his cause. He would immeasurably have added to his reputation as a man, and to his honor as a king. Strange to say, too, the report was in contradiction of the statements made in the manifesto which he left behind, at the time of his departure.

Marie Antoinette also supported the allegations made in the paper of the king, and declared that if it had been his intention to leave the kingdom, she would have persuaded him against such a course. The report, notwithstanding its inconsistent statements, had a great effect in allaying the public temper. The people accepted it because they were anxious to believe in the innocence of the king.

What would have been the result if the king had succeeded in his attempted flight? The royalists believed his escape would have produced a civil war, and that it ultimately would have led to the invasion of France by the allies, for the purpose of restoring the monarchy. On the other hand the radicals were of opinion that they would have had a free field for the building of a republic. The king's absence would have united

DANTON

all the factions in support of the new or provisional government that would have been set up until the republic was firmly established, and if the king had attempted to recover by force that which he voluntarily abandoned, he would have aroused against him the patriotic sentiment of the whole nation. Louis would surely have been weaker out of the kingdom than in it. He would not have inspired enthusiasm in a strange land any more than he did at home. He had not the spirit of the bold crusader and if he had escaped from his kingdom he never by his own efforts could have recovered it. He was the last man in the world, by his appeals and resolution, to arouse Europe in his cause. By the greatest stretch of the imagination it is not possible to picture him as flashing his sword and rallying his followers. Had he possessed the wit, the spirit, the resolution, the courage and the diplomacy of Henry of Navarre, he would not have been compelled to leave his kingdom.

The allies might have undertaken an invasion but it would have been for the preservation of their own thrones rather than for the restoration of a Bourbon king. The moving cause that would have induced them to act would have been a desire to destroy a dangerous republic, rather than to effect the re-establishment of the French monarchy. Had Louis escaped, his life would no longer have been in danger, and his personal safety being assured, a different question would have arisen for the consideration of the allies. For it is one thing to attempt to succor a king

THE FRENCH REVOLUTION

whose life is in peril, and another to undertake to restore the throne which he has abandoned, and judging from the feeble efforts made by the allies and their failure to relieve the king, there is not much assurance that they would have succeeded any better in effecting his restoration. His escape ought to have been, under the circumstances, a blessing to France and to have resulted in the establishment of a republic. The Revolution then, doubtless, would have been a different story.

Napoleon thought it was a great error for the National Assembly to order his return. It would have been far better had they directed that he be allowed to proceed on his way. They then could have declared the throne vacant, could have attained their great object, the establishment of republican institutions, and above all, would have avoided the infamous crime of regicide. " By bringing him back they encumbered themselves with a sovereign whom they had no just reason for destroying and lost the chance of getting rid of the royal family without an act of cruelty."

Danton was much enraged at the time of the king's flight, for he did not know how far-reaching were the plans, nor could he surmise the real purpose of the conspirators. But after the excitement subsided, he believed it would have been much better for France had Louis effected his escape, for then the republic would have been sooner and more firmly established. The voluntary abandonment of the throne would have united the factions in a common purpose, and if

DANTON

Louis had attempted by force of arms to recover his power, he would have had to assume the role of invader.

Danton at this time was the leader, the representative of the ultra revolutionists, and he boldly led the way in the direction of popular government. From this point there was no doubt in his mind, no hesitation in his conduct. He urged with all his might that the only logical issue of the Revolution was the founding of a republic. A reaction set in, after the return of the royal party, that favored the king, but it was of short duration. It was one of those golden opportunities of which the royalists failed to take advantage. The road to Varennes was the highway to the scaffold. Louis had sealed his doom by the attempted abandonment of his kingdom. There was, to be sure, an interval between his return and his final deposition, but it was only an intermission, a mere interruption, the final result was inevitable.

He had irretrievably ruined his cause, when he fled from his post and betrayed the nation. Because of his departure and the manner of it, he had lost the respect and the homage of his people. He possessed no longer " the divinity that doth hedge a king," and as time ran on, his presence in the capital became irritating. For the State had a monarch on hand who did not rule, and who, when the republic was established, became a menace to its existence, for he was the centre around which gathered all the forces in opposition to popular government.

CHAPTER XI

DANTON FAVORS A REPUBLIC—DANTON URGES DEPOSITION OF THE KING—REPUBLICAN SOCIETY PROCLAIMS REPUBLIC—THE ASSEMBLY DECREES THE INVIOLABILITY OF THE KING—THE CLUB OF THE CORDELIERS ISSUES PUBLIC ADDRESS—FUSILLADE OF THE CHAMP DE MARS

Danton was now determined, if possible, to destroy the monarchy. He was outspoken in his denunciation of the king. What valid reason, said he, has Louis to refuse to surrender that which he voluntarily abandoned? If he does not willingly abdicate, then he should be shorn of his title and power by force, but was not his abdication complete when he left his throne and attempted to flee from France? Before the return of the king from Varennes, Danton declared in the Club of the Jacobins: "Louis, after having sworn to support the Constitution, has become a fugitive, and yet I hear some one say that he has not forfeited his crown, but he has signed a paper in which he states that he is going to seek means of destroying the Constitution. The National Assembly should put forth its whole strength to provide for its safety. Confront him with this paper; if he acknowledges it he is a criminal, unless we are to take him for an imbecile. If he is an imbecile he can no longer be king."

Danton openly declared for a republic. He was one of the first among the leading revolutionists who took this stand. Robespierre, at this juncture, hesitated to announce his opinion. To explain his position, he said it was too soon to advocate a change in the form of government, as the people had not as yet been sufficiently educated on the question, and prematurely to make an effort, in that direction, would destroy the Revolution. Even the Jacobins, at this time, feared to advocate the overthrow of the monarchy. When Billaud-Varennes proposed in the club that the question: "Which is better for France, a kingdom or a republic?" should be discussed and considered, he was sternly rebuked by the president and threatened with expulsion.

"There were perhaps in July, 1789," said Danton, "not ten republicans in Paris, and what covers the Old Cordeliers with glory is that they began such an enterprise as the republic with means so small." Even as late as August, 1792, he declared in an address to the Council of Ministers, after Longwy had fallen, "*Vous ne pouvez pas vous dissimuler l'extrême minorité dans l'état du parti qui veut la republique.*"—"You cannot conceal from yourselves the very insignificant minority of the party in the country which is for a republic." Immediately after the overthrow of the monarchy, Barère is quoted as saying: "*Il y a une république—il n' y a pas de re-*

THE FRENCH REVOLUTION

publicains."—" There is a republic—but there are no republicans.

Danton thundered and raged against the men who, when every condition favored the establishment of a democratic form of government, hesitated to act but spent their time in arguing mere abstractions. He stood forth in this period of uncertainty and doubt as the herald of the republic.

On the morning of July 1, 1791, Thomas Paine, representing a Republican Society, startled Paris by having placards posted in conspicuous places throughout the city, and even on the doors of the National Assembly, announcing the advent of the republic. The proclamation did not mince matters, for it stated that the nation could have no confidence in a king who had broken his oath, had deserted his people and had attempted to join with traitors and foreigners in invading his country, with the purpose of subduing his subjects, abrogating the laws he had approved, and by force imposing upon the people the tyranny from which they had just been rescued.

No one knew how far-reaching was the influence of this society, but the audacious declaration that the republic was at hand, aroused the indignation of the conservatives and the monarchists and they demanded the arrest and prosecution of the members of this association, who dared to disturb the peace of the country by making so treasonable an announcement.

To quiet the agitation upon this matter, the

DANTON

Assembly decreed the inviolability of the king. This was at a time when a warrant was out for the apprehension of General Bouillé as the accomplice of the king in the conspiracy to escape, and when Madame Tourzel, governess of the children, the waiting women and the *gardes du corps,* were under arrest, held as co-conspirators in a crime in which the king actually was the principal, but in the eye of the law deemed guiltless. It was the application of the doctrine that " the king can do no wrong," one of the old sophistries and relics of absolutism. How in all reason and justice could it be argued that those who were acting under the king's orders and in his interest, should be held as criminals while he was wholly innocent?

It was not until long after the decree of the Assembly, declaring the king inviolable, that the prisoners were released under a general amnesty moved by La Fayette at the time of the acceptance by the king of the Constitution.

The decree of the king's inviolability aroused the anger and the scorn of all the radicals. The Club of the Cordeliers, nothing daunted, boldly declared for a republic and issued an open address to the Assembly. It smacks of Danton's style and no doubt he had a guiding hand in its preparation.

" We were slaves in 1789. We thought ourselves free in 1790. Legislators, you have signed away the power of the nation you represent. You have invested Louis XVI with unlimited authority. You have consecrated tyranny

THE FRENCH REVOLUTION

by constituting him an irremovable, inviolable, hereditary king. You have consecrated the slavery of the French by declaring France to be a monarchy. Good citizens have lamented it. There have been violent conflicts of opinion. But this was the law and we obeyed it. A healthier state of things we could only expect from the growth of intelligence and reason. This sham contract between a nation which surrenders all and an individual who gives nothing, it seemed necessary to maintain, and till Louis XVI showed himself an ungrateful traitor, we could only thank ourselves for spoiling our own work. But times are changed. This sham connection between people and king exists no longer. Louis has abdicated. Henceforth he is nothing to us, nothing unless he becomes our enemy. We are as we were after the taking of the Bastile, free and without a king. Is it worth our while to name another? This Society is of opinion that a nation ought to act either of itself directly or through officials removable and chosen by itself; that it is unreasonable that any one man in the State should possess such wealth, such prerogatives, as to be able to corrupt the administrative body. It is of opinion that no citizen of the State should be debarred from any State post, and that the more important the post, the shorter should be the term of its occupation. Impressed with the truth and importance of these principles, it can no longer be blind to the fact that royalty, above all hereditary royalty, is incompatible with liberty. Such is its belief, for which it holds it-

DANTON

self responsible to all Frenchmen. It foresees a host of antagonists. But was there no antagonism to the Declaration of Rights? In any case, this question is important enough to deserve the serious consideration of those who frame the laws. Once already the Revolution has miscarried owing to lingering regard for the phantom of royalty. That phantom has vanished. Therefore, without fear and without terror, let us do everything to prevent its resurrection. This Society would not, perhaps, have demanded the suppression of royalty so soon if the king, abiding by his oath, had regarded royalty as a duty; if the people, ever the dupes of this institution, so fatal to the human race, had not at length opened their eyes to the light; but to-day, when the king, free though he was to keep the crown, has of his own accord abdicated; to-day, when the voice of the nation has made itself heard; to-day, when all citizens are disillusioned; we make it our duty to act as the medium of its will by demanding the destruction at once and forever of this scourge of liberty. You, legislators, have a striking warning before your eyes. Remember that after what has happened you cannot possibly inspire the people with any confidence in any functionary named king. Accordingly, we conjure you by our common country either at once to declare that France is no more a monarchy but that it is a republic, or at least to wait till all the primary assemblies have expressed their will on this momentous question before a

THE FRENCH REVOLUTION

second time plunging the fairest empire on earth into the chains and fetters of monarchy."

There was no uncertain ring in the tone of this appeal. At the Jacobins, Danton moved that a petition signed by the people be presented to the Assembly, asking for the king's deposition. He argued that his flight was an abdication, and that the vacancy should be filled by the nation. This was revolutionary to a degree. But how should the people be given an opportunity to express their views on the subject, was the question. After much discussion, it was at last decided that the petition should be placed on the altar of the nation in the Champ de Mars, and Sunday, July 17, 1791, was selected as the day when the signing should take place. The altar of the nation, "*un tertre que l'on avait pompeusement décoré du nom d'autel de la patrie,*" was in the centre of the Champ de Mars and had originally been erected for the taking of the national oath on the 14th of July.

Public announcement was made by posters and in the columns of the newspapers that all that desired to sign, men, women and children, would be given an opportunity on the day named.

La Fayette was determined that this plan should not be carried out if he could prevent it, and he called upon the authorities to act with precision and to take every precaution against so flagrant a violation of the law. Bailly, the mayor of Paris, at once made proclamation that no crowd would be permitted to assemble in the

DANTON

Champ de Mars for the announced purpose, and that if the people collected in a multitude, he would give orders to disperse them, if conditions required it, by force. It was generally believed that these threats were not meant and that the authorities would not dare to carry them out.

On Sunday, July 17th, thousands of people, men, women, and children, gathered in holiday attire, not only to sign the petition but also to enjoy the excitement of the scene and the occasion.

The petition was laid upon the altar which stood on a wooden platform. Danton read it in a loud voice, and then called upon the people to fall into line and to come forward to sign.

Before the signing began, some one discovered under the platform two men. It was subsequently ascertained that one was a barber and the other an old soldier with a wooden leg; they had a basket of provisions and a keg of water. The two scamps had located themselves in this position that they might view the nether limbs of the female petitioners. They had bored holes in the flooring of the platform and evidently intended spending the day in this unseemly and indecent occupation. The discovery of these men created the greatest excitement. There was no time to ascertain whether their purpose was lubricity or treason, it was enough to know that they had been caught while concealed under the nation's altar. Rumors flew thick and fast, all sorts of diabolical plots were discovered, but the one that was quickly accepted by the people as the truth was that the two men were royalists whose intention it was to blow up the altar of the nation. The keg of water was soon, in the heated imagination of the people, converted into a keg of powder.

While the prisoners in the custody of officers were on their way to the Town Hall, after a preliminary hearing at the Gros Caillou, they were seized by the mob and literally torn to pieces; their heads were stuck on pikes and carried triumphantly through the streets. The people were greatly wrought up by the incident and in an angry mood made noisy demonstrations, defying in their rage even the officers of the law, who in the name of the mayor ordered them to disperse. The officers were howled down, stoned, and had to flee for safety.

Bailly, when the news was reported to him, raised the red flag on the city hall and proclaimed martial law.

La Fayette hastened to the Champ de Mars at the head of several battalions of the National Guards. The mayor read the riot act and three times commanded the crowd to separate. He, too, was insulted and defied. La Fayette straightway ordered the troops to fire, one volley went into the air, but the second cut into the ranks of the people, who, panic-stricken, turned to flee and in the crush, men, women, and children were thrown down and trampled under foot. The soldiers wheeled their cannon into position and made ready to fire upon the retreating multitude, but La Fayette, mounted on his white charger, ran in front of the guns and prevented further slaughter. The number of citizens killed was never officially announced; the radicals greatly exaggerated the figures and the authorities suppressed the real facts. St. Just said that the number killed was 2,000; other accounts varied, in some cases the number falling to a dozen. The reports were influenced by the purpose or the prejudice of those who made them. Not a soldier was killed or wounded. The rout was complete, but in the end it was a dearly bought victory. It was an important count in the indictment against Bailly, when he was arraigned in 1793, and materially aided in sending him to the scaffold.

The populace were maddened and rushed to the house of La Fayette to take vengeance by murdering his wife and children, but fortunately for them, a passing regiment of cavalry came to their rescue and routed the mob before any damage was done.

It will, perhaps, always be a mooted question whether or not Bailly and La Fayette upon this occasion acted hastily and without sufficient cause. It does seem as we look at the affair from this distance, that the massacre was unjustifiable. The object of the petition, the change of government from a monarchy to a republic, was clearly revolutionary, but the signing of the petition and its presentation to the Assembly were acts that in themselves were not unlawful.

The time was a holiday when men, women, and children in their best attire had gathered in a public square, surely with no intention of re-

THE FRENCH REVOLUTION

sorting to violence; the presence of the women and the children settles that question. The crowd was unarmed. To be sure the mob had violated the law when the barber and the old soldier were killed, but this act was not committed on the Champ de Mars, but while the prisoners, after a hearing, were being taken from the office of the Commissary of Police to the Town Hall. This was in the morning and the massacre took place in the afternoon, and some distance from the locality where the two prisoners had been murdered.

The affair, which was called the Fusillade of the Champ de Mars, caused for the time being a very decided reaction. The signing of the petition was abandoned; its leaves were scattered to the four winds. The Assembly passed a vote of thanks to La Fayette and tendered him its congratulations.

The department of the Seine instituted a prosecution against Danton, who left Paris when he found that his arch-enemy, La Fayette, was hostile and determined to bring him to trial.

He went first to the house of his father-in-law at Rosny sur Bois and then hastened to Arcis. While here in his old home and among his friends, he felt comparatively safe. "It would need a troop of cavalry to arrest him. Everybody was on his side." But La Fayette was vigilant and in pursuit. Danton took refuge in Troyes in the house of a friend named Millaud, and at last, to escape arrest, fled to England.

In Paris the journal of Desmoulins was suppressed and Marat suddenly disappeared from public view for a time. Madame Roland despaired and feared that the Revolution had received its death stroke. Robespierre in hastening from the scene of disorder was offered an asylum in the house of a carpenter named Duplay, and subsequently made this his permanent home. The mob was completely subdued. Even the Jacobins began to apologize for their errors. The blatant orators in the clubs tempered their eloquence. The curb-stone agitators sneaked out of sight and were as docile as a flock of sheep.

Danton while abroad did not lose his influence at home for he was in constant correspondence with his friends and watched with a keen eye the passing events, and was ready to take advantage of that change in public opinion he knew would come. While in England he had an opportunity to ascertain the real sentiment of the English people in relation to the Revolution and from his observations he was convinced that the government, as well as the people, was anxious to avoid any complications with France. In fact he found that the Whigs, under the leadership of Fox, sympathized with the Revolution.

When the reaction set in after the meeting on the Champ de Mars, the moderates rejoiced, but satisfied with their triumph and relying upon the protestations of loyalty to the monarchy by the radicals, failed to follow up their victory and thus lost an opportunity to secure the results that were so close at hand. This was a point at which, by

THE FRENCH REVOLUTION

the exercise of political wisdom, the Revolution could have been decisively stayed.

At the time the Jacobins moved to submit to the people the question of the king's deposition, La Fayette, Bailly, Barnave, Duport, the Lameths and their followers withdrew from the club and organized the Feuillants, an association composed of moderates and royalists, men who favored a constitutional monarchy. They signally failed to exert the power and influence they anticipated. By their withdrawal they thought they would weaken and perhaps destroy the organization of the radicals, but instead of accomplishing this end their conduct only strengthened their enemies, for the Jacobin Club now was relieved of dissensions and was composed only of ultra revolutionists. During this period, so decided was the reaction, that even the royalists began to assert themselves and in public wore their badges openly. The *fleur de lis* and the white cockade of the Bourbons were defiantly flaunted in the faces of the radicals. "The aristocrats," declared Madame Roland, "are actually growing insolent."

On August 5, 1791, Thouret made a report to the Assembly, announcing that the Constitution was completed. After careful revision it was presented to the king on the 3rd of September. On the 13th, he sent word to the Assembly that he would accept its provisions and that on the following day he would personally attend their session and take an oath to support it. Here was news indeed and the house rang with cheers. The Revolution had reached its consummation. The monarchy was re-established upon an enduring basis. France was now at peace and her future was radiant with promise. On the 14th, the king appeared in the Assembly and took the oath of allegiance to the Constitution. The queen and her children were in the gallery and they came in for a fair share of the applause. For the first time in months the air rang with "Long live the queen."

Everybody was in the happiest frame of mind. A new era seemed to be dawning upon the country, which had been torn and shattered by bitter strife and factional contention, for more than two long agonizing years. When Louis and his family returned to the palace, the deputies accompanied them as an escort of honor. The people joined in the procession and their voices rose in chorus, as they hailed in acclaim the king, the queen, and the dauphin. Better than the acceptance of the Constitution, should have been to the king the fact that he was once more enshrined in the affection of his people, but he did not seem to appreciate the influence of that invisible power of love, "the cheap defense of nations," that is in truth a stronger support to thrones and empires than are military glory and standing armies.

When Louis and Marie Antoinette reached the seclusion of their bed-chamber, they wept like babies over the loss of that power which they had always abused and which they did not know how to exercise. The nation believed the oath taken by the king was sincere and they in con-

THE FRENCH REVOLUTION

sequence applauded him to the echo, but as usual, he was playing a game of deception. A secret messenger sneaked into the palace that night and received from the hands of Louis a letter addressed to the Emperor of Austria begging him to render assistance in order to throttle the Revolution and to destroy that Constitution which Louis on the morning of that very day had voluntarily pledged himself to support.

It is perhaps not reasonable to suppose that a Bourbon king who had been kicked from pillar to post could have had much respect for the Revolution or the Constitution, but he should have had wisdom and sense enough as a politician to accept the inevitable, and honor enough as a man to keep his oath, or at least to have some regard for his word. There is no classification for his conduct other than that it was perfidious. " 'Tis not the king's stamp can make the metal better."

Count Fersen, who had been in constant communication with the queen and who in his zeal to serve her had abandoned his home in Stockholm and had taken up his residence in Brussels that he might be close to Paris, was much surprised at the queen's attitude to the Constitution. Her acceptance was apparently so sincere that he thought after all the Revolution might be at an end and that his services would be no longer needed, so he wrote to Marie Antoinette asking her specifically if she had accepted the Constitution in good faith. She answered at once: " Do not be alarmed. I am not going over to the fanatics. If I see and have communication with some of them it is only to make use of them. They inspire me with too much horror ever to go over to them. Be assured I will never espouse their cause." "Trust if you will," cried Marat, "the honor of kings and queens."

All Paris rejoiced over the adoption of the Constitution. There were festivities, illuminations, dancing in the streets and in the public squares. The Revolution was ended. France was rejuvenated and all was to go well. The Assembly was dissolved on the 30th and the king was present to take part in the event.

The deputies returned to their districts and provinces, and were warmly received by their constituents. La Fayette, upon reaching Auvergne, was accorded a most generous welcome. Robespierre was received at Arras with all the honor that could be paid a returning victor; he was carried on the shoulders of the people and extolled as the savior of France.

The whole country felt the inspiration of a new life, the past was forgotten, the future's prosperity was assured. Alas! how soon all this joy and glory were to dissolve, all the hopes and promises were to vanish like a mist.

The lauded and accepted Constitution had not yet been tested; it was to be put to the proof and it was soon discovered by the radicals to be too monarchical in its features and by the royalists too democratic. It was a makeshift and at last was torn to shreds by warring factions.

CHAPTER XII

CONVOCATION OF THE NEW ASSEMBLY—KING'S RETURN TO POPULARITY—REACTIONS IN HIS FAVOR—HIS ADVISERS—HIS DECEPTION—MARIE ANTOINETTE—RETURN OF DANTON FROM EXILE

The new legislative body was convened on October 1, 1791. Although Louis had gladly bade farewell to the retiring Assembly, he met and welcomed with no favor the new one. This was composed entirely of delegates without experience, for a decree of the last convention, in the nature of a self-denying ordinance, had provided that no member of that body should be eligible for re-election to the succeeding legislature.

"It was little more," said Madame de Staël, "than a council of village attorneys." In a total of seven hundred and forty-five members, four hundred and seventy were lawyers. The old leaders had been left at home and the people consequently did not have much confidence in the wisdom of the body nor much respect for its *personnel*. There were very few if any members with national reputations. The great majority were young, unknown, and untried, and in consequence discredited. "Among them,"

DANTON

says Watson, " were many brilliant talkers, men who had charmed the juries in the provinces by their eloquence, and the justices of the peace by their learning."

Capitals are great levelers of men with provincial reputations and Paris was no exception to the rule. The delegates, feeling their self-importance, assumed an imposing dignity which they thought was in keeping with their station, and thus disgusted the people and called down upon their heads the ridicule of the radical as well as the royalist journals. Unfortunately for them they stood in the place of men who had impressed the country with their greatness. Mirabeau, Siéyès, Barnave, Robespierre, and men of that class had been delegates to the prior Assemblies, and it required men of great ability to wear their mantles without inviting invidious comparisons. The fact that the Constitution had been made, and that a reaction had set in also greatly lessened their importance.

The welcome of the king had been so cold, he had treated them so cavalierly, that their pride was ruffled and they decided to retaliate. With this end in view, a measure was proposed, gravely considered, and solemnly enacted into a decree providing for the abolition of the title Sire. Such legislation was so mean in its conception, so paltry in character and so spiteful in its purpose that it provoked the ridicule of the people, and the whole town, from hovel to palace, rang with jeers.

As a consequence Louis now never appeared in

THE FRENCH REVOLUTION

public that he did not receive an ovation. The very populace that upon the king's return from Varennes had received him with an ominous frown and in silence now made the welkin ring with their plaudits and greetings. The monarch they had insulted and humiliated they now honored and exalted; yet it was the same king with the same mind and the same purpose.

There is nothing more fickle than public sentiment, so illogical and whimsical. During the Revolution it was like a weather vane that is turned by every wind that blows. The saying of Roscommon, "The multitude is always wrong," may be too sweeping in its generalization, but that the populace in those eventful times was capricious, inconsistent, and unstable goes without contradiction. From the days of Alcibiades and Marc Antony the demagogues have played with effect on the passions of the mob, but never in any age did they have so pliable a mass to mold as in France at the time of the Revolution.

If, at this period, Louis had exercised proper judgment and discretion, had adopted a conciliating policy, and had acted with firmness and decision, he might have made the reaction permanent.

"Even such a man, so faint, so spiritless," had he shown some resolution and courage, might have saved the monarchy. The tide had turned in his favor but he did not know how to direct nor to take advantage of the change. Accepting for granted that the future was now safe he was so improvident as not to provide precautions against a counter-reaction. This was the time when if he had played a skilful game, he could have won back his kingdom. He ought at once to have called to his side the ablest counselors in all France to advise him as to the proper plans to adopt under existing circumstances, but unfortunately for him he would not repose even in those advisers he called to his assistance that implicit confidence that was so necessary to enable them to render to him and his cause the aid that was required. Dumont, as we have already seen, attributed to him all the woes that fell to France and asserted that for his disasters he had no one to blame but himself.

Catharine II of Russia wrote: "The king is a good sort of man and I would like to aid him, but one cannot help a man who will not be helped." Lamartine says, "When we place ourselves in the position of Louis XVI and ask what could have saved him? we reply disheartened—nothing. There are circumstances which enfold all a man's movements in such a snare, that whatever direction he may take he falls into the fatality of his faults or his virtues. This was the dilemma of Louis XVI."

This was unquestionably the case after a certain period had been reached, but there were many times before he became so involved when he could have extricated himself and doubtless saved his crown. If, in the first stages of the Revolution, during the sessions of the States-General, he had insisted upon the meeting of the three orders in

THE FRENCH REVOLUTION

common it would have been a step towards the speedy settlement of pending troubles. There was a deal of time wasted here and much bad feeling engendered and the king controlled alone by the court party exercised no governing nor directing influence over the Third Estate. By his unwise conduct he lost their respect, whereas with a little tact he might have won over their affection. He was not well enough informed on the real issues to know what reforms were necessary, nor did he have any clear idea of what the revolutionary spirit meant. He was so loath to relinquish anything that at last he lost all.

One trouble was that he was controlled and influenced by men who deemed their own personal interests as of first importance and who would not brook the giving up of what they considered time-honored rights and privileges. The system they were defending had become so oppressive that it could no longer be endured and yet, in spite of all, they clung to every shred of it with rabid tenacity. These French Tories or Bourbons of the old school did not know that they were standing still while the world was moving on. They took no heed of the teachings of the philosophers. They sneered at the prophecies of seers. Their eyes were blind to the sufferings of the people, their ears were deaf to the appeals of the oppressed. They had no idea of surrendering their rights, exemptions and privileges. They opposed the destruction of any feature of feudalism, and so far as restricting the arbitrary

DANTON

power of the king was concerned, they thought that was a crime in violation of the decrees of God Himself.

Banished from France, their incomes and pensions cut off, their estates confiscated, their chateaux burned, reduced to poverty, to virtual beggary, they still took no lessons from their misfortunes. When the Revolution was over, they returned to claim their own; experience had not been to them a teacher, they were the same old Bourbons who, according to the witticism of Talleyrand, "had learned nothing and had forgotten nothing."

"Let wealth and commerce, laws and learning die,
But leave us still our old nobility."

These were the men who were advising the king.

Louis was so timid and suspicious by nature that he was afraid to commit his cause to the care of strong and energetic men. In the early years of the Revolution he retained Mirabeau and then would not follow his advice, and as for Bailly, his dislike for this official was so great that he would not even treat with him. He permitted his personal feelings to stand in the way of the safety and preservation of his empire. The reactions after the affair of Nancy, after the 17th of June, and after the adoption of the Constitution were all in his favor but by his inaction he lost the great chances they offered.

During all these periods the king's staunchest friends were importunate in offering assistance.

THE FRENCH REVOLUTION

La Fayette was more than willing to aid the king and queen, but they contemptuously declined his help. The Duchess d'Angoulême, daughter of Louis, upon one occasion in referring to the past troubles of her house feelingly exclaimed: "If my mother had been able to conquer her prejudices against M. de La Fayette, if he had been more trusted, my unhappy parents doubtless would still be alive." Fersen would have sacrificed his life for the queen, but she ignored his suggestions. She might have been safe in the camp of Bouillé had she allowed the general to arrange in his own way the details of her flight. Barnave gave her sound advice but she would not follow it. Dumouriez tried to gain her confidence but failed. It is said he threw himself at her feet, kissed her hand, and beseechingly exclaimed: "Madame, allow yourself to be saved!" Madame de Stael conceived an ingenious plan of escape that if carried out to the letter might have succeeded, but she met with a cruel rebuff.

After the adoption of the Constitution the reaction was so sudden and the change in public sentiment so great that the moderates became intoxicated with their success and foolishly provoked and defied the radicals. The conservatives flattered themselves that the Revolution was over; if they had been directed by prudence and wisdom they could have ended it, but uncertain in purpose, divided in action, and discounting the strength of their opponents, they lost their golden opportunities.

DANTON

The revolutionists were watching every move in the game and were ready to take advantage of every mistake. Danton from his retreat saw the weakness of the conservatives and directed from afar the plan of campaign.

The Constitution, that was supposed to be a carefully and solidly constructed foundation upon which the monarchy could securely rest, was soon found to be crumbling under the weight of the superstructure. The queen was beginning to lose her popularity because she declined to comply with its provisions in that she would not fill the household offices as provided for under that instrument. The king too, after his acceptance of the Constitution, provoked the people because he persisted in receiving the ministrations of only non-juring priests. Having sworn to support the Constitution he ignored its provisions by refusing to receive the offices of those prelates who had taken a similar oath.

Louis was never sincere and candid with the people. In his acceptance of the new order of things there was always present an apparent mental reservation. He was too shallow in character to play a successful game of deception. An honest, open avowal in his case, would have been worth a hundred subterfuges. At this very time he was corresponding with foreign courts. He knew the emigrants were making preparations to invade France, and that the armies of the allied kings were at a word ready to march towards the frontiers, yet he never boldly protested against their designs. A frank word from him

THE FRENCH REVOLUTION

would have quieted all France and disconcerted her enemies.

There was trouble, too, in the royal household. The king and the queen were at odds, they differed upon the policies to be pursued, their contentions and disagreements were so bitter that she one day exclaimed in despair, " Our domestic life is a hell." They were of one mind on one thing, and that was a dislike for the Constitution. While openly professing fidelity and obedience to its provisions, they never had an honest intention to accept a line of it. They were playing false and the result was a foregone conclusion. They were more anxious to avenge their wrongs than to accept safety under the new order of things. They apparently submitted to the present conditions, but with desperation they were still clinging to the old order that had been wrecked, and which they hoped in some way to re-establish.

The queen had a stronger mind than the king, but she lacked judgment, was without tact, and was at all times controlled by her emotions and prejudices. She had the haughty and intolerant spirit of the aristocrat and mistrusted all those that were not of her social class. It was impossible to make her believe that there was any reason for the Revolution. From her point of view there were no wrongs under the old *régime* that should have been corrected, no royal privileges that should have been abolished, no burdens on the people that should have been removed. In her opinion the king's right to rule

DANTON

was inviolable, was divine; his person was sacred; he could do no wrong, and the restriction of his authority was a violation of God's law. This, of course, was the result of her education and her environments. She had been trained in the school that taught these doctrines. The system appeared to her reasonable, she had been born into it; besides it had existed time out of mind and had the stamp and authority of age. She had never given attention to public matters but had frittered her time away in frivolous amusements and had devoted her life to pleasure and extravagance, with no sense of responsibility and with no imperative assumption of duty, so that when the Revolution broke she was not fitted by training or experience to cope with its conditions. How could it be expected that a woman born and bred and reared as she had been could know how to reign, especially in a period so tumultuous as to require the highest type of statesmanship? Perhaps after all she is to be pitied rather than condemned for the mistakes she made.

The Jacobins, acting with prudence and biding their time, were insidiously inflaming the temper of the people. Rumors were set in motion that the king was again making preparations to escape and that he was in constant correspondence with the emigrants and the allies. The radical journals which had not been suppressed or censored grew bolder in their expressions.

In November, 1791, Robespierre sold out his property in Arras and moved to Paris. Even

THE FRENCH REVOLUTION

Marat emerged from his place of concealment, and Danton returned from England more determined than ever to overthrow the monarchy. Since he left France conditions had greatly changed. The reaction in favor of the king that had set in after the meeting on the Champ de Mars had been followed by another change in public sentiment. The fires of the Revolution had been only temporarily smothered; the embers were still burning in the ashes and required but a breath to blow them into a flame.

CHAPTER XIII

THE FEUILLANTS—THE CLUB OF THE CORDELIERS WHERE DANTON RULED—THE GIRONDINS—MADAME ROLAND — WAR ISSUES — DANTON AFTER SOME HESITATION FAVORS THE WAR—VETOES — DUMOURIEZ — DANTON AND DUMOURIEZ

The Revolution was rapidly becoming a war for factional supremacy. Among so many discordant elements there could not be made a fair division of the raiment, and so it became a struggle for the survival of the fittest. It had already been shown, by the efforts that had been made, that it was impossible for the monarchists and the revolutionists to frame a constitution or to create a form of government that would be acceptable to both. It was like the question that afterwards confronted the American Republic, which, it was contended, could not exist half slave and half free. To establish a stable government either the royalists or the republicans had to be in the ascendancy, and so the bitter, bloody struggle for supremacy began in earnest.

The Feuillants, composed of La Fayette, Barnave, the Lameths, Bailly, Duport, Siéyès and other less distinguished men, having withdrawn from the Club of the Jacobins, had discarded the

THE FRENCH REVOLUTION

ultra-radical views of that organization. They represented the liberal nobles and the better educated of the middle class. They sincerely supported the Constitution and labored in every way to strengthen the foundations of the monarchy, but their efforts in a great measure were neutralized by the insincerity and the vacillating policy of Louis, and by the silly action and imprudent conduct of the emigrants at Coblentz.

To retain their popularity, which was fast waning, they attempted to arouse a war spirit, advocating the raising of armies to resist the threatened invasion of the allies. This policy they adopted to convince the people that they had no part in the negotiations that were supposed to be taking place between Louis and the Emperor of Austria, the King of Prussia and the emigrant princes.

Though the events of June 17th, which threw such terror into the ranks of the radicals, were still vivid in the public mind, the Jacobins began to express openly their views.

The Club of the Cordeliers at this time surpassed the Jacobins in turbulence and liberalism. Danton dominated there and he supported no half-hearted measures. He was in favor of the deposition of the king, and the establishment of a republic; he also advocated the raising of an army to repel the threatened invasion of the allies.

His voice rang out in no uncertain tones. Since his return from England his sentiments had grown more revolutionary than ever. His exile perhaps had embittered him against the conservatives and he fought them with a bitterness that was at times somewhat personal and vindictive in its character.

Perhaps the most interesting party of that historic period was that of the Girondins. It was originally organized by the deputies in the Assembly from the department of the Gironde, although all its members did not come from that district; in fact its leader or political chief, Brissot, hailed from Normandy.

The men who formed this party or faction were of the educated middle class. They were, in many instances, dreamers and illusionists but their purposes were sincere and their patriotism was unquestioned. Their heroism, their surpassing eloquence, and the courageous manner in which they met their doom, have created for them an admiration, a love, and an enduring sympathy everywhere and for all time in the hearts of men. So long as history shall be written their deeds will be recounted. Brissot, Vergniaud, Gensonné, Guadet, Isnard, Barbaroux, and Louvet were its most distinguished representatives.

Madame Roland was a ruling spirit in their conferences. Her *salon* was the rallying point of their clan. It, in time, became the focus of the Revolution or what has been appropriately called the Second Revolution. Here in charming conversation, animated and eloquent, the world was made anew and the liberty of man secured. It was not all illusion, however, for in

THE FRENCH REVOLUTION

the parlors of this remarkable woman were conceived many of the plans and the bloody projects that helped to overthrow the monarchy.

This woman, who played so important a part in the scenes of the Revolution, was born in Paris in 1754. Her father was a distinguished engraver, who lost his fortune by dissipation. She was a woman of deep sympathies, strong passions, and of an ardent and a loving nature. Her intellect was precocious and even in early childhood she acquired knowledge without an apparent effort. From her youth she devoted herself to a close study of the ancients and she lived in a world of her own creation, where the men were free and the women virtuous and where all were equal before the law. Her heroes stepped out of the pages of Plutarch and were as cold, as severe, and as precise as that austere biographer has described them. She readily acquired the polite accomplishments of women, yet at the same time her powerful mind took within its grasp and comprehension the abstruse principles of the sciences. She early became familiar with the writings of the English philosophers and studied with a full knowledge the works of Voltaire, Rousseau, and Montesquieu. She had the faculty of easily acquiring the correct use of foreign tongues and spoke them with remarkable fluency.

Such a woman, it might be supposed, was something of a blue-stocking, but she was anything in the world but that. It has been said that with her great knowledge, she was not even pedantic. Not only was she renowned for her animated and radiant intelligence, but also for her dazzling beauty. "A tall and supple figure, flat shoulders, a prominent bust raised by a free and strong respiration, a modest and most becoming demeanor, that carriage of the neck which bespeaks intrepidity, black and soft hair, blue eyes which appeared brown in the depths of their reflection, a look which, like her soul, passed rapidly from tenderness to energy, the nose of a Grecian statue, a rather large mouth, splendid teeth, a turned and well-rounded chin that gave to the oval of her features that voluptuous and feminine grace without which even beauty does not elicit love, a skin marbled with the animation of life and veined by blood which the least impression sent mounting to her cheeks, a tone of voice which borrowed its vibrations from the deepest fibres of her heart and which was deeply modulated by its finest movements." Such is the description we have of her.

In her twenty-first year she met M. J. M. Roland de la Platiere, inspector general at Lyons, a man many years her senior, "of antique manners, without reproach except for his passion for the ancients, his contempt of his age, and his too high estimation of his own virtue." He more closely approached her ideal than any one she had up to that time ever met. He asked her father for her hand, but the old gentleman, in view of the disparity in their ages and possessed with more worldly wisdom than his daughter, strenuously objected to the union. Her parent's

Madame Roland
From an engraving in the collection of
William J. Latta, Esq.

THE FRENCH REVOLUTION

stern refusal only increased her desire, and surrendering to her emotions, she straightway retired to a convent, destitute of everything. But this sacrifice on her part did not seem to affect M. Roland as she had hoped it would, and she was greatly disappointed in his conduct. She was somewhat like the maiden who to test the ardor of her lover threw herself into a torrent and was disappointed to find that his affection stopped at the shore. The philosopher had passed the ardent stage of youth and was not only too wise but too old to climb stone walls or force an entrance into a prison. Love with him was not a fire; it was a condition.

For some time after her departure he did not visit her and seldom wrote. After an interval of six months, however, he came to the convent, proposed, and was accepted. She was devoted and self-sacrificing, but as she soon discovered it was to a philosopher and not to a lover, that is a lover after her own ideals. She had been impressed by the lofty and profound views of this sage and mistook admiration for passion. "The one sought a disciple rather than a wife and the other married a master rather than a husband," and the union resulted in what might have been expected. She made the mistake of uniting herself with a man for whom she had a high personal regard but for whom she had not that ardent love, that continuing passion that alone binds closely man and woman.

Of a proud and lofty nature she endured that agony that tests the virtue of even an honorable woman. "I have not," she said, "for a moment ceased to see in my husband a most estimable person and to whom it was an honor to me to belong; but I often felt that similarity was wanting between us. If we lived in solitude I sometimes had very painful hours to pass, if we went into the world I was liked by persons, some one of whom I was fearful might affect me too closely." The temptation she endeavored to avoid she yielded to at last when she met the handsome Buzot and she broke her husband's heart when she revealed to him the secret.

In 1789 she was living in the country on the paternal estate of her husband. The tocsin of the Revolution rang in her ears like an alarm in the night and stirred all the emotions of her soul. During her residence in the country she had become familiar with the sufferings and the degradation of the poor peasants and she had labored hard to relieve their distresses. In her immediate locality she had essayed the role of Lady Bountiful.

Her heart having been touched, she longed for the coming of that day when tyranny would cease its exactions and when men would enjoy that state under the law that would enable them to realize the happiness that comes from opportunity and political equality. To her the excitements of the Revolution brought new life, new inspirations, new occupations, and what was better than all, a change in the irksome monotony of her existence. It furnished a stage upon which to play a distinguished role. "She adored the Revolu-

THE FRENCH REVOLUTION

tion like a lover" and she gave to it that devotion she would have given to a husband who responded to her heart's desires.

On the 20th of February, 1791, in the thirty-third year of her age and in the full bloom of her womanhood, she came with M. Roland to take up her residence in Paris. She had been absent from the capital for a period of five years. She at once took a leading part in public affairs and towards the close of 1791 was the mouthpiece of a party.

When her husband was in the cabinet she exerted a far-reaching influence and at times took too conspicuous a part in the business of the department. Condorcet, alluding to this matter, said: "When I wish to see Roland I can never get a glimpse of anything but the petticoats of his wife." "She occupied," says Barras, "with obstinate assurance the closet of the minister." She may have thought that she was fitted to lead a party but she really had not even the fundamental qualities of a politician. She was too visionary, too emotional; she often injured her cause by speaking too freely upon political questions and by criticising too severely her enemies and public men. Her sarcasm cut to the quick and her sneer was scorn itself. She would risk an empire rather than let pass an opportunity for a *bon mot*.

She did not possess that great faculty of accurate discrimination in judging character that is so essential to the success of the politician. Controlled by her prejudices, her ill-timed criticisms

DANTON

of men and measures often made enemies when a little tact could have made friends. The great trouble with her from a political point of view was that she talked too much and constantly involved her friends and party in explanations.

She sought in every way to strengthen her influence and to increase her power, for her ambition was boundless. She tried to win over to her cause even the icy heart of Robespierre. "She flattered Danton, but with fear and repugnance as a woman would pat a lion." She conceived for him a mortal dislike which she could not overcome. "I looked," she said, "at this repulsive and humble face and though I feel I ought not to judge a man on hearsay and that I know nothing against him . . . I could not associate an honest man with such a countenance. I have never seen anything so absolutely the incarnation of brutal passion and astounding audacity half veiled under an appearance of immense joviality and an affectation of great *bon-hommie*. Often have I pictured to myself Danton, dagger in hand, hounding on with voice and gesture a band of assassins more cowardly and less savage than himself." He must truly have seemed out of place in the parlors of the Roland mansion where his herculean form towered above the cultured, classical enthusiasts that paid court and homage to their plebeian queen. Bold, outspoken, and not always restrained by the precise etiquette of fashionable drawing-rooms, his rough, scarred features and his generous laugh made him appear *outré* in so polite and gallant an

THE FRENCH REVOLUTION

assemblage. Yet in spite of this she ought to have cultivated the real friendship of this man, for, as time will show, he was the one above all others who could have saved her party from destruction. In the end she was the evil genius of the Girondins as Marie Antoinette was of the royalists.

Madame Roland had an utter contempt for the queen. She was outspoken enough to declare that the time had come when "two illustrious heads," referring to the king and the queen, "should be brought to trial." In her denunciation of the queen she was always bitter and cruel, often alluding to her as a Messalina and intimating that her crimes were no less in number and of a character no better than those of that detested Roman empress.

When Madame Roland's affection for Buzot was made known, scandal played wild havoc with her name. Virtue was no longer her defense and she was attacked most bitterly from every quarter. Those enemies whom she had assailed with her vituperation paid her back in the same coin without discount. Marat, who spared neither man nor woman in his abuse, poured upon her head the vials of his wrath. He called her "Queen Coco" and Penelope. He subjected her to execration and held her poor husband up to public ridicule as a cuckold, the plaything of a wanton.

At this period, the close of 1791, the Girondins were in power, that is they were the strongest of the factions in the convention. The war was the

DANTON

sole absorbing theme. Its dire shadow fell athwart France and cast a gloom in every patriotic heart and home. As a party the Girondins were in favor of it. Marat argued with all his might against it. He predicted that it would be a field of glory for the rich and a hell for the poor and doubtless would result in the establishment of a military despotism and the overthrow of social order. Robespierre was opposed to it from partisan motives. He believed it would put the Girondins further in the ascendency. La Fayette declared that the Jacobins were influenced in their opposition by the fear that it would be directed by their rivals and also by the fact that several of them, like Danton, were interested financially in the secret negotiations with the court party. This was one of the suspicions of La Fayette for which at a later date he had to answer.

It is true that Danton at first hesitated upon the question of the declaration of war, for in the interest of France he would gladly have favored any honorable plan that would have avoided the conflict. He was ready at all times to repel invasion and would have been willing to shed the last drop of French blood in driving back a foreign foe, but he would not under any circumstances for the glory of his party provoke a war. From the very beginning, however, he thought that a foreign war was inevitable. "I know it must come," he said. "If anyone were to ask me, are we to have war? I would reply, we shall hear the bugles." When at last it did come no

THE FRENCH REVOLUTION

one gave it more ardent and loyal support. Brissot, as the leader of the Girondins, appealed to the nation to resent the insult offered to France by the allied kings who, gathering their armed hosts on the frontiers, not only menaced her peace but also defied the courage of her sons. The Girondins no doubt were actuated by a patriotic spirit, but they also clearly saw that a war would be to their advantage politically; and that unquestionably had its weight in controlling their action. The stand they took was popular and greatly strengthened them for the time being in public opinion.

War! War! was the cry everywhere. The revolutionary journals published the most inflammatory appeals while the orators harangued the people at the clubs, on the street corners and in the gardens of the Palais Royal.

The autumn of 1791 was dark and gloomy and gave every promise of a cheerless winter. In November the Assembly decreed that the emigrants would be deemed guilty of conspiracy if they still remained on the frontiers on January 1, 1792, and if captured it was further decreed that they would be punished by death and their lands confiscated by the government, which confiscation however, would not prejudice the rights of wives, children, and creditors. The king refused to sanction this act. The Assembly a few days later decreed that the priests who persisted in rebellion against the State should take the oath of allegiance; if they refused, they should be deprived of their salaries and driven out of their parishes.

DANTON

The king also vetoed this measure. How was it possible for him to retain the support and confidence of the people if he was determined to defeat those laws which provided for the punishment of traitors—for the emigrants were so classed by the people—and which required upon the part of the clergy the observance of a constitutional provision? And yet, to be fair, it was no easy thing from his standpoint to approve such legislation.

There was no violent outbreak following these vetoes and Louis congratulated himself that his action had seemingly received the approval of the nation, but he never made a greater mistake in his life. The silence of the people was but evidence of a sullen mood. Step by step he was paving his way to the scaffold. To appease the public temper he issued at the same time a proclamation calling upon all emigrants to return and promising them that protection which they claimed they could not secure.

From the people's point of view there was no sound reason for his disapproval of those measures he vetoed. The emigrants were plotting with the enemies of France and were menacing the peace of the country. They were endeavoring by every possible means to induce strange kings to start upon a march of invasion. Condé, himself, was enlisting men for this purpose and openly declaring his intentions. There was no concealment of these facts, they were known to the world. The emigrants had not renounced their citizenship and consequently were traitors.

THE FRENCH REVOLUTION

Many of them still claimed their pensions and were receiving rentals from their landed possessions.

When Louis was requested to consent to a decree requiring the German princes to disperse the emigrants, he was asked by Vaublanc if he thought his great ancestor, Louis XIV, would have permitted, after the revocation of the edict of Nantes, the assembling of armed Huguenots on the territory of German princes and under their protection. The king replied that he had notified the German princes that the continued gathering of hostile forces would be taken as cause for war, and that he had instructed the minister to move 100,000 men to the frontier to make ready to repel any invasion, and that the forts on the border had been garrisoned, supplied with ammunition, and put in a state of defense.

Leopold, emperor of Austria, the brother of Marie Antoinette, answered the note of Louis by saying that he would not tolerate any violation of the imperial territory. His letter was so belligerent in tone that it only intensified the war spirit throughout the country.

On February 7, 1792, a treaty was made between Austria and Prussia to quell the disturbances in France. Solemn conferences were held to consider plans for invasion and for the re-establishment of the old order. France had no controversy with the outer world, her troubles were all domestic; the question as to whether or not she should be a monarchy or a republic was one for her people to decide without any foreign interference. She had not offended any state or empire nor had she broken any law under the international code. What right then had these nations to league themselves against France?

The aristocracy had abandoned their country and had taken refuge on German soil where, under the protection of foreign princes, they had plotted against the home government. The French emigrants had virtually established a court at Coblentz. They advised on public questions, issued proclamations, made treaties, entered into negotiations with foreign states and rulers, insolently threatened to destroy the great results of the Revolution, placed rewards upon the heads of distinguished rebels, and arrogantly announced what they would do upon their re-entry into France. They divided the spoils before the battle was fought and sentenced men to execution before they were captured. They had simply transferred the court temporarily, as they supposed, from Versailles to Coblentz. They preserved all the customs and the etiquette of their former state. Envy and jealousy marked their conduct towards each other; gossip, as of old, was their diversion. They lavished on every hand ribbons, medals, titles, honors, and distinctions. They were the same silly, vain and insolent set they had been at home. It had made no difference in them to sit by the waters of Babylon instead of by those of the Seine; since their sojourn in a strange land they had learned nothing by misfortune or experience.

Germany had offended against France as well

THE FRENCH REVOLUTION

as against the laws of nations, in that she had permitted her soil to be used as a sanctuary by these fugitives and had allowed them to issue proclamations disturbing the quiet of a state with which she was at peace. Hostile armies were daily getting closer to the borders and the people anxiously asked, " Are the ministers to remain supine or are they to make preparations to repel these forces when they attempt to cross the line into French territory? Is France to be overrun by foreign hordes and no resistance to be offered? "

The Girondins assailed the ministry and denounced the king for his inertness. Under the strain Louis yielded, dismissed the ministers, and named as their successors, among others, Roland and Dumouriez.

Dumouriez was by all odds the ablest man among the new appointments. He was classed politically as a Girondin, but partisan classification did not bother him; he could serve or betray any party, if it were to his interest to do either. Prior to 1789, he had been a courtier, during the days of the first Assembly a constitutionalist, then he became a Girondin, and under the republic a red-capped Jacobin. Ultimately he betrayed his country and deserted his colors. His career as a soldier, however, was a record of bravery, of unexampled gallantry. " He was," says Lamartine, " of that middle stature of the French soldier who wears his uniform gracefully, his haversack lightly, and his musket and sabre as if he did not feel their weight."

DANTON

His body had been riddled with bullets in the Seven Years' War, but his wounds had not impaired his strength and, although when appointed minister he was approaching sixty years of age, he was as robust, as ambitious, and as enthusiastic as a boy. Even at that time of life he could leap into the saddle without putting foot to stirrup. He was one of those men upon whom time seems to make no impression. His life from youth had been one of adventure and, so far as real success was concerned, a failure. He was unscrupulous, fond of intrigue, and a diplomat of marked ability. No sooner did he secure a seat in the cabinet than he began to scheme, and he played his game most adroitly in attempting to win all parties. He almost succeeded in gaining the confidence of the queen.

Danton had a great admiration for his ability and for a long while implicit faith in his loyalty. At the time of the selection of Dumouriez as commander of the Army of the Rhein, although he was classed as a Girondin, Danton threw aside every factional consideration, gave him the most earnest support, and was most influential in securing the appointment. In this matter Danton considered alone the interests of France and was actuated and controlled by the most patriotic motives. The subsequent treason of the general cast a shade of suspicion over Danton, but he was absolutely innocent of any complicity in the designs and plots of the traitor.

CHAPTER XIV

DEATH OF LEOPOLD—ASSASSINATION OF GUSTAVUS III, KING OF SWEDEN—FRANCIS II MAKES PROCLAMATION—DANTON HURLS DEFIANCE—WAR DECLARED APRIL 21, 1792—DEFEAT OF THE FRENCH TROOPS—DEATH OF GENERAL DILLON—DEPUTIES FROM MARSEILLES PRESENT PETITION TO THE ASSEMBLY—DAY OF THE BLACK BREECHES—PÉTION

On March 1, 1792, the Emperor Leopold died. So bitter was the feeling in France against the Austrians that Marie Antoinette feared to go into mourning for her deceased brother; indeed she ought not to have felt it incumbent upon her to pay him any marked respect. He apparently had not troubled himself much about her safety. His indifference had provoked the criticism and censure of the queen's friends. The Count d'Allonville one day asked the Prince of Condé what the emperor would do if the mob should murder his sister: "Perhaps he would venture to go into mourning for her," was the sarcastic reply.

Gustavus III, king of Sweden, was assassinated on the night of March 15th, by a man named Ankarstrom, at a masked ball in Stockholm. Gustavus had been meditating upon a plan, in fact had been arranging its details, by which Catharine of Russia was to furnish the soldiers and Spain the subsidies in order to relieve by invasion the king of France. The sudden and unexpected death of the Swedish monarch, however, put an end to this formidable combination. The fact was not conceded nor even taken into consideration by these foreign potentates that the French people had any right to change their form of government or to establish a new one. " Who," cried Danton, " has authorized them to interfere in our domestic affairs? Who has made them masters or arbiters of our destiny?"

France was but acting upon the principles announced in America's glorious Declaration, " a Declaration," says Buckle, " which ought to be hung up in the nursery of every king and blazoned on the porch of every royal palace." The object of the institution of government is to secure the rights of the people, for it is alone from them that it derives its powers and " whenever any form of government becomes destructive of these ends it is the right of the people to alter or abolish it and to institute a new government, laying its foundation on such principles and organizing its powers in such form, as to them shall seem most likely to effect their safety and happiness."

Leopold's successor, Francis II, took a most decided stand in relation to the conditions in France. He demanded the restoration of the rights of the pope and the German princes; he further announced that the Church property which had been confiscated by the State should

THE FRENCH REVOLUTION

be restored, and that the government should at once be re-established upon the basis of the royal proclamation of June 23, 1789.

The demands were so insolent in character, so dictatorial in tone, that they aroused a feeling of indignation and resentment in every heart, stirred every patriotic impulse, and effected a unity of purpose throughout all France, in spite of factional differences, that nothing else could have accomplished. Such impertinence only added fuel to the flame. Boldly the challenge was accepted, and the nation rose like a giant in her strength to grapple with her foe. Danton thundered in the ears of the people and aroused their patriotic fervor. Defiantly he hurled the gage of battle into the teeth of the Austrian prince. Danton's robust and impetuous temperament made him the natural leader at such a time. The impending peril aroused the lion in his nature and he was a host in himself. He was a practical, far-seeing politician, not a blind, unreasonable fanatic, and with his political instinct he saw clearly that the Revolution could succeed alone by keeping alive the vehemence and energy of the insurrectionary spirit of Paris; it was this force that had to be depended upon to resist the invaders.

The insolent tone of the Austrian emperor's proclamation was the expression of tyranny—" The tree of liberty," exclaimed Barère, " only grows when watered by the blood of tyrants." Isnard in one of his impassioned flights stirred the emotions of the Assembly when he cried out,

DANTON

"If a war of kings be raised against France, we will raise a war of people against kings." In such a time eloquence is born of the occasion; it is the inspiration of passion, the utterance of the emotions.

The orators in the gardens and at the clubs moved the people to desperation. They declared that the country was being betrayed by traitors at home and threatened by enemies abroad. They openly asserted that the king and the queen were in correspondence with the emigrants and the allied kings and that the glorious results of the Revolution would be lost if the people did not rise in their strength to defend what they had secured. Foreign tyrants had impudently directed what should be the policies of France. Could a free people yield to a dictation so arrogant? France would not have been worthy the liberty she desired if she had complacently submitted to such an insult.

To meet public sentiment, the king at last, under the advice of his ministers, proposed to the Assembly the Declaration of War on April 21, 1792.

One great danger to the Revolution was the fact that the officers of the French troops were royalists; and as those at the head of the armies of the coalition were the brothers of Louis and the relatives of Marie Antoinette, this produced a state of affairs that surely gave no assurance of future success for France.

The first battle was a repulse for the French,

THE FRENCH REVOLUTION

who, greatly out-numbered at every point and poorly manœuvred, fell back in confusion. The retreating soldiers, believing they had been betrayed, cried "treachery," and in their fury murdered Théobald Dillon, one of their generals. Marat shrieked with joy when he heard of Dillon's death, for it proved to him, he said, that the troops were loyal even though their leaders were traitors, and it further convinced him that their officers could not lead them against Paris.

The Assembly passed a decree constituting itself in permanent session. It also directed the formation of a camp of 20,000 men near Paris. This measure the king vetoed. He further inflamed the public temper by dismissing the ministers, Servan, Roland and Clavières.

On the day that the king vetoed the decree providing for the enlistment of 20,000 men to defend Paris, several representatives from Marseilles appeared at the bar of the Assembly and presented a petition, which read: "French liberty is in danger but the patriotism of the South will save France. The day of the people's wrath is arrived. . . . Legislators, the power of the people is confided in you; make use of it. French patriotism demands your permission to march with an imposing force towards the capital. . . . You surely will not refuse the sanction of the law to those who are ready and willing to die in its defense." It was Barbaroux, the deputy from Marseilles, who instigated the presentation of the petition and whose purpose it was to reveal to the capital the patriotic spirit of the South and incidentally the popularity of the Girondins in the provinces.

Charles Barbaroux was a most enthusiastic revolutionist. He was one of the leaders of his party and, though of uncommon ardor, possessed wisdom and judgment of a high degree. He wielded considerable influence in the Assembly as well as in the councils of his party, and was an active partisan and a most pronounced republican.

Fearing that the Revolution was losing ground in the North, he proposed that preparations should be made to retire, in case of foreign invasion, behind the Vosges and the Loire, and if Liberty were driven from these defenses "she would still have left in the east the Doubs, the Ain, and the Rhone; in the west the Vienne and the Dordogne; in the centre the rocks and the rivers of Limousin and beyond these the Auvergne with its steep hills, its ravines, its aged forests, and the mountains of the Velay, laid waste of old by fire, now covered with pines, a wild country, where men plough amidst snow, but where they live independently. . . . Lastly, if all these points were forced, we should have Corsica left—Corsica where neither Genoese nor French have been able to neutralize tyranny; which needs but hands to be fertile and philosophers to be enlightened." He was determined that Liberty should not be driven from France, but if compelled to retreat she would not surrender but fall back step by step and die in the

THE FRENCH REVOLUTION

last ditch. It was Barbaroux who infused the ardor of the South into the Revolution and boldly led his cohorts into the capital to give it new life and vigor.

In spite of the ulterior purpose of the Girondins, which was to show the capital the power of the provinces, Danton believing that the enthusiasm of the Marseillais would arouse the patriotism of the Parisians gave the project his strong support. On the 16th of June the insurgents in the district of St. Antoine addressed a communication to the Commune requesting permission to assemble in arms on the 20th of June and to present a petition to the Assembly and to the king. The Commune referred the matter to the Directory and the municipal body. The Directory passed a resolution forbidding armed assemblages and enjoined the commandant general and the mayor to employ such measures as should be necessary to disperse such gatherings.

The ostensible purpose of assembling on the 20th of June was to celebrate the anniversary of the oath of the Tennis Court; the real purpose, however, was to strike terror into the hearts of the royalists, by the sight of fifty thousand pikes. The insurgents, in spite of the resolution of the Directory, were active in making preparations for the march. Their leaders gave them every assurance that, notwithstanding the order of the authorities, the National Guards would not fire and the mayor would take no steps to interfere with their right to petition the Assembly and the king and to celebrate the anniversary of an event that in its nature was historic. Here was anarchy in its very essence.

On the morning of the 20th of June, 1792, eight thousand men, in contemptuous violation of the law, marched out of the faubourgs Saint Antoine and Saint Marceau and directed their steps towards the Assembly. A grim, swarthy mass, terrible to behold, emerging from these seething centres of population burst forth upon Paris and spread on every hand the terror that is created by a great moving, undirected force. Some of the men were hatless; many wore the *bonnet rouge;* all were armed—the weapons, various in character, ranged from the hatchet to the scythe, from the bludgeon to the pike. They moved forward with that intrepidity that marks the multitude, conscious of the strength that comes from numbers. Strange were the banners of this army. One man carried on the end of a pike a calf's heart, under which were written the words: "The heart of an aristocrat;" another bore aloft on a tall staff a pair of black breeches, the motto reading: "Long live the Sans Culottes." It was this that gave the occasion its designation, "The Day of the Black Breeches."

The procession was led by Santerre, the rich brewer of Saint Antoine, and the rabid Saint Huruge, surnamed the Marquis. At every step crowds gathered and cheered the marchers on their way; women and children mingled with the throng and when the mob reached the hall of the Assembly their number had increased to 30,000.

THE FRENCH REVOLUTION

The National Guards, fearing a repetition of the scenes of the Champ de Mars if they should attempt to repulse this great multitude, opened their ranks and permitted the procession to enter the hall. It was the capitulation of law to anarchy. The spokesman appeared at the bar and in language both positive and threatening declared that the people had been patient too long but that they were now aroused and were determined to use that power vested in them by the Declaration of Rights and to resist oppression. He condemned the dismissal without cause of the patriot ministers and declared it was high time that the happiness of the people should not depend upon the caprice of a king. "Why should the monarch be above the law? The life and the rights of the people are as dear and as valuable to them as those of crowned despots. Let those of your body whose sentiments do not agree with ours, cease to pollute the land of liberty and betake themselves to Coblentz. We complain of the inactivity of the armies, if this inactivity be the result of the treachery or the incapacity of the executive power, then let that power be destroyed."

The president of the Assembly answered in a conciliatory tone that the requests would be considered. The crowd then marched through the hall and made the rafters ring as they sang the wild chorus of the *Ca ira* and cried: "*Vive la nation,*" "*Vivent les sans-culottes,*" "*A bas le veto.*"

Out into the street next swept the procession,

headed for the Tuileries to pay respect to his majesty. The people gathered under the windows of the palace and shouted their insults to the royal family, their favorite cry being: "Down with the veto." As usual Louis was complacent and accommodating, and gave orders to open the gates; immediately the crowd rushed into the court-yard, broke down the doors of the palace, and swarmed through the halls and the corridors like an army of rats. They ascended to the royal apartments, crying all the while: "Where's the king?" "Where's the Big Veto?" They even dragged a cannon up the marble staircase to the second floor.

The mob swept everything before them, overcoming all resistance, though in fact there was very little offered. The soldiers seemed to be utterly demoralized, paralyzed with fear. A man like Napoleon would have been worth a kingdom to Louis at this moment. Cold steel and the open mouth of a cannon were the only arguments that could convince such a rabble.

Bourrienne, in his Memoirs, says that he and Bonaparte had been in a coffee-room in the Rue St. Honoré and on going out they saw a mob of five or six thousand men, "all in rags and armed with every sort of weapon, vociferating the grossest abuse and proceeding with rapid pace towards the Tuileries." Bonaparte and Bourrienne followed the crowd and after a short walk reached the terrace from which they had a full view of the disgraceful occurrences that ensued. Bonaparte was surprised and indignant, says

THE FRENCH REVOLUTION

Bourrienne; he could not understand such weakness and forbearance. "When the king appeared at the window wearing the red cap, Bonaparte could no longer restrain his indignation and exclaimed: 'What madness! How could they allow these scoundrels to enter. They ought to have blown four or five hundred of them into the air with cannon; the rest would have taken to their heels.'"

Bonaparte would have been the man for the occasion but his day had not yet arrived. This "bronze artillery-officer," of clear-cut medallion face, out at the elbows, eager for opportunity, and ambitious for promotion, was in the near future to play his part when with a "whiff of grapeshot" he was to scatter the rabble of the sections, bring order out of anarchy, and "blow into space the thing we specifically call French Revolution."

After the mob rushed into the palace and reached the apartments, they began breaking down the doors with hatchets. Louis had sent away many of his friends whose presence he thought would tend to exasperate the mob. He retained at his side only the old Marshal de Mouchy d'Acloque, some of the servants of his household, and a number of the officers of the National Guards in whom he had confidence. When the mob began hammering at the door of the king's apartment he ordered it opened at once. He faced without trepidation a crowd of angry men armed with pikes and bayonets. "Here I am," he exclaimed; "what do you want with me?" Acloque, addressing the rabble, said: "Citizens: This is your king; pay respect to him. We stand ready to die at his side rather than let you hurt him." Louis was placed in the recess of a window and his friends formed a rampart about him. He was seated on a chair that stood upon a table. His demeanor was calm and firm. He had the patience of endurance; passive courage was his virtue, he could suffer heroically but could not resist.

For two long hours he had to submit to all manner of insults; women scolded and men upbraided him, while the crowd shouted in his ears: "No veto! No priests! No aristocrats!" One of the mob presented him a *bonnet rouge* on the end of a pike; the king put the red cap on his head and promised to support the Constitution. "So stands Majesty in red woolen cap; black Sans-culottism weltering round him far and wide, aimless with inarticulate dissonance, with cries of Veto! Patriot ministers!" Some one handed him a sword and demanded that he should wave it and at the same time cry: "Long live the nation!" He obeyed the command to the letter, although he did not evince much enthusiasm nor display much grace in the performance. A drunken fellow offered him a glass of wine, which he drank off without a moment's hesitation. Legendre, the butcher, stepped up before him and in a loud voice charged him with duplicity and treachery, warned him to beware the people's wrath, and in the name of the nation demanded the sanction of the decree pro-

THE FRENCH REVOLUTION

viding for a camp near Paris, to which Louis replied: "This is neither the time nor the place to discuss that question. I will do what the Constitution requires." This timely answer of the king gained the applause of the crowd.

Madame Elizabeth shared the dangers of the day with her brother, to whom she was devotedly attached. When she was seen at the window the crowd below took her for the queen and shouted: "There is the Austrian." Some of the soldiers surrounding the princess called out to the people: "This is not the queen but Madame Elizabeth." With that gentleness and self-sacrificing spirit that characterized her, she requested them not to correct the mistake. "Leave them in their error," she said, "and save the queen."

Marie Antoinette had not been able to reach the side of the king, for when the crowd entered the palace their first cry was for her, and she fled with her children to the Council Chamber where Mandat with two hundred National Guards gave her protection. Santerre, the brewer, stood at her side and persuaded the rabble to show her some respect. A hoodlum put a Jacobin cap on the head of the dauphin, but Santerre tossing it aside remarked: "The boy is stifling, it is too hot for him."

Hearing of the king's danger, a number of the deputies hastened to the palace and appealed to the people to withdraw, and after much persuasion the mob at last retired. Then forming in procession, they returned to their sections; their coarse and discordant cries gradually grew

DANTON

fainter but the echoes rang in the ears of the king long after the marchers had disappeared from view.

The royal family, worn out and humiliated, when at last united fell into each other's arms and wept. The king perceiving that he still wore the red cap impatiently tore it from his head and threw it to the ground. One of the deputies from the Assembly standing near was seen to have tears in his eyes and Marie Antoinette turning to him said: "You weep to see the king and his family so cruelly treated." "Understand me, Madame," he said; "I weep for the misfortunes of a beautiful, tender-hearted woman and the mother of a family, but there is not one of my tears for the king or the queen—I hate kings and queens." This was the distinction between the man and the revolutionist, and it was this sentiment that eventually overthrew the monarchy.

Pétion, the mayor, reached the palace long after the greater part of the rabble had deserted it. He mounted a chair and addressing the crowd said: "You have laid your remonstrances before the king; there is nothing now for you to do but to retire." The palace was cleared about seven o'clock in the evening. The mayor made some sort of excuse for his delay in arriving, but the king gave him a stinging rebuke and turned from him in disgust. Of course next day the royalists and the constitutionalists waxed indignant, cried aloud for investigations, and demanded that the ringleaders and those who, while remaining in the background, had instigated this

THE FRENCH REVOLUTION

outrageous attack upon the palace and the royal family, should be brought immediately to trial and punishment. As might be expected, however, the matter was never followed up.

After this day of violence and anarchy, a reaction set in at once. The Revolution, indeed, was made up of reactions. On the 21st, from morning until night, in marked contrast to the prior day's occurrences, crowds of people gathered around the palace and shouted their cries of loyalty to the king. The wonder was that they came so late; where were they the day before?

There was absolutely no excuse for the inertness of the authorities. The conduct of the mob should not have been a surprise to them. The people of the faubourgs Saint Antoine and Saint Marceau had given notice that it was their intention to arm themselves on the 20th of June and to proceed in a body to the Assembly to present a petition and to follow this proceeding with a personal visit to the king. Even after the authorities had resolved that such a gathering would not be permitted, the leaders of the mob openly continued their preparations. There was no attempt at concealment. As early as five o'clock on the morning of the 20th, the Directory again gave notice that it would enforce its resolution, but no steps were taken to protect the Assembly and the palace. The fact that the mob was to bear arms was of itself a menace to civil order and enough to reveal to the authorities the purpose of the leaders. Artillery with a firm commander would have been the only sure means of meeting such a condition and enforcing the law, and the cannon ought to have been posted so as to sweep the avenues leading out of the faubourgs before the mob began to march.

Outside of Paris the sentiment was strongly in favor of bringing the leaders and instigators of the mob to judgment and punishment. The department of the Seine preferred charges against the mayor and demanded a thorough investigation. Pétion ought to have been adjudged guilty, but so soon as the public temper subsided the whole matter was dropped. His attitude, or what may be called his masterly inactivity, can easily be explained. He was in spirit a Jacobin; he was a political or factional executive and had neither the desire nor the nerve to resort to positive measures. He was trimming; he stood between his duty as an official and his sentiments as a partisan. As mayor it was incumbent upon him to defend the king; as an individual it was his wish to see him overthrown. He was a demagogue fearing to lose the favor of the rabble, and consequently adopted no strong or severe measures to compel a compliance with the law.

CHAPTER XV

LA FAYETTE COMES TO PARIS—LA FAYETTE—DANTON AND LA FAYETTE

Hearing of the attack upon the Tuileries, La Fayette assigned a brother officer to his command and came post haste to Paris. He appeared at the bar of the Assembly and demanded the punishment of the insurrectionists. When upon the streets he was greeted most enthusiastically, and surrounded by his old comrades of the National Guards, who urged him to lead them against the Jacobins. Had he complied with their request the reaction might have lasted longer.

It is possible that if a strong mind had directed public sentiment at this point the Revolution might have ended in the firm establishment of a constitutional monarchy. The people were so incensed at the conduct of the mob and the weakness and inertness of the municipal authorities that they were ready to abandon the Revolution, to make secure the results that already had been attained, and to establish a government of peace and order.

When La Fayette called at the palace of the Tuileries to pay his respects to the king and the queen they gave him a very cool reception. With their usual want of wisdom and foresight they declined to accept and utilize the services of one who, a born monarchist, was willing to bare his sword in their defense, and who at this juncture could materially have aided them. In fact, the queen at this time told Madame Campan that she would rather perish than be saved by him.

After a few hours' stay in the capital, he departed, finding his visit had come to naught. He received cheers, applause and congratulations, but attained absolutely no results; and without further ado he trotted back to the army.

His sudden appearance in Paris had sent a cold chill down the backs of the Jacobins. His popularity and the hold he had on the affection of the National Guards were what they feared. Danton, with his keen political instinct saw that La Fayette had a great opportunity at hand, and he watched with the eyes of a lynx every move made in the game. He was soon convinced, however, that the conservatives could not unite their forces nor agree upon a plan of action and he rejoiced at the utter discomfiture of his archenemy.

In view of the public temper at this time, La Fayette would have made a most formidable leader; but the pride and the prejudices of the queen, as usual, stood in the way of any mutual agreement and frustrated his every effort. She could not understand how a born royalist could be a revolutionist or why a marquis of the old *noblesse* should be interested in enfranchising the rabble and in emancipating the peasant from the

THE FRENCH REVOLUTION

thraldom of feudalism. La Fayette was to her an apostate, guilty of treason to his order. She might have reposed confidence in a plebeian, but she could not trust, under any circumstances, a renegade patrician. The antipathy of Louis was also very great; he could never forget the prediction of Mirabeau that " La Fayette, if he could, would hold the king a prisoner in his tent."

It would have been a useless and a thankless task for the general to try to save those who preferred to be lost rather than be placed under obligations to him. It is said the queen herself notified Pétion and Danton of his purpose and thus made it impossible to carry out his plans. It was the last chance he ever had to serve the king. He missed a great opportunity and the royal family lost their strongest defender.

Marie Jean Paul Roch Yves Gilbert Motier, marquis de La Fayette, was born at Auvergne in 1759. He was left an orphan at the age of thirteen and inherited a princely fortune. When sixteen he married a daughter of the Duke d'Ayen, granddaughter of the Duke de Noailles, a member of one of the oldest and most aristocratic families in France. He enjoyed every advantage that birth, riches, and high social position could confer. He was received with favor at the court and was admitted to the exclusive set of the queen. The door of every fashionable *salon* was open to him, but the follies and the amusements of the gay world did not tempt him from his ambition. As between the court and the camp he preferred the latter, and at an early

DANTON

age, following in the footsteps of his father who was a soldier of some renown, he entered the Guards.

His ambitions were high and laudable; he was anxious to become famous and to win personal renown but only by honorable methods. His enthusiasm was so aroused in the brave struggle of the American Colonies for independence that he decided to offer his services to the American minister and to enlist in the cause. "At the first news of the quarrel," he wrote, " my heart was enrolled in it." His friends did all in their power to dissuade him from his purpose but without avail; the king forbade his departure but this only intensified his desire and strengthened his determination. He fitted out a ship at his own expense. The British ambassador protested and orders were given by the authorities to seize the vessel which was lying at Bordeaux, but it was quickly taken by its officers to a neighboring port in Spain.

Meanwhile La Fayette was arrested under a *lettre de cachet,* but escaped from the guards and in disguise reached his vessel and with eleven companions sailed for America. Two British cruisers were sent in pursuit, but he eluded them and, after a voyage of two months, arrived at Georgetown in South Carolina. He proceeded at once to Philadelphia where Congress was in session and was shortly assigned to a command as major-general with a stipulation upon his part that he should serve as a volunteer and receive no pay. He fought at Monmouth and was ac-

THE FRENCH REVOLUTION

tive at the siege of Yorktown, displaying great personal valor, but giving no special evidence that his soldierly qualites, in so far as commanding troops was concerned, were of a high order.

La Fayette's name is so closely linked with the story of American independence that it seems almost sacrilege to do aught but praise him. As the steadfast companion of Washington, as one who suffered with the troops at Valley Forge, as one who gave his purse, his pen, his sword, his services to the Colonies, his memory is embalmed in the heart of every American patriot; but it is the duty of the historian to measure men as he finds them and while judging them leniently he must at the same time criticise them fairly and justly.

No one can doubt La Fayette's sincerity. He abandoned the comforts, the delights, and the luxuries of an aristocratic home, to cast his lot with a struggling people. To say, as it has been said in certain quarters, that he did this simply for glory and personal fame is doing him a grave injustice. He may have been actuated by the ardor of youth; those ragged bare-footed heroes whose footprints marked with blood the snow they trod, battling without resources against a mighty empire, may have appealed to his imagination, but he was at all times so sincere, so consistent in his conduct, so self-sacrificing, that he is entitled to the highest praise and the ever-affectionate remembrance of an enfranchised and a grateful people. His sympathies were with the oppressed and his voice was ever heard ad-

DANTON

vocating the cause of political liberty and human freedom.

It is not surprising, then, that when the French Revolution arrived he at once, notwithstanding his aristocratic connections, boldly espoused the popular side. He unhesitatingly turned from his own order and in consequence subjected himself to the reproaches, sneers, and calumny of the court party, among whom of course were many of his old friends; but with a clearly defined purpose he pursued his way to the end.

In the violence and anarchy of the Revolution he at last saw his hopes turn to despair. He fled from his country to avoid arrest and certain death, took refuge in Austria, and was thrown into a dungeon at Ulm, where he languished for five years. Napoleon stipulated for his release; yet notwithstanding this fact La Fayette, true to his principles, voted against the life consulate and afterwards against the imperial title. He opposed tyranny and usurpation in their every phase and always favored constitutionalism and popular rights.

When we study carefully the part he essayed in the French Revolution I think it will be admitted that he was not equal to the occasion; he was not the man for that epoch. His vanity, his love of the dramatic, or rather the spectacular, his irresolution, his suspicions, his prejudices, his want of tact, and his poor judgment in measuring the qualities of men caused him to make many grievous errors. He was not a revolutionist of the stamp that directs events and that

THE FRENCH REVOLUTION

takes quick advantage of contingencies. He was not a politician of invention and resource, and had not the dominating spirit of the born leader. He was so anxious to retain the respect of the public and to maintain his honor that he would not resort to the means and measures adopted by his unscrupulous enemies and consequently in the game of politics he was often out-played. The Cæsars, the Cromwells, the Richelieus, the Dantons, the Napoleons, in accomplishing their ends, do not stop to weigh the niceties of a moral code. In a contest so fierce, in times so tumultuous as the French Revolution, the politician who relies alone upon virtue to win is like the commander in battle who depends upon prayer instead of his artillery.

The Count d'Artois described La Fayette as "*a scelerat et fanatique* in whom no one could confide, because no one could bribe him from his duty." Mirabeau had an utter contempt for him and sarcastically referred to him as "Grandison Cromwell." Napoleon, who thought any man was a fool who would allow his honor or his conscience to stand in the way of his preferment or ambition, called him a noodle.

Camille Desmoulins delighted to hold him up to public ridicule and he never lost an opportunity to humble his pride or to mock his vanity. He knew the sensitive points of the general and he played upon them as a satirist with consummate skill. He considered him a carpet knight and a soldier always on dress parade. He alluded to him ironically as "the liberator of two worlds," and dubbed him the "Don Quixote of Capet" and the "Constellation of the White Horse." La Fayette's consuming desire was to win popularity or as Mirabeau tersely put it, "he loved the glory of gazettes." Jefferson, who was a keen judge of men, said he had "a canine appetite for popular applause." He was at times given to boasting which made him appear somewhat ridiculous. Upon one occasion when Mirabeau through the influence of some friends was endeavoring to form an alliance with La Fayette, the general, drawing himself up to his full height, stoutly exclaimed: "I have vanquished the King of England in his power, the King of France in his authority; I will certainly not yield the place to Mirabeau." La Fayette was totally wanting in that personality that was possessed by Cromwell; and the attributes of such a leader were needed for the role he essayed. He had those qualities of heart that secure the love of men but not their confidence in a crisis; he could command their admiration but not their unreserved dependence.

In the French Revolution La Fayette played a most conspicuous part — he represented one phase of it; but in politics he was no match for Danton. One was vain, visionary, cautious, scrupulous; the other was natural, practical, resolute, audacious, and not hindered by any question of moral nicety in reaching his ends or accomplishing a purpose. Where La Fayette would hesitate Danton would dare. They were two distinct types representing the conservatism and the

THE FRENCH REVOLUTION

radicalism of that period. Both were sincere in their desires for reform and it was unfortunate for the cause of the Revolution that they could not form an alliance.

While desiring to do full justice to La Fayette I think it must be admitted that his capacity was far less eminent than his virtues.

A distinguished English author and statesman wrote: " Men of all parties join in testifying their absolute belief in La Fayette's inflexible integrity and men of more than ordinary sagacity and reflection have added that he alone passed unscathed through the revolutionary furnace; alone trod without a fall the slippery path of those changeful scenes." " It must be a great satisfaction to you," said Charles James Fox in a letter written to La Fayette, " that having passed through the scenes of the Revolution you have nothing wherewith to reproach yourself." " Stay, my dear man," said Napoleon. " Yours is a fine conduct. To lead in one's country's affairs and in case of her making shipwreck to have nothing in common with her enemies—that is the true course."

It is no small praise to say of a man that his honor was exalted, his integrity was inflexible, his ideals were lofty, and that he pursued his way through the most trying scenes and experiences with his truth and his character unsullied.

The radicals recovered very slowly from the reaction that set in after the 20th of June, but their spirits and their courage rose when they saw La Fayette leave the city. There is no question but that he could have closed the Club of the Jacobins and could have brought their leaders to trial and punishment if quick action had been taken and he had received the support of the court party and the constitutionalists. With the public sentiment in his favor he could have censored the radical journals and for their treasonable utterances could have suppressed them, for they had gone far beyond the limits of the law. They had become but the mouth-pieces of anarchy.

As stated before, it was quite possible at this point in the Revolution for La Fayette with his influence in the National Guards and with public opinion strongly favoring a reaction, to establish the throne on a substantial basis, but the queen would not have it so.

The radicals in Paris were not at rest; the dangers that surrounded them were appalling. They were greatly surprised when they ascertained that the king and the queen had refused to consider the propositions of La Fayette and they rejoiced beyond measure when he left Paris, but they still had their troubles for they were threatened by the armies of the allies from without and by the royalists at home.

It was rumored too that La Fayette would lead the troops against the capital and make short work of the Revolution by the establishment of a military dictatorship. "Keep your eye on La Fayette," cried Marat, "for he is more dangerous without than within Paris;" and the people knew that this wild fanatic was a pretty good

THE FRENCH REVOLUTION

judge of men and could fathom their purposes very accurately.

After the eventful 20th of June Madame Roland feared the Revolution was lost and she encouraged her friends to make the most strenuous efforts to save it. The future was so uncertain that all parties were in a state of suspense, bewilderment, and doubt. While Madame Roland was worried over the threatened destruction of the Revolution, the king and the queen were as much worried over the threatened destruction of royalism.

The emigrants at Coblentz, encouraged by the change in public sentiment, were making all sorts of threats and declaring they would be in Paris in six weeks, terrorize the revolutionists and avenge the ills they had suffered. No conduct could have been more imprudent and nothing could have put the king and the queen in greater jeopardy. Nor could any plan have been adopted better calculated to inflame the passions of the people and to unite them in a common purpose and a common defense.

The changes were rung upon these threats in every club and in the columns of every newspaper. It gave a great chance for the radical orators and journalists to recover lost ground and they did not fail to take every advantage of it. Danton was not idle in these days and his eloquence resounded throughout France; not only did he arouse patriotism but he formed public opinion. He looms up, at this period, as the foremost revolutionist in the nation.

CHAPTER XVI

THE MARSEILLAIS—THE MARSEILLAISE HYMN—LAMOURETTE KISS—THE DAY OF FEDERATION

In order to arouse Paris and to infuse some of the hot ardor of the southern provinces into the spirit of the Parisians, Barbaroux, as we have seen, at the time of the vetoing of the decree providing for a camp of 20,000 men near Paris, instigated the presentation of a petition to the Assembly and subsequently offered the services of a battalion of six hundred brave men from Marseilles who "knew how to die, and were not afraid to die."

It was in the dusty, hot, and sultry days of July, 1792, that these valiant volunteers began their march to the capital, dragging their two cannon by hand. All the countryside, the villages, and the towns through which they passed turned out to greet and encourage them. The air fairly quivered with weird songs and wild cheers. "It was the fire of the soul in the South coming to rekindle the revolutionary hearth."

The marchers enlivened their way and aroused the enthusiasm of loyalists by singing the Marseillaise, a patriotic hymn that, a short time before, had been composed by Rouget de Lisle, a young officer of artillery in garrison at Strasbourg. Originally composed as a war song for

THE FRENCH REVOLUTION

Lückner's army—"*Chant du guerre pour l'armée du Rhin*"—it acted on the heart of France like an inspiration; it made the blood tingle in men's veins, for it was the triumphant cry of a regenerated race. All the world took up the refrain and the words were sung in a hundred different tongues; like the tri-color it made the circuit of the earth. It was heard when the armies of the republic marched in serried columns against the enemies of France, and its echoes reverberated even after the victories of the republic were swallowed up in the glories of the empire. It will be heard in every land unto the latest generations of time wherever brave men make a stand for liberty. It will comfort the patriotic soul in despair and give courage, fortitude, and hope to those martyrs who, in the sacred cause of human freedom, languish in the dungeon, perish in battle, or die upon the scaffold.

Singing this hymn that "preserves notes of the song of glory and the shriek of death," the men of Marseilles marched triumphantly on their way through France. A swarthy crew indeed, "a black-browed mass full of grim fire, who wend their way in the hot, sultry weather, very singular to contemplate." Their faces were bronzed by the rays of the burning sun, their arms and bosoms were bared, their uniforms were covered with dust, their Phrygian headdresses were surmounted by the *bonnet rouge,* and they used branches filled with leaves as shades to shelter them from the heat.

DANTON

In the eyes of the royalists these revolutionists were looked upon as a band of pirates or brigands; they were but madmen on an errand of death; their war songs were but attempts to terrorize. Of course in a time of such excitement, stories greatly exaggerated as to their conduct, appearance, and numbers were put in circulation, and it was difficult in those days of tumult to verify facts. They have been described as a drunken, riotous band of bacchanals, that reeled through France on their way to the capital, where they were debauched with wine and blood.

The body, according to Lamartine, consisted of 1,200 to 1,500 men and was composed of Genoese, Ligurians, and Piedmontese, who had been "banished from their country and recruited suddenly on the shores of the Mediterranean; the majority sailors or soldiers accustomed to warfare, and some bandits hardened to crime."

Lamartine seems to have been mistaken in his description both as to numbers and as to character. According to the best authorities, they were not men such as he describes and they did not number at the most more than seven hundred.

Careful historical research has shown that they were picked men from the National Guards at Marseilles, the most hardy as well as the most revolutionary men of the city, and there is no reason to denounce them as a band of vagabonds. They were chosen for their loyalty and courage, and when they returned to their homes in October, 1792, they were welcomed with acclaim by

THE FRENCH REVOLUTION

their fellow citizens and accorded civic honor by the municipality. The pretext for their march was to fraternize at the Federation on the fourteenth of July, but it was not until the thirtieth that they arrived in Paris. The real purpose of their coming was to terrorize the royalists, to arouse the revolutionary spirit of the people, and to serve as the vanguard of that army of 20,000 men decreed to be enlisted by the Assembly.

The Girondins were bringing them to Paris for their own protection, to awe the Jacobins, and to show to the people of the capital what the provinces could do. These provincial delegates always had a feeling of antagonism towards the capital, and it was one of the things that ultimately wrought their ruin. They forgot that Paris was the heart of France and that all the arteries of the Revolution were vitalized with her blood.

Danton, time and again, warned them against the mistake they were making in drawing a distinction between the capital and the provinces; "they are but parts of one whole," he exclaimed, "and true patriots love all France, not only a portion of it." But they turned a deaf ear to his advice and disregarded his warnings.

While the men of Marseilles were marching up from the south the Girondins in the Assembly were denouncing the king openly, charging him with plotting with a foreign foe and with double dealing. They even went so far as to accuse him of treason and declared he feigned a love for the laws merely to preserve the power that would enable him to defy them. Vergniaud, one of the most eloquent members of the Assembly and perhaps the most polished orator of the Revolution, made an impassioned speech that thrilled the hearts of all patriots. "Every threat against liberty," he exclaimed, "is made in the name of the king. The armies of the allies are gathering on the frontiers and menacing the peace of France for no other purpose than to re-establish the throne, to maintain its splendor, to renew its extravagance, and to destroy the results of the Revolution. The empire, no doubt, will be dismembered to pay the expenses of the coalition and the people will be burdened by a heavy indemnity. To strike the allies with terror you must assail the king."

"Let us form ourselves into one and the same mass of freemen," cried the priest Lamourette, "equally terrible to anarchy and to feudalism. The moment the foreigner sees that we are united, will be the moment when liberty triumphs and France is saved." A wave of enthusiasm swept over the Convention, past enmities were forgotten, factional lines were obliterated, and as if by one impulse the deputies ran into each others' arms and embraced with the fervor of lovers. This remarkable exhibition of fraternity is known in history as the "Lamourette kiss." It was another one of those emotional scenes that happened so often during that exciting period. Jacobins and Girondins, radicals and conservatives, pledged to each other their loyalty. The king, hearing of the enthusiasm, entered the hall

THE FRENCH REVOLUTION

of the Assembly and was greeted with applause. There is no record, however, of his having exchanged kisses with any of the members of the congress.

On the 11th of July the Assembly solemnly declared the country in danger and authorized the enlistment and enrolment of 85,000 volunteers. The sittings were made permanent and cannon discharged at regular intervals announced to the citizens the impending crisis. The day of Federation, July 14th, had arrived, but it was not observed with its old-time enthusiasm. A large tree had been planted in the centre of the Champ de Mars upon which were hung, like toys upon a Christmas tree, the symbols of royalty, religion, and feudalism,—crowns, blue-ribbons, tiaras, cassocks, birettas, cardinals' hats, St. Peter's keys, escutcheons, titles of nobility, coats of arms, doctors' caps, bags, bundles of lawpapers and records. The king was to set fire to this tree, but after taking the oath he excused himself by stating that feudalism was dead already and the ceremony they asked him to perform was, under the circumstances, useless. It was refined cruelty for the managers of the celebration to assign him to such a task and he would have been a poltroon had he complied with their request.

This was the last time Louis appeared in public, until he mounted the scaffold.

CHAPTER XVII

ENLISTMENT—PROCLAMATION OF THE DUKE OF BRUNSWICK—MARSEILLAIS ENTER PARIS—BRUSH WITH THE FILLES ST. THOMAS

The volunteers under the enlistment decree of July 11th were enrolling themselves very slowly. The quota of Paris was 3,000, and up to this time, July 14th, only 200 had registered. Something had to be done to meet the emergency. The country had been declared in danger and her defenders must be aroused. Inflammatory speeches had availed nothing. The recruiting offices were as empty, as deserted, as the churches.

Accordingly Sunday, July 22, 1792, was named as a day for enlistment of volunteers. In the early morning cannon began to boom, drums rattled, bells rang out from every tower and steeple, horsemen galloped in all directions carrying banners announcing that the country was in danger. Bands were stationed at the recruiting booths around which swarmed great crowds of people. At every enlistment of a volunteer the drums rolled, the bands played, and cheers rent the air. Paris was in a fervor, and under such a stimulation her quota was soon raised.

THE FRENCH REVOLUTION

The decree that provided for the enlistment authorized the soldiers to select their commanders. Moreau, Pichegru, Soult, Massena, Jourdan, and Davoust were chosen. These men in time became marshals of France, following the star of Napoleon and the eagles of the empire. They were now to receive the training that was to fit them for their future greatness.

The volunteers encamped on the Champ de Mars and awaited marching orders. Agitators were at work among them and asked: "What will become of those you leave behind when you go forth to meet the armies of Austria and Prussia? Can any one say that the traitor royalists at home will not take advantage of your absence?" This was sowing seed that in due season was to bring forth fruit.

On July 20, 1792, the king of Prussia declared war and on the 28th the proclamation of the duke of Brunswick, commander of the Prussian army, was issued.

"To the People of France:
"Their Majesties the Emperor and the King of Prussia, having given me the command of the armies assembled by their orders on the French frontier, I have thought it well to tell the inhabitants of that kingdom the motives that have inspired the measures taken by the two sovereigns and the intentions that guide them.

"After having arbitrarily suppressed the rights and the possessions of the German princes in Alsace and Lorraine, troubled and overset public order and their legitimate government, exercised against the sacred person of the King and against his august family violence which is, moreover, repeated and renewed from day to day, those who have usurped the reins of the administration have at last filled up the measure by causing an unjust war to be declared against his Majesty the Emperor, and by attacking his provinces in the Netherlands.

" Several possessions of the German Empire have been drawn into this oppression, and several others have only escaped from a similar danger by yielding to the imperious threats of the dominant party and its emissaries.

" His Prussian Majesty with his Imperial Majesty, by the ties of a strict and defensive alliance, and himself a preponderant member of the Germanic body, has therefore been unable to excuse himself from going to the aid of his ally and of his fellow State. And it is under both these heads that he undertakes the defense of that monarch and of Germany.

" To these great interests another object of equal importance must be added, and one that is near to the heart of the two sovereigns: it is that of ending the domestic anarchy of France, of arresting the attacks which are directed against the altar and the throne, of re-establishing the legitimate power, of giving back to the King the freedom and safety of which he is deprived, and of giving him the means to exercise the lawful authority which is his due.

" Convinced as they are that the healthy part of the French people abhors the excesses of a party that enslaves them, and that the majority of the inhabitants are impatiently awaiting the advent of a relief that will permit them to declare themselves

THE FRENCH REVOLUTION

openly against the odious schemes of their oppressors, His Majesty the Emperor and His Majesty the King of Prussia call upon them to return at once to the call of reason and justice, of order, of peace. It is in view of these things that I, the undersigned, General Commander-in-Chief of the two armies, declare —

" (1) That led into the present war by irresistible circumstances, the two allied courts propose no object to themselves but the happiness of France, and do not propose to enrich themselves by annexation.

"(2) That they have no intention of meddling with the domestic government of France, but only wish to deliver the King, and the Queen, and the Royal Family from their captivity, and procure for his Most Christian Majesty that freedom which is necessary for him to call such a council as he shall see fit, without danger and without obstacle, and to enable him to work for the good of his subjects according to his promises and as much as may be his concern.

"(3) That the combined armies will protect all towns, boroughs and villages, and the persons and goods of all those that will submit to the King, and that they will help to re-establish immediately the order and police of France.

"(4) That the National Guard are ordered to see to the peace of the towns and country-sides provisionally, and to the security of the persons and goods of all Frenchmen provisionally, that is, until the arrival of the troops of their Royal and Imperial Majesties, or until further orders, under pain of being personally responsible; that on the contrary, the National Guards who may have fought against the troops of the allied courts, and who are captured in arms, shall be treated as enemies, and shall be punished as rebels and disturbers of the public peace.

"(5) That the generals, officers, non-commissioned officers, and privates of the French troops of the line are equally ordered to return to their old allegiance and to submit at once to the King, their legitimate sovereign.

"(6) That the members of departmental, district, and town councils are equally responsible with their heads and property for all crimes, arson, murders, thefts, and assaults, the occurrence of which they allow or do not openly, and to the common knowledge, try to prevent in their jurisdiction; that they shall equally be bound to keep their functions provisionally until his Most Christian Majesty, reinstated in full liberty, has further decreed; or until, in the interval, other orders shall have been given.

"(7) That the inhabitants of towns, boroughs, and villages who may dare to defend themselves against the troops of their Imperial and Royal Majesties by firing upon them, whether in the open or from the windows, doors, or apertures of their houses, shall be punished at once with all the rigour of the laws of war, their houses pulled down or burnt. All those inhabitants, on the contrary, of the towns, boroughs and villages who shall hasten to submit to their King by opening their gates to the troops of their Majesties shall be placed under the immediate protection of their Majesties; their persons, their goods, their chattels shall be under the safeguard of the laws, and measures will be taken for the general safety of each and all of them.

"(8) The town of Paris and all its inhabitants without distinction shall be bound to submit on the

THE FRENCH REVOLUTION

spot, and without any delay, to the King, and to give that Prince full and entire liberty, and to assure to him and all the Royal Family that inviolability and respect to which the laws of nature and of nations entitle sovereigns from their subjects. Their Imperial and Royal Majesties render personally responsible for anything that may happen, under peril of their heads, and of military execution without hope of pardon, all members of the National Assembly as of the Districts, the Municipality, the National Guards, the Justices of the Peace, and all others whom it may concern. Their aforesaid Majesties declare, moreover, on their word and honor as Emperor and King, that if the Palace of the Tuileries be insulted or forced, that if the least violence, the least assault, be perpetrated against their Majesties, the King, the Queen and the Royal Family, and if steps be not at once taken for their safety, preservation, and liberty, they, their Imperial and Royal Majesties, will take an exemplary and never-to-be-forgotten vengeance, by giving up the town of Paris to military execution and to total subversion, and the guilty rebels to the death they have deserved. Their Imperial and Royal Majesties promise, on the contrary, to the inhabitants of Paris to use their good offices with his Most Christian Majesty to obtain pardon for their faults and errors, and to take the most vigorous measures to ensure their persons and goods if they promptly and exactly obey the above command.

" Finally, since their Majesties can recognize no laws in France save those that proceed from the King in full liberty, they protest in advance against any declarations that may be made in the name of his Most Christian Majesty, so long as his sa-

DANTON

cred person, those of the Queen and of the Royal Family, are not really safe, for which end their Imperial and Royal Majesties invite and beg his Most Christian Majesty to point out to what town in the immediate neighborhood of his frontiers he may judge it best to retire with the Queen and the Royal Family, under good and sure escort that will be sent him for that purpose, in order that his Most Christian Majesty may be in all safety to call to him such deputies and counsellors as he sees fit, call such councils as may please him, see to the re-establishment of order, and arrange the administration of his kingdom.

"Lastly, I engage myself, in my own private name and in my aforesaid capacity, to cause the troops under my command to observe everywhere a good and exact discipline, promising to treat with mildness and moderation all well-meaning subjects who may show themselves peaceful and submissive, and to use force with those only who may be guilty of resistance and of recalcitrance.

"It is for these reasons that I require and exhort, in the strongest and most instant fashion, all the inhabitants of this kingdom not to oppose themselves to the march and operations of the troops under my command, but rather to give them on all sides a free entry and all the good-will, aid and assistance that circumstances may demand.

"Given at our Headquarters of Coblentz, July 25, 1792.

(Signed) "CHARLES WILLIAM FERDINAND,
"*Duke of Brunswick-Lunebourg.*"

A remarkable feature of the matter was that the proclamation dated at Coblentz on the 25th should have been in Paris on the 28th and pub-

THE FRENCH REVOLUTION

lished in all the royalist newspapers on the morning of that day. It at once created a suspicion that the friends of the monarchy in the capital were in possession of the paper prior to the date of its publication; and, if so, must necessarily have been concerned in its preparation.

Is it surprising that a proclamation so impudent should have fired the indignation of all France? It was so insolent in expression, so imperious in tone, that it aroused the anger of even the moderates. It was like a slap on the cheek, which makes every drop of blood in the body tingle. There are some insults a brave man must resent even though death stares him in the face, or else lose his self-respect. Could a proud and an independent people do aught but defy a challenge so arrogant?

The kings and the princes did not understand the spirit of the Revolution. At Coblentz the emigrants, believing that the day of deliverance was at hand, increased the anger of the people and the peril of the king by renewing their wild threats. They were coming back to France to reclaim their own; in this work of reclamation they were not only to terrorize the revolutionists, but if necessary to burn Paris to the ground and deluge the land in blood. The allied sovereigns declared they were advancing with their armies to put an end to anarchy, to crush out by force the violence of the Revolution, to re-establish the throne, and to rehabilitate the king.

It was generally thought, and there were many strong reasons for the belief, that the proclamation had been prepared by Louis and the princes at Coblentz and at their instance issued in the name of Brunswick. Its publication produced results entirely different from what its originators intended. Instead of terrifying Paris it aroused its fury and united the sentiments of its citizens. Foreign potentates, supported by their mighty cohorts, threatening to dictate the policies of France, was enough to inflame the patriotic ardor of the whole nation. " Do you ask, What is the news? " cried Demosthenes in an earlier age of the world's history. " What could be greater news than a Macedonian making war upon the Athenians, and regulating the affairs of Greece? "

The appeals of the Assembly amounted to nothing in stimulating the energy of the people as compared with the effect produced by the issuance of this paper. The capital rang with the cry of defiance, men sprang to arms, and the night skies were reddened with the glare of a hundred furnaces, where were being forged the implements of war.

On the 29th of July the Marseillais reached Charenton, a suburb of Paris. Barbaroux, Santerre, and other leaders of the Revolution went out to meet and welcome them. A banquet was given at which patriotic speeches were made and pledges of loyalty given. After the banquet Danton, Westermann, Desmoulins, Marat, and a number of conspirators withdrew to a small house in a retired locality to confer and decide upon a plan of action. It was long after mid-

THE FRENCH REVOLUTION

night before the conspirators were gathered together, each one having gone alone to the rendezvous, and having taken a different and if possible an unfrequented path or road.

It had been a day of intense heat, the atmosphere had been humid and sultry, and suffering humanity rejoiced when it saw the gathering of heavy clouds in the west, foreboding a coming storm. The rumble of distant thunder had been continuous all afternoon. The sun went down behind a bank of clouds as black as ink, and the evening closed in earlier than usual. About ten o'clock the tempest broke over Paris; the rain fell in torrents, and the streets were deserted immediately. The wind blew with the force of a hurricane; chimneys toppled over, tiles were blown from the roofs, shutters, doors and gates were wrenched from their hinges. For eight hours the tempest raged with unabated fury. During this time it was unsafe to be abroad. The next day, the oldest inhabitant declared that Paris had never, within his recollection, been visited by so terrific a storm.

Yet during the continuance of the fury of the elements, the conspirators were arranging the details for the destruction of the monarchy—a fit season for work so dark. It was decided at the conference that on the 10th of August, or thereabouts, after arousing the sections, an attack should be made on the Tuileries and the king deposed.

On the 30th of July the Marseillais entered Paris singing their " impressive and terrible songs." The populace turned out to greet the brave and swarthy men from the South and a warmer welcome was never given in the capital to a visiting delegation.

It was not everyone in Paris that rejoiced at their coming. Baron Thiébault in his description of them says: "On July 30th those hideous Federals, spewed forth by the city of Marseilles, arrived at Paris. I do not think anything more horrible can be imagined than those 500 madmen, three-quarters drunk, almost all in red caps, bare-armed and bare-chested, followed by the dregs of the people, constantly re-inforced by crowds that swarmed out of the slums, fraternizing from one public house to another with bands no less dreadful than their own." They marched through the streets with a defiant air, "their keen black eyes seeming to seek out aristocratic victims."

They at last reached the Champs Elysées, where a repast was spread and served under the direction of Santerre. While the feast was in progress, a battalion of the National Guards, distinguished as the Filles St. Thomas, were dining a short distance away. The men composing this command were royalists. The rabble, eager for excitement and riot, could not forbear insulting the soldiers of the king; a clash took place and the mob was sent scattering in every direction. Running to the Champs Elysées they called on the Marseillais for protection. Heated with wine and wrought up by the enthusiasm of the occasion, the soldiers of the South responded

THE FRENCH REVOLUTION

promptly, by charging upon the royalists and putting them to flight, killing one and wounding several others. Some of the fugitives covered with blood did not stop running until they reached the Tuileries; here they were protected by the National Guards stationed at the palace and it was said the ladies of the queen attended to the needs of the wounded. Such humanity was in the eyes of the rabble a crime and the town rang with stories about the court giving protection to the enemies of the people. It was the first act of violence on the part of the visitors and in the eyes of all law-abiding citizens their conduct was without any justification. It was that of a crowd of drunken street bullies rather than that of a band of men who boasted of their soldierly qualities and who proudly declared they were not afraid to die. It was riot, not revolution. The National Guards petitioned for the removal of the Marseillais, but the tribunes sneered at the proposition, and refused even to consider it.

CHAPTER XVIII

THE TENTH OF AUGUST

During this time Danton was hard at work arousing the sections, encouraging the weakhearted, and intensifying by his ardor the spirit of the brave. He comprehended to the full the importance of the campaign he had on hand. It was no child's play; it was revolution in its sternest mood. It meant the sacking of the palace, the deposition of the king, the destruction of an ancient monarchy. He had assumed the responsibility of the enterprise and defeat or failure meant to him personal destruction.

In the midst of his preparations he hastened to Arcis to say farewell to his mother and to convey to her his property, thus making provision for her in case he should lose his life in the adventure he had on hand.

The revolutionary leaders made no secret of their purpose. There was no concealment of the fact that they had laid their plans to overturn the throne. Even the details could have been ascertained if the court party had sent out agents or spies to secure information. The very air was charged with revolt. The orators in the clubs expressed themselves without any reservation. The radical journals day after day urged

THE FRENCH REVOLUTION

the people to prepare for the event. "Everyone in Paris from the king to the poorest street boy," says Stephens, "knew that a revolt was being planned." It was an open declaration of war against royalty.

The sections were petitioning the Assembly to dethrone the king. At every session the galleries were packed with the rabble from the slums, who interrupted the proceedings from time to time by calling on the deputies to vote for the abolition of the monarchy They jeered and hooted the members who spoke conservatively. Some of the mob armed with pikes intimated that the representatives who defied the people's will might find their heads a public spectacle.

The king was without the kind of leader that was needed for such an exigency and personally he did not know what to do. The emissaries of the court were bribing the leaders of the insurrection, but judging from the results they evidently did not place the money where it accomplished much good. General Mandat, in command of the National Guards at the palace, seemed to be the only one near the king who had a clear head and he was mobilizing all the loyal troops that could be found and succeeded in gathering 6,000 men, tried and true, to defend the Tuileries against attack, a pretty formidable force if properly handled, but we shall see.

The sustaining hope of Louis during all these hours of suspense was that Brunswick would march directly to Paris. The royalists and the revolutionists alike believed that the undisciplined

DANTON

French levies would not stand before the trained armies of Austria and Prussia. So great was the fear of the Parisians in this regard that they would not have been surprised at any moment to see the soldiers of the retreating French army pour through the gates of the capital followed in close pursuit by the enemy. Every hour was burdened with rumors concerning the advance of the allies. There was no telegraph in those times to flash information from the seat of war and men's fears and imagination took the place of news. The journalist was as sensational then as he is in the present day and the bulletin board was an hourly alarmist. The public mind was wrought up to the highest state of excitation, but there was no change in the purpose of the insurrectionists; the throne was to be overturned even in the face of invading armies.

La Fayette was a power to be reckoned with for he too might turn upon the capital; so on the 8th of August the Assembly considered the question of his accusation, but by a strong majority it was decided that there were no substantial grounds upon which to prefer a charge. While this matter was under consideration great crowds gathered outside the doors of the Assembly and insulted, and in some instances even maltreated, those deputies who had absolved the absent general. The Jacobins burnt him in effigy in the Garden of the Tuileries and denounced him as a traitor.

On the 9th of August when the members, who had been insulted and attacked, complained of

THE FRENCH REVOLUTION

the treatment they had received, they were howled down and mocked with peals of laughter, the laughter that bites with its scorn.

The evening of the 9th was clear and starlit; all Paris was out of doors. The palace of the Tuileries was lighted up and the windows were open to admit every breeze that was blowing, for the weather was hot and sultry. Great crowds of people strolled in the gardens and upon the terraces. It was a serious, not a noisy crowd; the shuffling of feet could be distinctly heard above the subdued conversation of many voices. There was no merriment, no loud laughter. The people spoke in whispers, and the silence at times was oppressive; it seemed almost ominous. Paris stood in apprehension of some great uncertain event; the air was filled with rumors; and no one knew what a day would bring forth. Towards midnight the crowds dispersed, the palace lights were extinguished, and Paris waited for the dawn.

In some localities the night was one of terror and excitement. Two of the sections, at least, were in a state of increasing agitation; Santerre and Westermann were in the faubourg Saint Antoine, and Fournier was in the faubourg Saint Marceau. Danton, Desmoulins, and Carra were at the Cordeliers with the Marseilles battalion. Robespierre, who was not a man of iron and blood, nor "framed for warlike deeds," was somewhere in hiding, waiting for the storm to blow over. Marat, it is said, was concealed in a cellar. Now that the moment was approaching

DANTON

for decisive action, men, even brave men, lost their resolution.

This was not so with Danton; his courage and daring increased proportionately with the dangers. It was his resolution and decision of character that carried the plans through. There was nothing dim nor shadowy in his conception of what should be done and he did not for an instant waver in his purpose. After having made up his mind that the deposition of the king was necessary to the Revolution he never stopped until he accomplished his object. On the night of the 9th he mounted the tribune of the Cordeliers and thundered against the crimes of the court. He charged Louis with duplicity, declaring that his promise to support the Constitution was not sincere and only given to secure time to overthrow it; that his oath was taken with a mental reservation and that his conduct belied every promise he had made; that he had been conspiring with foreign princes to invade France and to enslave her people. "Citizens," he cried, "you can not depend upon your king, he has deceived and will betray you. Rise in your might and strike down the usurper! Lose no time, for this very night satellites concealed in the palace are to sally forth upon the people and to slaughter them, before they leave Paris to repair to Coblentz. Save yourselves then! To arms! to arms!"

At this moment it was approaching midnight; a cannon was fired in the Cour du Commerce, and the *Generale* beat to arms in every quarter of

THE FRENCH REVOLUTION

the city. Camille and others ran through the sections appealing to the people to rise, but there was nowhere the zeal of the district of the Cordeliers. Lastly the ringing of the tocsin was ordered, that dismal, terrifying sound startling the quiet of the night, making the timid quake and women and children cower in their beds.

"Ring out, wild bells, to the wild sky."

Steeple after steeple took up the alarm until at last the dreadful tones were borne to the palace; they awoke the sleeping king and announced the threatened destruction of his throne.

"You hear the alarm bell," said Danton in addressing the Marseillais, "it is the voice of the people. You have hastened from the extremity of the empire to the head of the nation which is menaced by despotism. May that bell sound the last hour of kings! To arms and *Ca ira!*"

Men pouring out of their homes in every quarter answered the summons; the streets were soon crowded with an excited multitude and their voices gradually grew into a hoarse sound like unto the roar of wild beasts, suddenly roused from their lairs. The sections were ready for the fray.

Danton and Desmoulins after a day of great excitement, fatigued with the arduous work of preparing an insurrection to overthrow the ancient and time-honored monarchy of France by the dethronement of its king—a task of no mean proportions, hurried home to get an hour's sleep before the bloody work began. Their wives, who had been waiting anxiously for their return, welcomed them as if from the dead, for they had heard the booming of the cannon, the ringing of the bells, and the rolling of the drums, and dreaded what such sounds might portend. Danton threw himself upon his bed and Camille slept with his head resting on Lucile's shoulder.

In the early morning Danton hastened to the Cordeliers, again harangued the Marseillais, and prepared them for the day's work. Shops were closed and business ceased; throughout the city, all was suspense and terror. General Westermann had been chosen leader of the attacking party.

Mandat, a brave and competent soldier, was in command of the troops at the palace. He was ordered by the Commune to appear at the Town Hall. At first he refused to answer the summons, but the king directed that he should obey the authorities. Appearing at the bar of the Commune he was questioned as to his conduct and, upon giving satisfactory answers, was dismissed. On his way back to the Tuileries he was arrested and carried before the Insurrectionary Commune, and after a short hearing was ordered to prison; while standing on the steps of the Town Hall he was treacherously shot down by Rossignol, a friend of Danton's. His head was severed from his body and placed on a pike. This murder deprived the king of his leader, his bravest defender, and immediately everything at the palace was thrown into confusion. Santerre was straightway chosen com-

THE FRENCH REVOLUTION

mander of the National Guards and it was left to him to disarrange the plans of defense adopted by Mandat.

The insurgents were now under marching orders. Santerre was at the head of the armed rabble. Westermann led the disciplined troops with the Marseillais holding the position of honor, the vanguard of the column.

The death of Mandat and the news that the mob was advancing from the sections threw the royal family into a panic. The king was urged by Roederer, the *procureur syndic,* to take refuge in the Assembly. The queen vehemently opposed this plan. "Madame," said Roederer, "you endanger the lives of your husband and children by remaining here. Think of the responsibility you take upon yourself." "Sir," said the queen, "you answer for the lives of the king and my children." "Madame," was the reply, "I answer for it that I will die by their side, but I promise nothing more."

Mirabeau at one time said that the queen was the only man the king had about him. She surely was the only person at his side who at this time displayed any real courage. She boldly declared that she would rather be nailed to the walls of the palace than retreat, and she thought it was high time to ascertain whether the king or the factions ruled. If Louis had possessed some of her nerve and spirit he might even at this crisis have saved his crown. He seemed to let his power slip away and by his impassiveness lost every chance of safety.

DANTON

Had he mingled with his troops his presence would have encouraged them. The Swiss were loyal and enthusiastic; a compliment from him would have put them upon their mettle. He had military force enough to make a strong defense and to protect the palace from capture, for a regiment of trained soldiers could have defended it against the assaults of ten thousand undisciplined men.

The entire number of defenders in the palace at the time Mandat was shot was close to 6,000. There were about seven hundred, fifty Swiss, brave and thoroughly drilled. Their officers were capable and confident in their ability to repulse any attack made by the mob. The Baron de Viomenil had assured the queen that with these men alone he would drive back the rabble to their slums. In the morning before the attack was made, Louis went out into the garden of the Tuileries to review his troops, but instead of warming their enthusiasm he chilled it. The cries of "Long live the king" were given liberally at first, but they grew fainter every minute. A few enthusiastic words, an appeal to their loyalty and patriotism, a display of resolution, would have turned lukewarm supporters into valiant defenders. The queen, who was watching the review from a window in the palace, exclaimed: "All is lost! the king has shown no energy."

Although the queen at this time evinced unusual courage, she unfortunately lacked judgment. When the commandant of the National

THE FRENCH REVOLUTION

Guards intimated that the nobles who were in the palace should be sent away as their presence irritated the people, she offended him and his command by pointing at the nobles and declaring that they were the men who would show the Guards how to fight.

But now the insurgents were drawing near and there was no time to be lost; already could be heard the discordant cries of the rabble when the queen reluctantly consented to leave the palace.

So the royal family left the Tuileries and strolled through the gardens to the hall of the Assembly. On the way the dauphin amused himself by kicking the dead leaves in the path. "The leaves fall earlier this year than usual," remarked the king. O! yes, Sire, a throne is to fall before the day is over. Who would have been thinking of dead leaves, at a time like that, except Louis?

When the Assembly was reached, Vergniaud was in the chair and the king addressing him said: "I have come here to prevent the commission of a great crime; I do not know any place where I can be safer than in your midst." The chairman assured him that the Assembly would maintain the rights of the people and the constituted authorities.

A deputy objecting to the presence of the king in the house during the debates on public questions, he in consequence was requested to retire with his family to a box back of the president's chair. This space was usually occupied by the reporters of the *Journal Logographique,* which paper claimed to give the most accurate reports of the speeches and the proceedings of the Assembly. For seventeen long, weary, harrowing hours, the king, his family, and his friends occupied these cramped quarters; a space about twelve feet square.

After the king left the palace to go to the Assembly, some of the courtiers, the "*Chevaliers du Poignard,*" because of his desertion tore from their breasts their crosses of St. Louis and broke their swords in rage and disappointment.

While the king was on his way to the Convention a body of royalists disguised as National Guards endeavored to reach the Tuileries to offer their services to the royal family. They were discovered, arrested, and confined in a building that stood between the palace and the hall of the Assembly. News was spread abroad of their arrest and a mob soon gathered, threatening to slaughter them. Baron Thiébault, commandant of the National Guards appealed to the crowd and had about succeeded in allaying their anger when suddenly a beautiful young woman, Théroigne de Méricourt, wearing a black felt hat with a black plume, and dressed in a blue riding habit with a pair of pistols and a dagger in her belt, pushed her way through the crowd, leaped upon a cannon, and called upon the men to carry out their threats, exclaiming, "How long are you to be fooled by the chatter of Thiébault?" The mob, stirred to fury by the burning eloquence of this beautiful demon, forced the doors of the building, ascended to the second floor, and made short work of the prisoners, throwing the bodies

THE FRENCH REVOLUTION

out of the windows to the pavement below. The mob, cheering the work of the murderers, danced around the victims of their fury like a band of red savages. The heads were hacked from the bodies and borne aloft on pikes. Later, street gamins amused themselves by tossing the heads back and forth and catching them on pointed sticks. Among the prisoners was Sulleau, the witty royalist journalist, who, time and again, had assailed Théroigne in the columns of his paper, in the most bitter and malignant terms. It is said she took dire vengeance on her enemy by cutting him down with her own sword.

The Place du Carrousel was crowded as early as seven o'clock on the morning of the tenth, but this was no part of the assaulting army; these people were idlers who came to watch the attack. The terraces were covered with a mass of humanity, every inch of ground was occupied. Through this multitude pressed the insurrectionists. They expected to meet with a sharp defense, for they did not as yet know that the king had deserted his post.

The repelling force at the palace at this time consisted of six hundred Swiss, two hundred gentlemen, and one hundred National Guards. One hundred fifty Swiss had accompanied the king to the Assembly. The Swiss were drawn up on the grand staircase of the palace under the command of Captain Durler, a brave, cool, and most competent officer.

Westermann led the attack and made straight for the gates of the Tuileries; he found them open and without delay entered the court-yard. A short parley took place between him and the Swiss. The general was an Alsatian and was able to speak in German. He appealed to them to desert their ranks and to fraternize with the people, who really were their friends. Some of the soldiers attempted to abandon their colors, but were instantly ordered back into line by their officers. At last a shot was fired, but by whom it will never be known. The soldiers stationed at the windows, taking it for a signal, opened fire on the crowd below. Captain Durler at once charged the mob and cleared the court-yard in a few minutes.

The king, hearing the discharge of musketry, quickly dispatched Captain d' Hervilly to order the Swiss to cease firing. D'Hervilly for some reason or other delayed serving the notice and the fighting continued for upwards of three-quarters of an hour. Westermann, having reformed his lines, led them a second time to the attack. It was at this point, unfortunately for the defenders of the palace, that d'Hervilly delivered the message of the king. The brave Swiss were thus left to the mercy of the mob. They massed and retreated slowly under a heavy fire. They attempted to force their way into the Assembly, but were ordered by the king to retire, so took refuge in the neighboring church of the Feuillants.

A number of Swiss soldiers had been left in the palace, not having heard the order of the king. Hemmed in by the advancing assailants

THE FRENCH REVOLUTION

they charged the mob, drove them back, and then marched across the gardens of the Tuileries until they reached the Place Louis XV. Here they formed a solid square under the statue of that king, determined to sell their lives at a dear price; but they were attacked by cavalry in superior numbers and cut to pieces.

A few remaining Swiss who could not escape climbed upon the marble monument, but the insurgent soldiers pricked them with their bayonets rather than deface the statuary by firing and when the poor fellows jumped to the ground they were brutally put to death. "An instance of taste for art mingled with revolutionary cruelty unparalleled in the history of the world."

The rabble now finding no resistance swarmed into the palace and destroyed right and left, like an army of Huns. Some loyal, devoted servants of the king, who were stationed on guard at the doors of the royal chambers, refused to quit their posts and were cruelly slaughtered.

A story is told to the effect that a workingman found a sum of money in the royal apartments, carried it to the Assembly, and handed it to Louis, saying: "If you had found my purse perhaps you would not have been so honest!" The palace was looted from cellar to garret, but the bandits who did the work of destruction were not the soldiers of the attacking columns, but the riff-raff of the slums who at last, drunk with blood and wine, turned upon each other and reveled in carnage. The army of insurrection consisted of the National Guards, the working men of the sections, and the battalion from Marseilles. These men were not of the lawless or criminal classes; the vast majority of them were industrious, law-abiding citizens.

The scenes in the French Revolution were so violent that we are apt to judge the participants unfairly and unjustly, and to group them all under one head, or to class them without discrimination among the lawless. We are describing a revolution, not a riot, and there never was a revolution in the world's history more justifiable. Its purpose was to relieve a people from oppression and tyranny that had been long continued. Royalty was so firmly entrenched and abuses were so deeply rooted that it required force, terrific force, to wrench them from their foundations. The wrongs of centuries had to be righted, and the struggle from beginning to end was bitter, relentless, terrible. "Revolutions are not made with rosewater," says Champfort.

To dethrone a king who would not abdicate was a task that required shot and shell, but we must distinguish between the patriot who assailed the palace and the bandit who looted it, between the revolutionist and the rioter.

When the king took refuge in the Assembly he may have thought that the mob would not assail an abandoned palace, but he was greatly mistaken if this was his conjecture. He heard the shouts of the combatants, the cheers of the victors, and the shrieks of the dying. He signed an order for the Swiss to cease firing and thus ex-

THE FRENCH REVOLUTION

posed them to the fury of the mob, and signed this order without even ascertaining the facts of the case; thus his ill-timed, inconsiderate act resulted in the slaughter of his sworn and most loyal defenders. They could have made a strong defense and perhaps might have saved the day if all the plans had not been disarranged by the withdrawal of Louis. By his cowardly desertion and by his order not to fire he left them naked to their enemies and they were ruthlessly massacred. The beautiful monument of the wounded lion at Lucerne, dedicated to these brave men, is pathetic in the story it mutely though eloquently tells of their sacrifice and destruction and moves to compassion the hearts of all that love loyalty and admire courage.

While in the Assembly Louis employed himself from time to time in pointing out to the dauphin the distinguished deputies, seemingly indifferent to the bloodshed and suffering at the palace. Even during the continuance of the firing, while men were dying for him, it is said he contentedly munched an apple and sucked an orange. The queen was greatly humiliated at the insensibility of her royal spouse to the suffering of his defenders, and was much chagrined at seeing him at meal time eat his chicken with as robust an appetite and drink his wine with as keen a relish, as though safe in his own dining-hall. And this while his monarchy was crumbling to pieces!

After the insurgents had massacred his troops and the mob had looted his palace, Louis saw the Assembly, on motion of Vergniaud, vote unanimously for his deposition. They compelled him to witness his degradation while they mercilessly stripped him of his power and humbled him in the presence of his queen and heir. How much rather would the queen have been nailed to the walls of the palace than to suffer such humiliation!

It was not until two o'clock on the morning of August 11th that the royal family were permitted to depart from the Assembly. They did not return to the palace of the Tuileries, as the mob had made that ancient and historic mansion almost uninhabitable, but were escorted to the convent of the Feuillants. Worn out with anxiety, suspense, and excitement, the king and the queen sank upon their beds exhausted.

The evening of the 10th of August was clear and calm. The people came in great numbers to the gardens of the Tuileries to view the ruins and to hear the recital of the exciting events of the day. The broken furniture and rubbish that had been taken from the palace were piled up in heaps and set on fire; the flames from the burning piles were so furious that both banks of the Seine were lighted up and the sky for miles was illumined with the glare. The blaze at times even threatened to destroy the palace itself. Death-carts under the direction of the Commune gathered the dead bodies of the combatants that had been piled in heaps,—Swiss, Marseillais, National Guards, *fédérés* and citizens,—and car-

THE FRENCH REVOLUTION

ried them away without ceremony, to a common burial.

The events of the 10th of August destroyed the monarchy. The king had surrendered so ignominiously and his conduct while in the Assembly had been so indifferent and undignified that he lost the respect of the deputies and the sympathy of his friends. He seemed to regret so little the fall from his throne that he made it easy for his enemies to deprive him permanently of that which apparently he so little valued.

The 10th of August was the people's day. They believed that Louis was false to them, that he was conspiring with the enemies of France, and in consequence foreign kings were leading their armies on a march of invasion. These strange monarchs already had directed what the domestic policy of the French people should be and had declared that it was their intention to strengthen kingly rule and to revive the monarchy as it had been before the adoption of the Constitution. It was to be a restoration of the old order and this, too, under foreign dictation. The time had come when either the king had to be deposed or the republic made impossible. "*Le 10 août*," said Danton, "*a divisé la France en deux partis, dont l'un est attache à la royauté et l'autre veut la republique.*" But the capture of the Tuileries and the vote in the Convention for the deposition of the king, put in ascendancy the popular cause and made certain its ultimate supremacy.

CHAPTER XIX

DANTON'S ACTIVITY—LONGWY CAPITULATES—DOMICILIARY VISITS

The insurrection of the 10th of August was Danton's work. The plan of campaign was his, the leaders had been selected by him, the people had rallied to his call. It was his courage that had inspired the insurgents, it was his nerve that carried the enterprise to a success. Even when the sections faltered his eloquence and his confidence aroused them.

General Santerre, the brewer, and the leader of the mob from Saint Antoine, who had nothing of Mars but his beer (" *Qui n' eut de Mars que la biere*"), trembled in his boots as the conflict approached and his courage had to be stiffened by a sharp word from Danton. Fréron despaired of success and Barbaroux was so fearful of the result that he had poison in his pocket to be used in case of failure.

Not so with Danton; the greater the danger, the greater his courage. He risked all in the cast and he won because his spirit was unconquerable. He never loomed up in bigger proportions than during this period. " *Si j' eusse été vaincu*," he said when it was over; " *je serais criminel. Le cause de la liberté a triomphé.*"

THE FRENCH REVOLUTION

On the 11th of August Danton was made minister of justice by a vote in the Convention of 222 out of a total of 284, and he declared in his characteristic way that he had entered the ministry through the breach made by the cannon of the 10th of August. During this period he was in supreme control; he was virtually dictator.

Condorcet, a distinguished philosopher, a member of the faction of the Girondins, and one of the purest men who took an active part in the Revolution, in commenting upon the selection of Danton for this office said: " They have reproached me for voting for Danton for minister of justice. Here are my reasons: It was necessary to have in the government a man who had the confidence of those who had just overturned the throne; a man who by his ascendancy could keep in order the many unruly instruments of a Revolution which undoubtedly was useful, glorious and necessary; a man with such talents and character that he would be agreeable to his fellow-ministers and the members of the Assembly. Danton alone had these qualities. I chose him and I do not regret it. Perhaps he referred too much to popular ideas and carried into public affairs too much the people's notions; but the only thing which in times of revolution can save the laws is to act with the people by directing the course of events, and all parties who have separated themselves from the people have ended by ruining themselves and the people at the same time. Besides, Danton has that precious quality, which ordinary men never have, of neither hating nor fearing those who are wise, talented, and virtuous."

The Revolution now took on a new phase; the government at once became more democratic in its features. The common people were in power and the *bourgeoisie,* who had awed the nobility, were in turn now terrorized by the rabble.

The Girondins met as usual in the *salon* of Madame Roland and haughtily boasted of their deeds, claiming credit for having overthrown the monarchy. The future to them was bright with hope; it was to be an era of freedom. In their imagination they had created an ideal republic and they were already living in its atmosphere. Their illusions so obscured the future that they could not read its signs. They did not for an instant appreciate the fact that coming to the front and supplanting them were men of stronger fibre; not idealists, not dreamers, not sentimentalists, but men of practical views, and of an audacity that stopped at nothing in attaining ends.

Marat's demoniacal features leered at these pedantic statesmen who danced in attendance upon Madame Roland and crowded her parlors discussing abstract questions and dreaming of Utopias. The fanatical doctor was bent on riot and the murder of all aristocrats. Politeness, courtesy, genteel manners, were sure indications of good breeding and consequently they were anathema to him. He had been hunted to the cellars, the vaults, the sewers, and the garrets, as well as to foreign lands and nothing so provoked his enmity as a fashionable *salon,* especially when

THE FRENCH REVOLUTION

its receptions were attended by those who professed to be revolutionists or republicans. But there was a special reason for his hatred of the Rolands. After the 10th of August he petitioned the Assembly to give him permission to use four of the royal presses in place of those belonging to him which La Fayette had destroyed away back in January, 1790. The Assembly refused his request. He then made application to the town council and that body acquiesced; Marat straightway took possession. Roland severely rebuked him for his conduct and declared that the council had no right to make such disposition of public property. This stirred the doctor's gall, but when Roland refused to give him any portion of the money voted by the Assembly to be used in disseminating revolutionary literature his anger knew no bounds and the columns of his paper teemed with abuse. There was nothing too vile for him to print and he unquestionably greatly injured the reputation of the Rolands in the estimation of the common people.

Though the events of the 10th of August terrorized the royalists, they did not stop the advance of the allied armies. On the 20th Longwy was invested, and on the 24th it fell into the hands of the enemy. Brunswick immediately pressed on to besiege Verdun; if this city should fall the road to Paris would be open. Of course the capital was thrown into great excitement; terror ruled all classes, and the minds of many were paralyzed with fear.

There was one man, however, whom these

dangers did not frighten and whose defiance and courage failed him not. This man was Danton. At a meeting of the ministers it was proposed by some that the government should retire to Blois; others suggested that an army of citizens be at once enlisted or conscripted and that a stand be made under the walls of Paris; but Danton, resolute and unperturbed, disregarded all such propositions. "I have brought my old mother here," he cried; "my children also. If the Prussians take Paris, let it be a Paris burnt to ashes." Then turning to Roland he said: "Take care, Roland, do not talk too much about flight; the people might hear you."

On the 28th of August he attended an evening session of the Assembly and created the greatest enthusiasm by one of his inspiriting speeches. "There is no time to be lost," he said. "We must prepare for action and go forth to join the army of the Fatherland. It is not safe for the loyal citizens to leave Paris, to meet the approaching armies of invasion, while traitors lurk in the capital; the royalists would incite the populace and strike the patriots in the rear. We would be between two fires. You cannot conceal from yourselves the very insignificant minority of the party in the country which is for a republic. It is necessary to strike terror to the royalists. Frighten them. True, the enemy have taken Longwy, but Longwy is not France. When a vessel is in a storm, threatened with shipwreck, the crew throw overboard all that endangers its safety; in the same way all that imperils the na-

THE FRENCH REVOLUTION

tion must be cast out. We must shut the gates of Paris, and all conspirators against the republic must be seized. We cannot delay, every minute counts; we may be surprised at any moment by hearing the drums and the foot-beat of the enemy. We must make house to house searches, and it must be done to-morrow. We must seize all arms and whatever else is of use to the nation in this, her hour of supreme peril. All belongs to the Fatherland when the Fatherland is in danger. *Pour vaincre que faut-il? De l'audace! Encore de l'audace! et toujours de l'audace!—et la France est sauvée."*

Here was a man who did not waver in the face of danger. Approaching armies could not daunt him. Foreign foes, invading and desecrating the soil of France, aroused his rage and indignation, but not his fears. Almost within sound of the enemy's drums he shouted out his defiance. There have been few stronger men than Danton, even in the most heroic periods of the world's history. We forget his methods and his short-comings in our admiration of his dauntless courage.

The decree for the domiciliary visits, in accordance with the suggestions of Danton, was passed and posted throughout the city, and arrangements were made to carry it into immediate effect.

The barriers were closed for forty-eight hours from the evening of the 29th of August, 1792, and no one was allowed to leave the city on any account during that interval of time. Even the country people, if they lingered beyond the hour, were not permitted to pass out of the gates. As daylight waned and just as the early shadows of night began to fall upon the city, the din and confusion of business ceased; streets that had been crowded with pedestrians and all sorts of vehicles, suddenly became as quiet as the grave; people scurried home from every direction to await the arrival of the patrol, for householders could more easily identify themselves in their dwellings than abroad; cafés and places of amusement were closed; and a hush fell upon the city that was not only oppressive but terrifying. Picture, if you can, a capital in the rush of life, with its activities in full swing suddenly, instantly, becoming as motionless as if it were dead, its inhabitants cowering with terror in their homes.

It had been directed by the authorities that after a certain hour every house should be lighted up in order that the search might be more quickly and effectively made. It was not until about midnight that the visits began. Patrols consisting of sixty pikemen were in every street. The tumult created by these armed men soon disturbed the quiet of the night as the searchers knocked upon the house doors and broke down those that did not open. No one felt safe, for informers and spies had been at work and the authorities offered inducements to those who had information to give. It was a great opportunity for the low-minded to satisfy revenge and to settle old grudges, and many innocent people were made to suffer Nobles, priests and enemies of the Republic were seized and cast into prison. All

THE FRENCH REVOLUTION

persons that had belonged to the late court, or had been in any way connected with the palace, or had even expressed themselves in favor of any royalist measure or movement, fell into the class of the proscribed and were arrested. Every word ever uttered, every opinion ever expressed, every act ever done in behalf of royalty or against the Revolution was remembered and became the basis for denunciation and investigation.

All places were searched; closets, wardrobes, chimneys, cellars, garrets, roofs, gardens, woods, promenades, even the boats on the Seine. Any person found in an abode other than his own was arrested unless he could give a satisfactory explanation for his presence. Hiding places were at a premium, and the loyalty of friendship was put to the test by the risks and dangers it was willing to assume in affording protection to those who were suspected. There were many instances of noble and heroic sacrifice, for hospitality was considered treason and affection was no excuse for the sheltering of traitors. Men were concealed beneath piles of rubbish, under floors, and in excavations made in walls; every stratagem that fear could invent was resorted to by those who expected arrest to avoid detection.

The " suspects " were taken to the committee of the section in which they were found and then to the Commune; here they were questioned, and, if detained, were committed to prison.

CHAPTER XX

THE SEPTEMBER MASSACRES

Some authorities state that from twelve to fifteen thousand persons were arrested as a result of the domiciliary visits. Rumors were immediately put in circulation that the prisoners were conspiring to overthrow the Republic. The armies of the coalition were gradually approaching. Would it be prudent, it was asked, for the patriots to go out into the field to meet the allies and leave the enemies of the Republic in the capital? Would the women and children be safe when their defenders were absent? " Can we go to war and leave 3,000 prisoners behind us in Paris who may break out and destroy our property and slaughter our wives and little ones?" There was a sickening suggestion in these questions.

The Revolution was already sniffing the blood of the unfortunate prisoners and their massacre was decided upon without delay. Maillard, a rabid revolutionist, was selected to perpetrate the bloody work. He had organized a band of blood-thirsty desperadoes ready for any enterprise, no matter how diabolical. He had figured prominently in the events of the 5th and 6th of October when the women marched to Ver-

THE FRENCH REVOLUTION

sailles. He considered himself quite a political leader and was a demagogue of the lowest order, a representative of the riff-raff. Aristophanes, in his inimitable vein of satire in picturing an Athenian leader of the rabble, describes one of his ilk: "You possess all the requisites for a politician—a vulgar tongue; you are of mean birth, a low fellow."

Maillard was an idol of the mob, and supreme in the faubourg Saint Marceau. Loud in voice, bold in manner, and of an inflexible purpose; he was naturally a leader of the canaille. It is said of him that "he loved blood, he bore about heads, he displayed hearts, he cut up corpses." He had just taken part in another massacre, one which he had organized and conducted successfully, so that he was fitted by experience for the work in hand. He was given notice to hold himself in readiness to act immediately upon a given signal, and was ordered to prepare bludgeons, to take precautions for preventing the cries of the victims, to procure vinegar, holly brooms, quick lime, and covered carts.

Vague rumors were in circulation and fear and anxiety possessed the minds of the prisoners. Many of them were in communication with the outer world and were kept posted as to passing events. The royal family in the Temple trembled for their lives.

The sections were wrought up to great excitement by the circulation of reports that the prisoners had made arrangements to break out of the dungeons at night to spread themselves through the city, to destroy certain portions of it by fire, to carry off the king, and to throw open the gates and welcome the allies. This was a startling enough plot, yet no one seemed to consider the impossibility of its accomplishment. People in those days of excitement did not weigh such matters nicely, and they believed the rumors because it was stated that the information was obtained by the confession of one of the condemned.

An unfortunate incident only added fuel to the fire of frenzy. On the afternoon of the 2d of September sixteen priests in four hackney coaches were on their way from the Hotel de Ville, where they had been interrogated, to the Abbaye, where they were to be detained as "suspects." A crowd gathered on the Rue Dauphine, began to hiss and, drawing closer to the coaches, interfered with their progress. One of the priests, unable to restrain his temper, because of the insults, put his arm out of the window and struck a soldier or *fédéré* with his cane; the latter sprang upon the steps of the vehicle and, drawing his sabre, plunged it thrice into the body of the offending prelate. This was the signal for slaughter and only three of the priests escaped the vengeance of the mob; among these was the abbé Sicard, teacher of the deaf and dumb, whose life was saved by the courage of a watch-maker named Monnot. This massacre increased the ferocity of the multitude and whetted their appetite for blood.

The rabble marched through the streets and

THE FRENCH REVOLUTION

demanded the extermination of the prisoners; "to the sword with all aristocrats," was the cry. Danton's eloquence had already lashed the passions of the mob into a fury and they were ready for any deed of violence.

It was then that the signal was given and three hundred butchers, under the leadership of Maillard, began the inhuman slaughter known as the September massacres. The prisoners were conducted one by one from their cells and, after a short examination before an improvised tribunal of twelve judges, were delivered over to the executioners, who stood at the door armed with bludgeons, daggers, pikes, swords, cutlasses, pistols and guns to strike, shoot and cut them down. Old and young fell before the vengeance of these assassins. That the work might be expedited courts were held also in the prisons. The definition of Blackstone, "a court is a place wherein justice is judicially administered," had no application to these tribunals. Witnesses and rules of evidence went for naught. Hate sat in judgment and Vengeance pronounced the doom.

All the tribunals were very similar. Around large tables, littered with papers, records, bottles of wine, glasses, pipes, and sabres sat the judges. They were not men learned in the law but were of the laboring classes, their woolen caps, hobnailed shoes, and coarse aprons revealing this fact. Many of them took off their waistcoats and rolled up their shirt sleeves. They smoked and drank during the proceedings and ignored every feature of judicial demeanor and decorum.

DANTON

When a prisoner was acquitted a voice cried out: "Let the man be set at liberty." If condemned the sentence was: *"A la Force."* The door was then opened and the victim fell dead at the threshold.

For three days the cruel work continued; the gutters ran blood, the mob reveled in slaughter until the prisons were emptied. A squad of butchers did the work; besmeared and bespattered with blood they gloated with ghoulish glee over the task. Hatless wretches, their arms bare and covered with gore, cut down the prisoners without mercy. The mob cheered and encouraged the assassins at their work. The soul of pity was out of France. Night and day the horrid work went on. The murderers succeeded each other at the tribunal and at the wicket and became by turns judges and executioners. All this time they kept on drinking, placing their blood-stained glasses on the tables. Intoxication increased a ferocity that at best was unnatural.

When they grew tired or hungry, the cutthroats rested from their task, seating themselves on stools or boxes near the wickets and eating their meals without even washing their blood-stained hands. They joked and chatted and compared notes, except when their voices were drowned by the shrieks of the victims and the cheers of the mob.

In the midst of the slaughter one of the committee members begged to be heard; he was granted an audience and the noise temporarily subsided. He mounted a chair and said: "Com-

THE FRENCH REVOLUTION

rades and friends, you are good patriots, your resentment is just. Open war to the enemies of the common good, neither truce nor mercy; it is war to the death! I feel like you, that they must all perish. And yet if you are good citizens you must love justice. There is not one of you but would shudder at the notion of shedding innocent blood." "Yes! Yes!" cried the people. "Well, then, I ask of you, if without inquiry or investigation, you fling yourselves like mad tigers on your fellow men—" Just here the speaker was interrupted by one of the butchers who with a bloody sabre forced his way through the crowd and said: "Tell us, Monsieur le Citoyen, would the Prussians and Austrians if they were at Paris investigate for the guilty? Would they not cut to the right and left as the Swiss did on August the tenth? I have a wife and five children whom I leave with my section when I go to war, and it is not my bargain that villains in this prison, for whom the doors will be opened by the other villains outside, shall kill my wife and children in the meanwhile. Die here or die on the frontiers, I am sure enough to be killed by these aristocrats one day, but I mean to sell them my life at a high price, and be it I or be it others, this prison shall be purged of these rascals. I am no speaker; I cannot stuff the ears of anyone, but you now know my views." The appeal for mercy for the innocent was lost and the slaughter was at once renewed.

The reasons given by this assassin for his conduct were those that reconciled the community to the massacres. The cruelty displayed by the butchers proves, however, that their actions were prompted as much by hate as by fear. Even many citizens who condemned the brutality of the murderers believed that the massacres were a necessity.

At the Abbaye the executioners complained that the foremost alone got a stroke at the prisoners, and that those who were not close to the wickets were deprived of taking any effective part in the slaughter. It was ordered, in consequence of this complaint, that those who were in a position to deliver the first blow should strike with the backs of their sabres, and the condemned, being able to run the gauntlet, thus afforded an opportunity for all to have a hand in the murder. The prolonging of the agony of the victim was not considered.

In some localities formal requests were made to the Commune to furnish lights that the massacres might be witnessed by night; in compliance with these demands lamps were placed near the wickets, where seats were reserved for both men and women. More than once women forced their way through the crowd and, getting close to the executioners, beat out the brains of the dying with billets of wood.

Although the scenes witnessed showed the utter depravity of the human heart, yet on the other hand in some instances there was a display upon the part of the prisoners of a most exalted courage. Among the first victims condemned to death were the Swiss soldiers that had been im-

THE FRENCH REVOLUTION

prisoned since the 10th of August. There were one hundred and fifty of them and, as they appeared *en masse* before the tribunal, many sank upon their knees and begged for mercy. Some little time was lost here and the crowd outside were kept waiting. " Come on and end this matter one way or another," called out one of the executioners, opening the door and addressing the judges; " the people are growing impatient." The Swiss recoiled as they heard the shouts of the rabble and huddled together still appealing for clemency. " Enough of this," exclaimed one of the judges, " who will be the first to go? " A young and handsome soldier stepped out from the midst of his companions and, standing apart, alone, with his arms folded across his breast, turned to the judges, saying: " I will go, show me the way." The door opened, and throwing his cap into the air and shouting gayly a last farewell to his comrades, he sprang forward as if dashing himself against the lines of an enemy in battle. It was soon over, sooner than it takes to tell the story, but his memory is embalmed in history and treasured in the hearts of all men that admire heroic resolve and true manly courage.

M. Thierry, the king's valet, after a pike was run through his body, kept crying out: " God save the king." The assassins then burned his face with torches, but he still persisted in asseverating his loyalty.

One of the prisoners, the Count de St. Mart, had a spear run entirely through his body, and while he was bent almost double with pain, the wretches, because he would not renounce his loyalty to the king, compelled him to crawl on his hands and knees; his terrible sufferings and writhings induced the jeers and the laughter of the heartless mob, until at last, to relieve his agony, they cut off his head.

Masaubré, a young man at the *conciergerie*, had hidden himself in the chimney. Thinking he had escaped, the assassins determined to hold the jailer responsible. The latter, believing that the prisoner had not escaped but was concealing himself, fired a gun several times up the chimney; one of the balls struck Masaubré on the wrist, but he had sufficient fortitude to endure the pain in silence. The jailer then set fire to some straw on the hearth and the smoke soon so suffocated the prisoner that he fell to the ground. The executioners carried him out into the street and threw him on a heap of dead bodies, where he lingered in agony for about a quarter of an hour, until some one, perhaps out of compassion, put an end to his sufferings by shooting him five times through the head.

The venerable Sombreuil, governor of the *Invalides,* was brought forward to the tribunal. His daughter perceived him from the prison and, rushing through the crowd, putting her life in peril every step of the way, reached the side of her father, threw her arms around his neck, and with tears streaming down her cheeks, besought the murderers to save his life. So impetuous, so intense, was her manner, so sincere her affection,

THE FRENCH REVOLUTION

that she softened the fury of the butchers. "Drink," they said, "the blood of the aristocrats," and they handed to her a pot of blood. Without a moment's hesitation, so the story goes, she put it to her lips, and her father's life was saved.

The daughter of Cazotte, when he was about to be cut down, threw herself on his neck and presenting her bosom to the swords of the assassins, cried out in desperation: "You shall not touch my father until you have forced your way through my heart." A shout for mercy went up from the crowd and the old man's life was spared. This faithful daughter, whose name was Elizabeth, in the exuberance of her joy embraced the butchers, covered with human blood, and then conducted her father to his home.

At La Force was confined the beautiful Louisa of Savoy, Princess de Lamballe. She was to have been saved, her ransom had been paid, but for some reason or other the plan miscarried. She was subjected to a mock trial, and as she stepped over the threshold of the door, upon leaving the court-room, she was struck a severe blow on the back of the head with a hanger. Almost fainting from loss of blood she was led over dead bodies until at last the fiends completed her murder by running her through with spears. She was then stripped and her naked body exposed for two hours to the insults of the rabble. Men were placed at her side to wipe off the blood when it oozed from her wounds and to call the attention of the spectators to the whiteness of the skin. Modesty would blush to read the recital of the acts of lustful indecency with which the corpse was defiled, and these indecent acts were done in the presence of men, women, and children without the slightest protest from the authorities. Cléry states that the mob attempted to rush into the Temple to carry the naked, bleeding body of the princess to the apartments of the queen, but some municipal officers prevented the intrusion.

Her beautiful form at last was torn to pieces and the fragments divided among her executioners. Her head and heart were carried through Paris on the points of spears, the trunk of her body was trailed through the streets by a troop of drunken cannibals who were naked to the waist and smeared with blood. It is said a cannon was charged with one of her legs. Even her bloody chemise was waved in the air from the point of a pike like a trophy. The brute who carried the head on a pike suggested it should be taken to the foot of the throne. Accordingly, with a shout, the mob started for the Temple and the ghastly trophy was held before the window of the queen's chamber, but fortunately she fainted and was thus saved from witnessing the horrible spectacle. Later a drunken wretch took her head into a tavern, placed it on the bar amidst glasses and bottles, then washed its features, combed the hair, and called on all present to drink to the health of Madame Veto's friend.

Such ferocity is almost unparalleled; such scenes were never enacted in any other capital

PRINCESS DE LAMBALLE
From an old engraving

THE FRENCH REVOLUTION

in modern times. Perhaps never in the history of the world has there been among a civilized people such a display of savagery and of indecency. Men and women became fiendish in their desire to inflict cruelty.

The Commune protected the butchers and the government took no action to restrain the crimes. Indeed, the assassins openly demanded the promised reward for their work; they thronged to the doors of the committee of the municipality and threatened the members with instant death if they were not immediately paid. "Look, I have only twenty-four francs," said a young baker, "and I have killed forty aristocrats with my own hands."

The massacres continued for three days, the victims numbering from two to three thousand at least. Some authorities place the number as high as ten thousand. "The ditches of Clamart, the catacombs of the Barriére St. Jacques alone know the number." The most remarkable feature of all is that the butchers did not exceed three hundred, and yet this handful of men actually terrorized the whole city. These crimes were committed in the very heart of the capital, under the eyes of the Assembly and the municipal authorities. Fifty thousand National Guards were enrolled and could have been called into action at a moment's notice. Yet nothing was done to prevent this useless and inhuman slaughter.

From where did the men come who heartlessly indulged in such cruelty and brutality, who

DANTON

struck down their fellow creatures without compassion, compunction or remorse? They came from the everyday walks of life and in times of peace would have followed their legitimate vocations. They were made inhuman by the conditions that surrounded them and after the Revolution was over, many of them doubtless returned to their callings and spent the balance of their lives in useful pursuits. No question but that most of them were ashamed of the part they had taken in those scenes of violence and in after days thought of them with a shudder. Every community, perhaps, holds a similar class, that with a revolution would come to the surface. Like the dregs in wine, they need but agitation to bring them to the top.

The description of those dreadful scenes may not be pleasant reading, but it is necessary if one is to understand and comprehend to its full meaning the French Revolution. Such hatred was not engendered in a day nor in a generation; it required centuries of tyranny, of cruel, insolent oppression to create and develop such a spirit of savage vindictiveness.

CHAPTER XXI

PARIS DURING THE REVOLUTION—MANNERS—CUSTOMS—CONDITIONS—THE GUILLOTINE

While these terrible scenes were being enacted the life of Paris went on as usual; shops were busy, theatres were open, cafés were crowded, the streets were thronged with pedestrians. The farmer brought his products to market, fishwomen scolded each other in the ordinary slang, hucksters and peddlers were as vociferous as ever in calling their wares, children went to school, the baker delivered his bread, the newsboy cried his extra, the doctor visited his patient, the lawyer prepared his brief, the curate—well, to tell the truth, there was not much for him to do. Religion was out of fashion. The cassock of the priest was regarded as the habit of treason. "To the lamp-post with all the bishops," was the frenzied cry of the rabble. The churches were closed, their great doors barred and bolted, the altars overturned and the faithful dispersed. "Where, through the long drawn aisle and fretted vault," had once been heard "the pealing anthem (swelling) the note of praise," now all was silent and dismal as the tomb. The bells, instead of calling the faithful to prayer, now summoned the citizens to arms. They no longer

DANTON

intoned the melting notes of the Angelus, but rang out the wild shriek of the tocsin. The State had endeavored to legislate religion out of existence, forgetting that its abode is really in the hearts of men, and that the Church is but the symbol of their faith.

The population of Paris in 1793 was about 600,000. It was the largest and most important city on the continent. The cafés had greatly grown in favor, had increased in numbers, were frequented by both men and women, and were the meeting places for all classes, from the proletairiat to the aristocrat. Each café had its separate group. One known as the Hottot was a resort for the women of the slums and another called the Corazza was the favorite of the Jacobins. The Café Foy, in the Palais Royal, was the oldest in the city and was renowned as the place where Camille had called the people to arms on the 12th of July, 1789. The visitors began to drop into these resorts about 11 o'clock in the morning, but they were crowded the most at 5 o'clock in the afternoon. On holidays the gardens and public walks were filled with well-dressed people; Parisians were always fond of fine clothes and fresh air. Powdered wigs and queues were not so common as in the past, although Robespierre never abandoned his. Men as a rule wore trousers and top boots, instead of knee breeches, silk stockings, and buckled shoes.

A real Jacobin of the people was known by his attire. He wore a coarse red woolen cap called a *bonnet rouge,* on the side of which was

THE FRENCH REVOLUTION

fastened his tri-color cockade—the symbol of the Revolution; his shirt was cut low at the neck, exposing his throat and sometimes even a portion of his chest; he wore a long-sleeved waistcoat, known as a *carmagnole,* trousers extending to his ankles, and his feet were either bare or encased in wooden clogs (*sabots*). His hair was cropped short at the temples. This livery of the Revolution was considered very vulgar in the eyes of the fops who were designated Muscadins—so nick-named by Hébert, the editor of the *Pére Duchesne,* because of a kind of perfume they carried called *musk-pastilles.*

The dandies were as daintily dressed as in days agone. They wore high-crowned hats with broad rims; frock or long-tailed coats, generally green, gray, blue or olive in shade; vests of most brilliant hues; cuffs and frills (*jabots*); great scarfs that covered the throat and were arranged in some cases so as to reach above the point of the chin; short or knee breeches (*culottes*); silk stockings and buckled shoes. They cultivated the moustache and their hair was allowed to grow long, being either brushed back so as to fall loosely to the shoulders or else done up in a queue and powdered. They wore jeweled pins in their scarfs, carried large round eye-glasses, scent bottles, snuff boxes and heavy walking sticks. The last they did not hesitate to use in a fracas. They frequented certain cafés and well-known gambling houses. They were not Jacobins and their *béte noir* was Marat. Sons of brokers, bankers, merchants and the well-to-do of the middle class, they may be considered as the fore-runners of the *jeunesse dorée.*

The apparel of women underwent a great change during the Revolution. The fashions that had obtained at Trianon, at the court of Versailles, or during the days of the ancient *regime,* were out of date as not in keeping with democratic simplicity. Waists were discountenanced and instead of stiffened skirts and narrow bodices, women wore short loose robes, after the style of the Greek *chitons,* which they draped gracefully in imitation of the Athenian Aspasias. Girdles *a la* Cleopatra were also much in vogue among a certain class. High-heeled shoes were displaced by sandals and in many instances, among the ultra fashionable, the feet were without stockings, if the feet were small, pink and dimpled. The hair instead of being dressed in towers, or *a la* Pompadour, was allowed to hang loosely down the back. For ornaments gun metal and steel instead of gold and silver were used, for it was presumed that every loyal woman had sent her jewelry to the National treasury.

All titles of nobility were abolished. There were no coats-of-arms, crests, escutcheons, or heraldic designs to be seen even on business or shop signs. Tailors, shoemakers, and haberdashers no longer proudly announced that they were makers to his majesty, to his excellency, to his highness, or to duke so and so. People familiarly addressed each other in the second person — a custom known as *tutoyer* — and as Citizen and Citizeness. Madame and Monsieur as terms of

THE FRENCH REVOLUTION

address were too aristocratic. A most peculiar custom grew into favor, that of dropping the Christian or baptismal name and adopting in its place a classical designation; especially was this the case with those rampant republicans who were called Louis. This name was too suggestive of royal relationship; so it was discarded and appellations were seriously chosen from a Greek or Roman nomenclature. This custom, however, was not confined alone to everyday people and to those who were named Louis, for many men of distinction accepted it as the proper thing to do. Coffinhall, president of the Revolutionary Tribunal, adopted the prefix Mucius Scævola; Chaumette chose Anaxagoras as specially appropriate and the wild Clootz called himself Anacharsis. Pitou, the witty royalist poet, ridiculed the fashion; one of his favorite songs was about a cobbler, "Cujus," and his wife, "Cujusdam."

Even games were changed. Kings, queens, and knaves disappeared from playing cards and their places were taken by figures or designs representing *Fraternité, Egalité, and Liberté*. In checkers it was deemed treason to crown a king. I have not been able to ascertain what disposition was made of the king, queen, and knight of the royal game of chess. It would perhaps have cost a patriot his reputation if he had been found indulging in so aristocratic an amusement.

Equipages were not so sumptuous and luxurious as in the past. If the coachmen and footmen were liveried, they were in very plain and

DANTON

sombre habits; even the horses seemed meeker and the harness was less ornamented with gold and silver than in the days when the nobles recklessly dashed with their prancing steeds through the streets, utterly regardless of the rights and the lives of pedestrians.

Occasionally a crowd of hoodlums, shrieking like demons, would rush through the shopping districts of the city, bearing a ghastly head upon a pike or dragging at the end of a rope a bleeding, muddy corpse. Women would shriek, bury their faces in their hands, as they have done when frightened from time immemorial, and run into the adjoining stores; business would be temporarily suspended, but was resumed as soon as the tatterdemalions disappeared.

There was of course great excitement in the immediate vicinity of the prisons when the massacres and lynchings were taking place. Great crowds gathered, and necessarily at these points there was wild commotion, but really outside of these localities the everyday life of Paris revealed but little if any change. True, the death carts rumbled through the streets carrying the victims to execution. Some of the prisoners would be singing, some praying, others wildly appealing to the people, but these processions became so common, so frequent, that in time if the condemned were not distinguished they attracted as a rule only passing notice. The busy man, after watching them for a moment, would turn on his heel and hurry away to keep his engagement.

Many of the scenes of the French Revolution

THE FRENCH REVOLUTION

were so terrible that we marvel how a man of peace could have existed during that period; but it must be borne in mind that history describes only the extraordinary or abnormal events, and between them were great stretches or intervals of time in which life flowed on in its ordinary channels. "The 'Reign of Terror' in Paris," says Stephens, "seems to us a time unparalleled in the history of the world; yet to the great majority of contemporaries it did not appear so. They lived their ordinary lives, and it was only in exceptional cases that the serenity of their days was interrupted or that their minds were exercised by anything more than the necessity of earning their daily bread."

The Revolution interfered only with those who took part in it. The citizen who kept up his show of loyalty to the Republic, who quietly attended to his own affairs, without too plainly expressing his views, and who refrained from taking too active a part in public matters could pursue the even tenor of his way and avoid having his head taken off. Of great convenience was the *carte de sureté,* a guarantee of loyalty to the government which every person, whether man or woman, was compelled to obtain from the Revolutionary Committee. This card had to be produced whenever called for by any citizen, and failure or refusal to show it would subject the person so offending to arrest and investigation.

Executions were so frequent, blood was so cheap, and men had grown so familiar with death, that in a great measure it had lost its terrors, and with this insecurity of life there developed a fondness for all kinds of sensual enjoyment. Men and women endeavored " to bury anxiety in the delirium of pleasure." Paris never was gayer than during the " Reign of Terror; " from September, 1793, to July, 1794, according to Mercier there were twenty-three theatres and sixty dancing saloons open every night. The Parisians were like those people who reside in an active earthquake zone, or at the base of a volcanic mountain, who give no thought to the imminent peril, or else indulge in gayety and dissipation to forget it. In a prolonged siege it is said that the inhabitants of the beleaguered town or city become defiant and reckless in the face of continued danger. Where a shrieking shell at first blanches the cheeks of the bravest, it fails at last to make even the timid shudder.

Time was no longer reckoned as Anno Domini, in the year of Our Lord, but as Anno Republicae, in the year of the Republic. The Julian Calendar was out of date and the Christian Sunday was abolished. Every tenth day instead of every seventh was a holiday. The year was divided into twelve months, but to each month were assigned thirty days. This left in each year five days to be disposed of and it was decided that these should be observed as festivals and called *Sanscullotides*. The additional day in leap year was added to this list. The year had its four seasons, three months in each season, but to each month was given a new poetical

THE FRENCH REVOLUTION

designation. *Vendémiaire, Brumaire,* and *Frimaire* were the autumn months of Vintage, Fog and Frost. *Nivose, Pluviose, Ventose* were the winter months of Snow, Rain, and Wind. *Germinal, Floréal* and *Prairial* were the spring months of Buds, Flowers and Meadows. *Messidor, Thermidor* and *Fructidor* were the summer months of Harvest, Heat and Fruit. The new almanac began to compute time from the 21st of September, 1792, which date was marked as the beginning of the first year of the Republic.

During all the time of Revolution the Assembly was the centre of attraction. " Here swarmed, jostled, challenged, threatened, fought and lived all those combatants that are to-day but phantoms." Here occurred scenes such as were never before witnessed in any legislative body in the history of the world. Here were enacted laws that breathed the very spirit of liberty as well as laws that outraged every principle of justice and offended every sentiment of humanity, whose every sentence was written in blood.

The delegates were divided into factions and parties, the principal among them being the Dantonists, the Jacobins, and the Girondins. These had their platforms well constructed. There were also other groups that professed to be independent; they ignored party allegiance and their political principles were as dim as dreams.

The seats in the hall were arranged in the form of an amphitheatre. The top rows on the left were occupied by the Jacobins which location was called the Mountain, and the delegates occupying this eminence were designated the Mountaineers. The moderates and conservatives were on the right. The seats on the lower rows and the ground floor were known as the Plain or the Marsh, and the deputies were often referred to, sometimes jocularly, sometimes contemptuously, as the Frogs of the Marsh. The sessions were frequently tumultuous. Party spirit ran high and was bitter; controversies were hot and vehement; and the orators bandied epithets from one to another without reservation. The galleries were crowded with a noisy rabble who interrupted the proceedings of the Assembly, and, in the later days of the Revolution, controlled in a great measure the deliberations of that body. A threat from them to an offending deputy was not a thing to be ignored. The president used a bell instead of a gavel to call the convention to order, and at times the din was so great that the bell could scarcely be heard.

During the "Reign of Terror," the aristocrats and royalists confined in the convents and prisons endeavored to make life as comfortable and as agreeable as possible under the circumstances. All the amenities and the etiquette of polite society were practised in precise form. Conversation was as brilliant, wit as lively, satire as keen, and gossip as delightful as they had been in the drawing-rooms of the past.

The names of the condemned were called every day and the partings between friends were in

THE FRENCH REVOLUTION

many cases very sad, but in nearly every instance the courage shown was superb. Men and women went to the scaffold with as nonchalant an air as if going to dinner. Much of this apparent lightness of heart may have been mere bravado, but it nevertheless was a display of fine nerve. Lord Byron, commenting upon this, says: "It became the fashion to leave some 'mot' as a legacy and the facetious words spoken by the victims on their way to execution would make a jest book of great size and of considerable interest." The prisoners whiled away the time in playing games, and some, it is said, even indulged in sly flirtations—" the ruling passion strong in death." One favorite amusement was rehearsing the part they would enact if chance brought them to the scaffold. Gracefully and with a haughty demeanor ladies would approach and mount the steps of an imaginary guillotine and with perfect *sang-froid* lose their heads. Those who played the role with the greatest skill would be rewarded with the plaudits and congratulations of admiring friends. People living in apprehension of constant peril grow careless and indifferent, especially in such a time as the Revolution.

It was bad enough for the noble who remained in the country to suffer imprisonment and death, but his condition was not much worse than that of the noble who fled. The latter was an exile, a wanderer in strange lands, or "hovered disconsolate over the Rhine with Condé." His chateau was burned, his income cut off, his money gone; he must either work, live on charity or starve. His pride urged him to suffer the last rather than attempt the first. He was truly a pitiable object, born to luxury, to ease, to indolence, to extravagance, and taught that labor was menial and beneath him, he was too proud to be anything but a pauper.

The death penalty inflicted by the instrument known as the guillotine was a cruel, an inhuman method of punishment; it was only one degree removed from the block and axe, and these all civilized nations now considered barbarous. This fatal instrument was named after its inventor, M. Guillotin, a physician of great respectability, born in Paris in 1738. Strange as it may seem, he was of a most kindly and sympathetic nature. He was a member of the States-General in 1789, and was appointed on a committee to revise the Penal Code; from sentiments of humanity alone he proposed as a substitute for the hangman's noose or the sword of the headsman, the knife of the guillotine. He thought it would end the sufferings of the victim sooner than any other method of execution known. "With my machine, Messieurs, I whisk off your head in a twinkling and you have no pain." Poor doctor! he is "doomed by a satiric destiny to the strangest immortal glory . . . his name like to outlive Cæsar's." He reached a good ripe age and died a natural death; fortunately for him he was not called upon to test the efficiency of his invention. The horrible use made of the machine which he had originated, and which was sometimes called his daughter, haunted him to his dying hour.

Dr. Guillotin
From an engraving in the collection of
William J. Latta, Esq.

THE FRENCH REVOLUTION

His name being so inseparably connected with this dreadful instrument he was looked upon by many as a monster, but he was one of the gentlest and most inoffensive men of the Revolution. No one deplored more than he the use to which his invention was put.

When the guillotine was originally suggested as an instrument of execution, it was laughed at in all quarters. At first it was called "*la Mirabelle,*" so christened by Rivarol, the royalist editor of the *Actes des Apôtres,* in ridicule of Mirabeau. It seems strange that an implement that was to deluge the land with blood should have been a butt for the wits, satirists, and comic poets of the day.

At supper parties, among the upper classes, it was a fad to set a small wooden guillotine upon the table when dessert was served. The ladies then amused themselves by placing little dolls under the knife and when the heads were severed a stream of cologne would flow, into which the fair ones dipped their handkerchiefs.

In 1790 the Assembly decreed that the death sentence should be executed only by decapitation, and in 1792 the guillotine was accepted by the government after Samson, the headsman, had explained that beheading by the sword was most unsatisfactory and that the guillotine would remove the difficulties incident to that oriental method of inflicting death.

It is a grewsome, harrowing sight to witness the human head severed from the body, and yet this butchery went on day after day in the view of the public. Men, women and children witnessed the executions, and the whole community was brutalized by the spectacle. To complete the bloody performance the executioner, when the head fell into the basket, would lift it up by the hair and, while the eyes were still open, the muscles quivering, and the blood was streaming from the throat, would show it to the multitude, who shouted their approval by cries of "Long live the nation," "Long live the Republic!"

Such a scene ordinarily would make a brave man shudder and a tender woman faint; yet the people became so familiar with it that they would stand for hours to watch the executions out of mere idle curiosity, and at times would applaud the courage or jeer the craven spirit displayed by the unfortunate victims. One man who never missed an execution and who regularly followed the carts to the scaffold, called it "going to the red mass."

There was quite a trade in blond perukes made from the hair of guillotined women, and at Meudon, according to Montgaillard, there was a factory where were tanned such of the skins of the guillotined "as seemed worth flaying." The skin of the men was tough and answered certain commercial demands; it made "good wash leather for breeches and other uses;" but that of women was "so soft in texture that it was good for almost nothing."

The minds of men were so affected by surrounding scenes and circumstances that their sensibilities became warped or blunted, and by their

THE FRENCH REVOLUTION

conduct they exhibited an indifference to the decencies of life that was cruel and inhuman. They practised in a civilized community the customs of the savage who adorns his belt with the scalps of his victims. The habits of the North American Indian and the South Sea islander were in vogue in Paris. Men and women, it is said, wore as ornaments miniature guillotines made of gun metal; children played with toy guillotines, and in the candy shops were sold sugar figures representing human beings, from which, when the head was severed by the knife of the toy machine, a red jelly or syrup resembling blood would ooze. Even the mob, when they struck down their victim, began immediately to hack and chop off the head, a sickening and cruel operation. They did not deem their work as complete until they effected the decapitation and mounted the head on a pike to be carried in triumph through the public streets. This idea was due in part, no doubt, to the example set by the guillotine. The custom brutalized the nation and made the Revolution tenfold bloodier than it otherwise would have been. Had it not been for this terrible instrument the Revolution might have been a different story.

Women took an active and a prominent part in the Revolution and exerted a most potential influence. Marie Antoinette and Madame Roland played conspicuous roles in the drama and without doubt, because of their prejudices, indiscretions, and unwise utterances, did more harm than good to their respective causes. Madame de Staël and Madame Condorcet in the early period of the Revolution entertained extensively, and in the opinion of their followers spoke on political topics with almost oracular power. It was an army of women that on the 5th of October marched to Versailles and brought back with them the king to his capital. Théroigne de Méricourt, a young and beautiful woman, a leader of the demi-monde and the proprietress of the most notorious "*maison de joie*" in Paris, rode astride a cannon on the 5th of October on the march to Versailles, and on the 10th of August with her own right arm helped to cut down the royalists that had taken refuge in a deserted building close to the Tuileries.

In every violent scene women were present marching in the processions, mingling with the crowds, and urging the men to desperate deeds. They cheered and encouraged the butchers at work during the September massacres. These hags were as cruel as fate, as pitiless as hell itself. Women were employed by the insurrectionary committee to follow the tumbrils, and howl their imprecations at the condemned from the prison to the scaffold.

A number of female societies were organized after the manner of the Jacobins. They held meetings, discussed public questions and sometimes attended the sessions of the Assembly in a body. They were presided over by well-known female revolutionists and among their most distinguished leaders were Rose Lacombe, Renée Andu, and Marie Louise Bonju. Crowds of

THE FRENCH REVOLUTION

noisy women from these clubs would parade through the streets and insult on every hand well-dressed and respectable looking people. In time they became such a nuisance and such disturbers of the public peace that by order of the Great Committee they were driven from the highways and excluded from the galleries of the Convention. When they insisted upon their right as citizens to attend the sessions they were told that the Republic had no need of Joans of Arc, and that, until the State required their services, they could devote themselves to their household duties which, because of their active participation in public affairs, they had long and sadly neglected.

The knitters, *" les tricoteuses,"* sat in the shadow of the guillotine and kept tally of the executions by dropping a stitch every time a head fell into the basket, not a very decent or seemly occupation for women. The authorities specially assigned them seats for this purpose in recognition of the part they had taken in the events of the 5th and 6th of October. The women of the markets, *" les dames des halles,"* gathered around the house of Target and threatened to mob him because he had declined to represent the king at his trial. Charlotte Corday murdered Marat, but thereby doomed her friends to destruction. Rose Lacombe, " a daughter without a mother, born by chance in the *coulisses* of a provincial theatre," young, beautiful, stately, and with an eloquence somewhat declamatory, took a part not inconspicuous. She had considerable influence with the Commune and was popular with

DANTON

the masses. She scolded and berated the Convention and many of the deputies bent before her; the only one who closed the door in her face was Robespierre. Olympe de Gouges and Saint-Amaranthe, the latter better known, perhaps, as Egeria, wielded some political power through the influential and distinguished men they seduced by their charms.

In order to understand or to account for the excesses of the Revolution it is necessary to study its causes; otherwise it will appear to be an orgy of crime in which the passions of men indulged in the shedding of innocent blood without excuse or justification. When one calmly and without prejudice reviews the causes, however, every excess, no matter how cruel, seems to be in the nature of retributive justice; it was but the avenging of the tyranny, the crimes, and the agony of centuries.

The "Reign of Terror" was possible only with a people that had broken away from the restraints of religion and the humanizing influences of Christianity. The Church, by its avarice, corruption, hypocrisy, skepticism, imposture, bigotry and base superstition, had destroyed the faith of men in its teachings and when the Revolution broke forth almost the first thing it did was to raze to the ground that venerable edifice which from time immemorial had shielded and nurtured the virtues of mankind. Its influence over men was gone, and, released from its restraint, they gave way to their lowest passions.

CHAPTER XXII

WAS DANTON RESPONSIBLE FOR THE SEPTEMBER MASSACRES?—LA FAYETTE ABANDONS HIS COMMAND—DUMOURIEZ NAMED HIS SUCCESSOR—CANNONADE OF VALMY—DANTON'S ENERGY—DUKE DE CHARTRES—DUMOURIEZ IN PARIS

Who was responsible for the September massacres? The whole community might be held guilty as accomplices, but that is out of the question in the opinion of Edmund Burke, who declared that it is impossible to indict an entire people. Prudhomme, in his "History of Crimes," says: "This terrible demagogue, Danton, with frightful unconcern arranged everything for those unparalleled murders."

Without doubt, Danton was in a great measure instrumental in bringing them about. He had aroused the fury of the rabble and openly declared that the royalists must be terrorized. In an address before the Assembly he had argued for the domiciliary visits; in fact it was at his suggestion that a decree was passed authorizing them. It was his plan that had filled the prisons and his inflammatory speeches that had whetted the appetite of the mob for blood. "We must throw over the useless luggage in a storm, the ship will founder if you do not lighten it," he had said. There was a dreadful suggestion in these words. During the continuance of the massacres he never raised his voice against these monstrous crimes. It is said that when some one spoke about the cruelty practised he coolly answered, " Damn the prisoners; let them take care of themselves." Yet he showed much humane feeling when he saved Duport, the Abbé Berardier, and Charles Lameth; and his conduct in these instances proved that he had the courage to defy even the butchers, for depriving them of their victims was like snatching prey from a pack of hungry wolves.

Danton never attempted to excuse the part he had taken in the events from the 10th of August to the end of the September massacres. In answer to a charge flung into his teeth by the Girondins that he was responsible for these murders, he boldly declared: " I looked my crime steadfastly in the face and I did it." The overthrow of the monarchy, the establishment of the republic, and the extermination of the royalists constituted a drama in three acts. They were but parts of one scheme, and the dominating spirit in all these terrible scenes was Danton. His gigantic figure looms up out of the din and smoke of that period and, with a commanding air, moves unscathed and defiant through blood and flame, like one of the mighty souls in the lurid glare of Dante's Inferno.

It was indeed Danton who inaugurated the " Reign of Terror." It was his resolution, his audacity, his great courage that enabled him to

THE FRENCH REVOLUTION

strike blow after blow until the monarchy crumbled and fell into a heap of ruins. If it were necessary to resort to this violence and bloodshed to secure the establishment of popular government, then he truthfully may be called the Father of the Republic. When the butcheries were over he exultantly exclaimed: "We have rolled between the Revolution and its enemies a river of blood."

Lacretelle says of Danton: "Terror indeed was his system, but he thought of securing its effects with a sword suspended, not incessantly plunged into the breast of a victim. He preferred a massacre to a long succession of executions." "He was an exterminator, but without ferocity," says Mignet.

"The greatest blot of his administration," in the opinion of Stephens, "was his indifference during the massacres in the prisons, for his power could have stopped them at once. But," continues the same author, "he regarded these measures as an advantage to France and believed that they cleared the way for a new and more energetic government."

Madame Roland contended that it was Danton's duty to suppress the massacres, but she so expressed herself out of a hatred for Danton and at the same time for the purpose of shielding her husband, who as minister of the interior had been accused of criminal inactivity.

On September 3d Roland wrote: "Yesterday was a day on the events of which we should perhaps cast a veil. I know that the people is terrible in its vengeance, yet tempers it with a sort of justice, not indiscriminately immolating the objects of its fury, but directing it against those who have been too long spared by the sword of the law, and whose immediate death is demanded by the dangers of the hour. But I know that it is easy for wretched traitors to abuse such an effervescence. I know that we owe it to all France to declare that the executive have been able neither to foresee nor to prevent these excesses." This was the defense of a weak man, who, in an attempt to excuse the executive, put the blame on the people without offending them.

After the massacres began perhaps neither the minister of justice, the minister of the interior, nor the entire executive could have altogether stopped them, but there should have been power lodged somewhere that could have avoided such infamy and such disgrace to France and the Revolution. It was the beginning of the deluge of blood in the "Reign of Terror" that overwhelmed throne and altar, king and priest, aristocrat and bourgeoise, and at last engulfed the factions in its vortex.

The belief that it would be unsafe to leave the royalists in Paris to plot, to scheme, and to conspire while the patriots were in the army facing the allies may have been well founded and may have created a genuine fear in the minds of the revolutionists. The domiciliary visits and the arrest and imprisonment of the royalists may have been a necessity, the safety of the Republic

THE FRENCH REVOLUTION

may have required these measures, but there was no excuse for the horrible lynchings. The methods of trial and execution were cruel, barbaric; the utter disregard of all forms of law and the brutal butcheries were without any excuse. Such conditions and such scenes as were witnessed were a disgrace to a civilized state and people.

Without, however, in any way attempting a defense for this slaughter of unarmed men and women, let us draw one or two comparisons to see if they will not in a measure soften the judgment.

The proscriptions of the patrician Sulla in Rome were bloodier and more numerous a thousand fold than those of the plebeian Danton in France.

In August, 1572, upon a memorable night in the reign of Charles IX, the kennels of Paris ran blood until the Seine was reddened. The massacre of the Huguenots under a king was more cruel and treacherous than that of aristocrats under the Republic. Religious intolerance had its St. Bartholomew, and the Revolution had its September the Second. Let any fair-minded reader after a careful study of the facts, pronounce judgment as to which was the worse.

The Church had its Reign of Terror in the days of the Spanish Inquisition, and perhaps it may be alleged in all truthfulness that the cruelties practised by the Church while Alva was in the Netherlands were even a shade darker than those which disgraced the Revolution. It is

DANTON

difficult to improve on the rack, the stake, and the iron-maiden as instruments of torture.

But let us return to the events of 1792. After the 10th of August La Fayette saw that his fortunes had waned; the Revolution had gone beyond him, so he mounted his steed and galloped across the borders. Through the personal influence of Danton, Dumouriez was named his successor and at once put in command. The future looked dark and gloomy. Paris was thrown into a spasm. " France with all its frontiers open had for security nothing but the small forest of Argonne and the genius of Dumouriez."

Fortunately for the Republic the enemy was not well commanded. Brunswick was a parlor soldier; he advanced by easy stages, rain overtook him, and his troops and artillery were stuck in the mud. His army fed on unripe grapes. Mire and the dysentery sapped not only the strength but also the courage of his soldiers.

The emigrants had predicted that the invasion of the army would be a triumphal march, that the towns would throw open their gates to them, that the people would welcome them every step of the way, that all France outside of Paris was opposed to the Revolution and would gladly aid and greet the invaders, whom they would embrace as deliverers. The outcome showed that they had been sadly mistaken.

The Prussians had engaged in the invasion as a sort of outing. They had made no preparations sufficient for a lengthy or a severe campaign. At times they marched in mud up to their

THE FRENCH REVOLUTION

knees, and once for nearly a week had nothing to eat but boiled corn.

On September 17th, Valmy was reached and here occurred an engagement. From a military point of view it amounted to nothing, but in its final effect it was a most important one, for from this battle may be dated the beginning of that glorious military career that carried the standard of France into every continental capital from Berlin to Vienna and at last to the Kremlin.

The Prussians began cannonading the defenses of the town, to which the French replied sharply. The Prussians then advanced their line of battle, but the French, to the great amazement of their assailants, held their ground and gave no sign of retreating. The Prussian commanders called a council of war and after careful consideration it was decided under all the circumstances there was nothing left to do but to withdraw. It seems never to have occurred to them to charge the redoubts or to begin a lengthy siege. "The cannonade of Valmy" came suddenly to an end. About a thousand men had been killed on both sides. It is said the Prussians bribed the French not to molest them while on the retreat. There is a story to the effect that they were tired of the campaign, and only too glad to turn their backs upon the town. Other reasons given in explanation of their conduct are that they felt they had been deceived by the emigrants, that they had no real interest in the war, and further that they could not successfully co-operate with the Austrians. One rumor that seems to have some foun-

DANTON

dation is that the Princess Lichtenau, mistress of the king of Prussia, was bribed by one of the agents of Danton to induce her royal lover to withdraw from the invasion; for it is well known that at this time Danton was using extensively the secret service funds. Be this as it may, for some strange reason the Prussians abandoned the campaign.

The victory aroused an ardor so patriotic and a desire for military glory so great in the heart of France, that her sons sprang to arms all over the Republic, and her armies in time became, under the leadership of the modern Cæsar, as invincible as the legions of Rome.

It was the spirit inspired by the Revolution and the enthusiasm born of the Republic that made them the most dauntless soldiers of their day and generation. Their victories stretched from the Tiber to the Nile, from Arcola to Aboukir. They fought on the sunny plains of Italy and in the shadows of the everlasting pyramids. And when alas! the Republic, which had cost in its creation so much blood and agony, was merged by usurpation into the empire, they followed the victorious eagles of Napoleon until at last, defying the elements, he led them into suffering and defeat in the depths of a Russian winter. Hurled back by fire and frost, their retreat was marked with blood and death from Moscow to the Beresina. Overwhelmed at Leipsic, the lion writhing in his toils made the final struggle at Waterloo, and then came the bleak story of St. Helena. This closed the last scene of the Revolution. It

THE FRENCH REVOLUTION

was the period of which we are speaking that prepared the way for that great military career, before which the whole world stood in amazement.

The French troops met with further success under General Custine, and the Assembly announced to the world that the Republic was fighting to free all nations, all peoples, from the tyranny of kings. The gates of several German cities were thrown open to welcome the French troops and this was hailed by France as the dawning of a new era in the world's freedom.

Danton's energy, at this time, was indefatigable. He was the Revolution. No leader in any period of its existence exerted so potential an influence, did so much, and stood for so much as he. His imperial will dominated his colleagues; his superb audacity terrorized his enemies. He was not in any wise particular about the means he adopted to accomplish his ends; an object had to be attained, and he did not hesitate to bribe, subsidize, or resort to any method that would enable him to gain his end. He drew extensively upon the public treasury and lavishly spent money through the secret service. There was no economy practised in his negotiations. If gold could accomplish his purpose, the amount was of minor consideration. His agents and spies were out in every direction. They mingled with the emigrants at Coblentz, sat at the counsel table of the allies, and were in close touch with the royal courts of Vienna and Berlin.

In this time of turmoil, Danton rose in grand,

in magnificent proportions above all around him. The work he had in hand required measures that were drastic; no half-hearted policy would have met the conditions. No timid, hesitating or halting man would have been equal to the occasion. He was the leader, the factor, the controlling influence of that decisive period, and his efforts resulted in making the Republic a fact. The Girondins were already supplanted. These philosophers moralized over the passing events, but they did and could do nothing to change the prevailing policy. In the wild swirl of politics they were being wrecked and cast ashore. Their remonstrances were not heard. They sipped tea in the house of the Rolands and talked eloquently in the Assembly, but Danton, with his overpowering energy and robust methods of administration, was making history while they were only making speeches.

A short time after the September massacres, the Duke de Chartres, son of the Duke of Orleans, afterwards Louis Philippe, king of France, came up from the army to Paris to complain of some injustice which he claimed he had suffered. Among his friends and in the clubs he expressed openly his abhorrence of the events of August 10th and the massacres of September. Danton had an interview with him and in the course of it said: "Well! young man, I hear that you have been murmuring your disapprobation, that you have even denounced the government for its policy, and that you have expressed a sympathy for the victims and a hatred for the

THE FRENCH REVOLUTION

executioners. Beware lest your complaints reveal a lack of patriotism and your moderation be taken for treason." The young prince answered that the army looked with horror on the shedding of blood, save on the field of battle, and that the September massacres appeared in his eyes to dishonor liberty. "You are too young to judge of these events," replied Danton. "You cannot understand from your point of view what is necessary to be done; in the future be silent. Return to the army, fight bravely, but do not needlessly, in a spirit of heroism, risk your life—you have many years before you. France does not love a republic; she has the habits, the weaknesses, the need of a monarchy. After our storms she will return to it either through her vices or necessities; and you will be king. Adieu, young man; remember the prediction of Danton."

This is truly a remarkable forecast, if the story of the interview be true, and it reveals too the desire that was ever present in Danton's mind of enthroning the family of Orleans in case the republic should fall by the way. He looked into the future with the eye of a seer and he distinctly saw the shadows of coming events. He knew that this convulsion, in the nature of a spasm, could not last forever, that out of this condition would evolve a settled order of things, and that France in due season would return to her religion and that form of constitution which best suited her character and disposition. He was not a fanatic, he was a reasonable politician, whose vision was not clouded by illusions; he was far

DANTON

more practical than Robespierre, who was constantly dreaming of establishing an ideal government of his own creation.

About this time Dumouriez also came to the capital. His return was a triumph. He dined at the Rolands' and was welcomed by the Girondins with every expression of joy. In the evening he went to the opera and was received with the warmest demonstrations; he sat in the box with Danton, who shared with him the applause of the audience. Madame Roland and Vergniaud arrived at the theatre later in the evening, and were about to enter the *loge* when Madame Roland, perceiving Danton at the side of her hero, started back with aversion, and clutching the arm of her escort hastily withdrew. Her illusions were again dispelled; her hero had passed under the sinister influence of her arch-enemy, the man above all others whose power she dreaded. She it was, in her opinion, that should have presented Dumouriez to the public and should have shared with him its applause; but she was too late.

CHAPTER XXIII

GIRONDINS AND JACOBINS—LOUVET'S ACCUSATION OF ROBESPIERRE

The National Convention met on the 20th of September, 1792. Many of the old leaders were returned, and the first act passed by the new legislative body was one providing for the abolition of the monarchy. This was done on motion of Collot d' Herbois, and immediately on motion of the Abbé Grégoire, the Republic was proclaimed and thus dated its existence from the 21st day of September, 1792. "There was nothing left now for the king," remarked Manuel, "but the right of justifying himself before the sovereign people."

Now that a popular government was established it was hoped that dissensions would cease among the radicals and that they would unite in a common effort to strengthen it and make it a success, but from its very creation the Republic was vexed with factional contention. The Revolution had accomplished its purpose, the destruction of the monarchy, but instead of moderating its bitterness it continued with unabated fury.

At this time the Girondins had a majority over the Jacobins in the Convention. Between these two factions the struggle now began in earnest, and so far as the latter party was concerned it

DANTON

was a war to the death. The members of both organizations were republicans and it was unfortunate for the sake of France and for free institutions that they did not reconcile their differences and labor for one end. But every day drove them further apart; the bitterness as time ran on grew so intense that it became personal as well as political, and the desire or ambition for party supremacy rose above every other consideration and made men partisans rather than patriots, often blinding them to the welfare and the real interests of the country. During all this period Danton argued in favor of moderation, toleration, and unity. He was not possessed by a spirit of hate and envy and his personal ambitions never menaced the integrity of the Republic.

The Girondins were more aristocratic than the Jacobins and held themselves aloof from the rabble. They were not as close to the common people nor as popular with them as were their opponents. They were conservatives, men of education and cultivated manners. There were no Héberts and Marats in their midst. The Revolution in time outstripped them; they kept on dreaming and their enemies kept on scheming and at last the control of public, of political affairs fell into the hands of the Jacobins, the leaders of the rabble. The Republic was for all, not for a particular class, and in the evolution of events the great masses of the people had come to the top.

One thing that made the Girondins weak politically was the fact that they did not present a

THE FRENCH REVOLUTION

solid front on all questions. The individual members were independent in character and not always controlled by party discipline. They were broken into several groups and, although under one flag, they were not always united in policy nor in action. They were no match in practical politics for the hardy, audacious, unscrupulous men who had the mob at their backs. It is a question whether or not, even if they had been united, the Girondins, who were conservative in their methods, could have triumphed and saved the Revolution. " How could they have done with just laws what the Mountaineers effected by violent measures? How could they have conquered foreign foes without fanaticism, restrained parties without the aid of terror, fed the multitude without a Maximum, and supplied the armies without requisition?"

Between the Girondins and the Jacobins there were some well-defined differences in political principles, but the variance was not so great as to have precluded a complete reconciliation. The truth was that the contest was not over the question of policy or principles, but for political power and supremacy, and the Republic in consequence became the booty for which the factions fought; the matter of its political control, in the eyes of the warring partisans, being of far more importance than its welfare.

As a party the Girondins advocated a distribution of political power rather than its centralization. They strongly favored a government based upon the forms of the British Constitution. In-

DANTON

deed Robespierre declared that "*La Gironde* had long formed a project to separate itself from France, to become again *La Guyenne,* and to unite itself to England." An idea so unpatriotic found its conception in the imagination of Robespierre rather than in any thought or purpose of the Girondins; for the latter, no matter what else may be said of them, were Frenchmen to the core and really had no more intention of attaching their province to England than to a shooting star. But partisan or factional spirit was so blind and bitter in those days that mere suspicion usurped the place of proof.

One reason why the Girondins specially fell out of favor with the Parisians was because it was believed they desired to remove the capital; in fact Fabre d' Eglantine declared that he had heard Roland suggest either Tours or Blois as being suitable for the purpose. Such a rumor as this, even if it had but the slightest foundation upon which to rest, would naturally arouse the ire of the Parisians, than whom no people were ever so sensitive upon the question of their city's importance.

The Jacobins, as a political party, believed in the centralization of power, a strong executive, and state control of property and persons. They also favored universal education, freedom of the press, and religious toleration. They advocated the taxing of the rich alone for the maintenance of government. Their policies were absolutely democratic and their intention was to elevate the masses at the expense of the classes. They

THE FRENCH REVOLUTION

desired the creation of a republic where all men were to be equal before the law, a state in which all class distinctions, in so far as the enjoyment of political rights was concerned, were to be obliterated.

We may say that there was just the difference between these two factions, the Girondins and the Jacobins, in so far as their political policies and principles were concerned, that distinguishes an aristocratic from a democratic form of government.

The Girondins had no more bitter enemy among all their opponents than Robespierre, with the exception perhaps of Marat, whose antipathy was boundless, ferocious, and unreasonable. For some time the leaders of the Girondins had been waiting for an opportunity to attack Robespierre, to destroy, if possible, his popularity with the masses, and to deal him a political death-blow.

There was nothing in those days that so injured a politician in public estimation as a well-founded belief or suspicion that he sought to usurp absolute authority. Accordingly rumors were set afloat reflecting on the ambitious designs of Robespierre, and, after the public mind was excited in relation to these matters, the Girondins on the 10th of October, 1792, openly in the Convention charged him with aspiring to a dictatorship. The chamber was thrown into confusion; the friends of Robespierre, taken unawares, were greatly disconcerted and as a last resort they forced an adjournment. The attack was renewed unexpectedly on November 3d, the enemies of Robespierre assailing him from all sides. He ascended the tribune but in the tumult his voice could not be heard. Danton, seeing his discomfiture, came to his assistance and urged him to go on, saying that there were many good citizens present to listen; but it seemed impossible for Robespierre to recover his nerve. At last, in a moment when quiet had been partially restored, he shrieked out in desperation a defiant challenge; immediately he was assailed in a speech of remarkable power by a young deputy named Louvet, who demanded his public accusation. Robespierre, not having yet recovered his composure, thought it advisable to secure time in which to prepare an answer, and an adjournment was taken.

When the day arrived for him to reply to Louvet's fiery philippic he was prepared to meet the occasion. He had in the meantime written an elaborate speech and had taken the precaution to fill the galleries with his supporters. He answered *seriatim* the personal charges. The applause was all his that day, and when at the conclusion of his speech Louvet attempted to continue the debate Barère made a motion to postpone indefinitely further consideration of the question and then moved successfully the order of the day. The Girondins, strange to say, supported the motion. "They committed one fault in commencing the accusation and another in not continuing it."

The man from Arras had a close shave, but he

managed to effect his escape in good form; indeed he emerged from the conflict in triumph and when he appeared at the Jacobins' he was welcomed as a veritable conqueror.

It was not wise for the Girondins to make this attack on Robespierre without following it to the very end. They had aroused the resentment of a relentless, an implacable, foe and by their conduct had created in his heart a burning desire for vengeance. In referring to this matter Allison says: "The Girondins flattered themselves that a simple passing to the order of the day would extinguish Robespierre's influence as completely as exile or death, and they actually joined with the Jacobins in preventing the reply of Louvet—a fatal error which France had cause to lament in tears of blood."

During the progress of the debate on the motion of Barère, Marat ascended the tribune to come to the assistance of Robespierre, but just at this point Vergniaud asked permission of the chair to read a circular which had been sent by Marat and some municipal officials to the towns and cities throughout France defending the September massacres and advising them to adopt a like method for the extermination of the aristocrats. After the reading of the letter the deputies turned with hisses upon Marat, and one of them moved his accusation, which motion, however, was lost. All this while Marat occupied the tribune and quietly awaited the result of the vote on the motion to accuse; when it was announced he drew forth a revolver and pointing

DANTON

it at his head exclaimed: "Citizens, if the fury you displayed on this occasion had carried you to the length of an accusation against me, I should have blown my brains out."

CHAPTER XXIV

VICTORY OF JEMAPPES—GIRONDINS PROPOSE OPENING OF THE SCHELDT—EDMUND BURKE—ENGLAND JOINS COALITION—DANTON VISITS BELGIUM—DEATH OF DANTON'S WIFE

Dumouriez overthrew the Austrians at Jemappes on November 6, 1792, and on the 16th entered Brussels. The Austrian lines fell back to Luxembourg, where they were supported by the Prussian army. The victory was hailed with delight throughout France, and Dumouriez became the hero of the hour.

The Austrians and the Prussians were thrown into consternation. The victory was decisive; it was a fairly, a stubbornly contested battle and the raw levies of France had repulsed and routed the scarred veterans of Germany. For the first time the French battalions, while moving into battle and charging the enemy, sang the "Marseillaise," which from this date became the battle hymn of the Republic. Its effect upon the spirits of the soldiers was electrical and they dashed against the lines of the Austrians with a determination, a desperation that would brook no repulse. The Round-heads and the Puritans of Cromwell went into battle chanting their psalms, and under the spell of religious fervor became invincible. So the armies of France, feeling the impulse of a new-born patriotism, marched into the conflict singing the "Marseillaise." Thousands of voices joined in the chorus of that inspiring hymn that was already awakening the spirit of liberty throughout the world, and its strains were heard far above the din and the roar of battle. The mercenary troops of Germany had not been drilled to combat such enthusiasm. It was a new phase of warfare to them, and they threw down their arms and fled, panic-stricken, in all directions. The soldiers of the Revolution were receiving the training that was to enable them to secure the glory of the empire. The raw recruits of Dumouriez were yet to be the veterans in the armies of Napoleon. Valmy and Jemappes were but the skirmishes that were preparing them for the greater fields of Austerlitz and Jena. The victory aroused unbounded enthusiasm throughout the country and greatly increased the enlistments.

England, at this time, was friendly to France, and scouted every idea of joining the coalition. The Girondins, however, elated by the victory of Dumouriez, became too confident of their power and, instead of holding the friendship of England, lost it by insisting upon opening the river Scheldt and thus making Antwerp a commercial rival of London. It was simply a sentiment upon the part of France, but was taken by England as a breach of international law and the ignoring of old treaties to which the French had assented for upwards of a century.

THE FRENCH REVOLUTION

The foundations of the commercial greatness of Antwerp were laid early in the middle ages and she became in time one of the great commercial cities of the world. Her merchants were princes and her argosies freighted with merchandise sailed every sea and touched at every port. The renown and reputation of the Flemish trader were known the wide world over. At the height of this prosperity England, having rendered a service to the house of Orange, insisted upon closing the river Scheldt. An agreement to this end, a solemn pact signed and sealed, was entered into, and the glory of Antwerp vanished like a dream. Many of her merchants were ruined, some even abandoned the city; the great warehouses were closed and her wharves fell into decay. Where all had been bustle and animation, where the fleets of the world's commerce had ridden at anchorage, now all was emptiness and desolation.

The policy of England was selfish, even cruel. There was no question but that the Girondins were right in so far as sentiment was concerned; but it was not the time to play that kind of politics. To Frenchmen the interests of France were paramount, and until her own peace and liberty were secured she ought not to have embroiled herself in quarrels with other states or attempted to relieve at her own risk the burdens of other peoples. It was unfair and unjust that Antwerp should not have the same opportunities in commerce that were enjoyed by London, but the Girondins were disregarding contracts between foreign states, which contracts in no wise affected the interests or the commerce of France, and in so doing they aroused the anger of a great nation whose friendship they might have retained and whose enmity they could not afford to provoke. Their conduct was fatal to France in that it brought on a series of wars that lasted until Waterloo closed the scene. Nor, when all is told, were they actuated by the best and most patriotic motives in the world, for, believing that Dumouriez was classed in their faction, they thought his victories would give them political prestige and enable them to overthrow their opponents in Paris and to strengthen themselves in popular favor. They advocated that policy which would appeal to the people as just and they claimed that the opening of the Scheldt was the direct result of the victory of Jemappes.

Danton, anxious at all odds to retain the friendship of England, inveighed against what to him was an unwise and a short-sighted course to pursue, but his protests were of no avail. Robespierre also labored against this policy of the Girondins, but without effect for they had at this time the popular side of the question. Danton and Robespierre both saw where legislation so sentimental would lead the nation.

Let us now glance at the condition of affairs in England. Pitt was still averse to war and it required all his influence and his masterly skill to control public sentiment and the House of Commons. He succeeded, however, until matters were made still worse by the step taken by

THE FRENCH REVOLUTION

France. On November 30, 1792, the Convention by decree directed Dumouriez to invade Holland. This precipitated the trouble with England. Dumouriez, with the keen vision of the statesman, knowing what the withdrawal of England's neutrality would mean, sent a secret agent to London to confer with Pitt and to assure him of his support. But Pitt could no longer stem the tide of public opinion and at last had to yield. It was Edmund Burke who led the opposition.

The British Tory possessed the qualities of a Bourbon of the old *régime*. He was as intolerant, as unprogressive, and as conservative in his political views. Existing conditions suited him and a threatened change or innovation was in itself revolutionary. He saw nothing in the French Revolution but a rising of the rabble and the attempted destruction of time-honored institutions.

Edmund Burke, however, was in no sense of the word a Tory; he was a statesman of the most liberal type, characterized by a tolerance that was born of a love of humanity itself. His sympathies were always enlisted in the cause of the oppressed. The slave in chains or the insolvent debtor in prison never appealed to him in vain. He defended the proscribed Catholic and the reviled dissenter. Religion to him was a benefaction, not a superstition. He espoused the cause of the American colonies and was ever their steadfast friend in the House of Commons; but, when the French Revolution broke forth, from the very beginning he was so intolerant that he saw in it nothing but the supremacy of atheism and anarchy. Its purest and bravest leaders were in his view but rascals,—miscreants bent on the destruction of both Church and State. The Declaration of Rights he declared was "a sort of institute and digest of anarchy." The cry from France "fell upon his ears like the fire bell at night," and startled him to such a degree that he grew bewildered.

"I pardon something to the spirit of liberty," he said, in referring at one time to the American colonies, but he displayed no such sensibility towards France. "It must be confessed," wrote Scott in his Life of Napoleon, "that the colors he has used in painting the extravagances of the Revolution ought to have been softened by considering the peculiar state of a country which, long laboring under despotism, is suddenly restored to the possession of unencumbered license." This eminent reformer, this philosophical statesman, became fanatical in his opposition to the French Revolution. "He used arguments," says Dumont, "so alarming to freedom, that on many points he was not only plausibly, but victoriously refuted." He foresaw its terrors and horrors, and as one by one his predictions fell true, men marveled at his prescience. As the excesses increased, in the same ratio did his reputation as a prophet increase, and his word in England became almost oracular. "No political prophet," says Sir Walter Scott, "ever viewed futurity with a surer ken."

THE FRENCH REVOLUTION

When Danton declared that the National Convention was the "Committee of Insurrection of all Nations," Burke shrieked out his imprecations against this buccaneer who would incite riot and revolution in every state in Christendom. But when the Convention, in December, 1792, decreed that, "Wherever French armies shall come, all taxes, titles, and privileges of rank shall be abolished, all existing authorities shall be annulled, and provisional administrators shall be elected by universal suffrage," Burke cried out in defiance and called upon all nations to accept this as a belligerent challenge, and to resent it as an insult and a threat to the world's law and order.

England at last "let slip the dogs of war," and all Europe was deluged with blood and became for nearly a quarter of a century the battle-field of the nations, shaken to its very centre by the clash of contending armies. The English government supplied the sinews of war and added, under the administration of William Pitt, 32,000,000 pounds to her public debt. No one in all England was more responsible for this than Edmund Burke. "Mr. Pitt," says Hazlitt, "has been hailed by his flatterers as 'the pilot that weathered the storm,' but it was Burke who at this giddy, maddening period stood at the prow of the vessel of state and with his glittering, pointed speer harpooned the Leviathan of the French Revolution."

The Whigs, led by Fox, Sheridan, and Romilly, welcomed the French Revolution as the dawn of a day of freedom and as an effort to abolish the iniquitous system of feudalism and its attendant evils. They did everything in their power to avoid the war, but they were powerless to stem the tide of public opinion.

Without England the coalition would have melted away and France could then have had an opportunity to inaugurate a popular government that perhaps would have been so well established that it would not have fallen subsequently into the grasp of a usurper.

England gave the war a fresh impetus. She was a power in herself as mistress of the ocean, and her mighty fleets at once ruffled and spread their white wings and covered the seas, while her treasury, seemingly inexhaustible, poured its gold into the laps of the allies. She entered upon the war with a fervor that was almost religious in its fanaticism. She thought the so-called "Principles of the Revolution" endangered social and civil order and even the existence of the Christian religion, and, judging from what had occurred in France, it was not strange that she so believed. Even when Napoleon came upon the scene he was looked upon as the embodiment of the French Revolution or, as Pitt called him, "the child and champion of democracy," and the contest was continued for a generation.

When the ardor of the allies cooled, the British minister aroused it by increasing the subsidies, and through his agents bribed, cajoled, and persuaded them to keep alive the coalition. England poured out her treasures and Europe her blood, and all for the purpose of compelling France to

THE FRENCH REVOLUTION

restore the monarchy, a form of government of which her people had grown tired and which because of its extravagance, corruption, and tyranny they had every right and reason to destroy.

After the victory of Jemappes, Danton and several other members of the Assembly, who with him had been appointed commissioners, were sent into Belgium to examine the condition of the army, to reorganize the Austrian Netherlands, and to report to the Convention whether Belgium wished to be united to France or to be formed into a separate republic.

On this visit Danton had an opportunity to fathom the designs of Dumouriez, and he was soon convinced that although he was an ambitious, a self-seeking man, he was a great general as well as statesman, and absolutely, at this contingency, necessary to France. He found, too, that he was a keen politician and that he had his eye on political preferment in Paris. He had won the affection and the admiration of his troops and he was just the man to march on the capital and proclaim himself dictator. " He menaces Paris," said Robespierre, " more than he does Belgium and Holland."

Already the radical journals were beginning to intimate the treason of the rugged little soldier and to apply to him the title of Cæsar. Their policy was that of suspicion. They continually dangled before the people's eyes the dread of Cæsarism and Cromwellism. They maintained a close watch on their generals and by suspecting them of treason kept them constantly asseverating and proving their loyalty. The great fear of the Revolution was a military dictatorship, and in those days of acute suspicion a commander in the army if unsuccessful was looked upon as a traitor, and if successful he was feared as ambitious. Dumouriez was so wrought up by the attacks made upon him, and angered too, perhaps, because his designs were discovered and his plans frustrated that he declared that the inefficiency of the home government was a reason for its overthrow.

Danton saw clearly the evil results that would follow the identification of Dumouriez with any faction in the Convention and he made up his mind to thwart any dangerous political ambitions and to counteract any personal schemes. He made several visits to Belgium during these negotiations, always urging the annexation of that state to France. It was while on one of these visits that he had a domestic affliction that seemed to change the whole tenor of his life. When in the midst of his important labors he suddenly received news of the death of his wife.

Camille's journal contains the following in reference to her demise which really more than intimates that she died of a broken heart, because of the attacks made by enemies upon her husband while away from the capital. "Danton is down in Belgium, and the cowards have profited by that absence. They have represented him as pointing out during the days of the second and the third of September the victims that should

THE FRENCH REVOLUTION

be assassinated. His wife has received her mortal stroke from reading in the papers this atrocious invention. Those who know how much this woman loved Danton can form an idea of her sufferings. Danton was absent but his enemies were present in the miserable sheets that tore her heart." As there is no allusion made elsewhere to indicate that the death of Madame Danton resulted from shock due to attacks upon her husband's character, the statement may perhaps have found its origin only in the emotions of Camille.

Immediately upon receiving word of his wife's death, Danton dropped all the matters he had in hand, took a light carriage, and hastened to Paris. Upon his arrival, the coffin, at his request, was taken up that he might look once more upon the face of the woman he devotedly loved, for he had ever been to her a true and faithful husband. He embraced the body, kissed the lips, and sobbed aloud in his anguish. It was the sorrow of a strong man of deep emotions. He could not abide within his home; the memories and the associations were too sad. The house was empty and cheerless; it had been vacant for a week and seals were upon the furniture. His children, both young, had been taken to the home of their grandmother, and he felt that he was entirely alone.

In order to forget his sorrow and gloom he plunged at once into active life, and summoned all his energy to sustain him. His labors were herculean, and he never displayed greater talent in the dispatch of business. What he accomplished we shall learn later.

CHAPTER XXV

FINDING OF THE IRON CHEST—LOUIS SUMMONED TO THE BAR

The Revolution had a dethroned king on its hands. The monarchy had been destroyed, the Republic had been established and proclaimed, but so long as Louis was a prisoner in what had formerly been his own kingdom he would simply be a menace to the Revolution. His imprisonment and detention would arouse the enmity and resentment of every royal potentate in Europe against the Republic.

The question at once occurred as to what disposition should be made of him. To detain him as a prisoner separated from his family was to induce the sympathy of the whole world. Besides this could not be continued indefinitely; it was cruel and unreasonable. To furnish and maintain a separate establishment for a crownless king and his family in semi-confinement could not be considered; such a place would become but a nest for conspiracy. To set him at liberty would lead to infinite trouble. To banish him would give him the opportunity he had sought when he attempted to desert his kingdom, that of reclaiming his throne at the head of an invading army of traitorous nobles and foreign allies.

THE FRENCH REVOLUTION

Robespierre hit the nail on the head when he declared the execution of the king was a political necessity; the questions as to whether or not this was strict justice, and whether or not he was guilty under specific charges, were not to be considered. It was urged that the safety and welfare of the country alone should be weighed. And this was the opinion not only of radical, blood-thirsty revolutionists, but of "many great and good men, who mournfully inclined to the severer side from an opinion of its absolute necessity to annihilate a dangerous enemy and establish an unsettled republic."

Carnot, one of the most conservative among the revolutionists, a man of distinction and of superior abilities, but a most ardent and conscientious supporter of the Republic, voted for the death of the king; but when he did so he openly declared that never did word weigh so heavily on his heart.

During this period of agitation in November, 1792, Gamain, the locksmith who had taught Louis the secrets of his trade, went to Roland and revealed to him the location of a safe which he had helped Louis to build in a wall of the palace of the Tuileries. The safe was found; Roland took it to his office, examined the contents, and the secret was out that Louis had been playing double and that he had been corresponding with the enemies of the Republic. It was also discovered that some prominent men, who in the past had been popular favorites, had been in negotiation with the court to aid in the restoration of the monarchy. Mirabeau's bust was veiled.

It was immediately after alleged by the Jacobins that Roland had destroyed some papers that he found which reflected upon the patriotism of several members of his own party. The Jacobins rang the changes upon this for all it was worth and the people were in the frame of mind to accept as truth all such rumors. In corroboration of this charge Bozé, a royalist, informed the Jacobins of a letter that had been written by Vergniaud, Guadet, and Gensonné to Louis just prior to the 10th of August pledging themselves to do all in their power to maintain the monarchy. This was grist to the mill and the Jacobins chuckled over the discomfiture of their political foes, for it not only divided the ranks of the Girondins, but furnished their adversaries with a conclusive argument against their loyalty as a party and rendered them most unpopular.

On December 6th a committee of twenty-one was appointed by the Assembly to prepare charges against Louis and on the 10th its report was submitted to the Convention. On the 11th Louis was summoned to appear at the bar of the Assembly. Barère was in the chair. "Citizens," he said, "the eyes of Europe are upon you. Posterity will judge you with inflexible severity. Preserve then the dignity and the dispassionate coolness befitting judges. Recollect the awful silence which accompanied Louis when brought back from Varennes."

When Louis arrived, the president directed

THE FRENCH REVOLUTION

him to be seated and to answer the questions that would be propounded to him. In referring to the conduct of Barère at this time, Madame de Staël wrote: "When the presiding officer of the Convention says to his king, '*Louis, asseyez vous,*' we feel more indignation even than when he is accused of crimes which he never committed. One must have sprung from the very dust not to respect past obligations, particularly when misfortune has rendered them sacred; and vulgarity joined to crime inspires us with as much contempt as horror."

Louis was charged with all the faults of the court: with having entertained the life-guards who insulted the national cockade and trampled it under foot; with having refused to sanction the Declaration of Rights and several other constitutional articles; with having made speeches of reconciliation and promises, which promises were not sincere; with having entered into secret negotiations with Mirabeau to effect a counter-revolution; with having furnished money to bribe delegates; with having assembled the "Knights of the Dagger"; with having corresponded with the *émigrés;* with having negotiated with the allies; with having attempted to flee the kingdom; with being responsible for the "Fusillade of the Champ de Mars" on the 17th of June, 1791; with having continued the pay to the emigrant life-guards; with having assembled an insufficient force of troops on the frontiers; with having refused to sanction the decree providing for a camp of 20,000 men near Paris; with having disarmed the fortresses; with having reviewed the Swiss and the troops composing the garrison of the palace on the morning of the 10th of August; and with having caused the shedding of blood in consequence of these military dispositions. The bill contained many other charges more or less insubstantial. To these and all of the above charges Louis made answer. He showed much impatience when held responsible for the shedding of blood on the 10th of August and emphatically asseverated his innocence. He denied the existence of the iron chest and his denial produced a most unfavorable impression, for it was an admitted fact that it had been found and its contents examined. He asked permission to select counsel to represent him at the trial. This right was accorded him and at once he requested the services of Target, one of the most distinguished members of the French bar, chief author of the Constitution of 1791, and president of one of the Paris tribunals. Target declined the honor, evidently controlled in his conduct by fear; he gave as his reasons, however, old age and infirmity. His seeming cowardice subjected him to insult and derision, and history will ever record him as a lawyer faithless to his oath. Cambècéres declared that "his example endangered public morality." Target attempted to repair the disgrace by afterwards publishing a full defense of the king, but it was too late to recover his former standing.

After the refusal of Target, Louis selected the venerable and illustrious Malesherbes, who

THE FRENCH REVOLUTION

was assisted by Tronchet and De Séze. Malesherbes, when his name was mentioned in this connection, wrote to the president of the Convention: "I have been twice called to be counsel for him, who was my master, in times when that duty was coveted by everyone: I owe him the same service now that it is a duty which many people deem dangerous." When Louis met his lawyer he embraced him tenderly, and with tears in his eyes, said: "Your sacrifice is the more generous since you endanger your own life without saving mine."

Malesherbes was afterwards pursued relentlessly by his enemies and his grand old spirit suffered all sorts of indignities, but at last he bravely met his doom and went to the scaffold in 1794. His family was almost extirpated by their merciless persecutors in those days when the Revolution was but "the madness that dwells in the hearts of men."

Ten days were allowed the king and his counsel to prepare the defense. In the meantime the public mind was inflamed by the radical journals demanding the death of Louis. The details of the campaign were well organized. Prior to the trial and during its continuance, blatant orators and loud-mouthed demagogues sent out by the clubs as apostles of murder harangued the people in the public gardens, and at the street corners upon improvised and portable rostrums. They demanded the execution of Louis to satisfy the vengeance of the people and as an example to kings. Under the influence of this fiery crusade

DANTON

the passions of the multitude were wrought up to the highest state and the opposition to Louis became most bitter. Patriotism at this period was measured by the degree of earnestness displayed in a desire for the king's death, lukewarmness or moderation was taken as a proof of treason.

As the day of trial approached, bands of ruffians paraded everywhere, brandishing their weapons and singing revolutionary songs. For expressing views of clemency men were cut down in cold blood upon the public streets. The crowd went to the Church of Vol de Grâce, and taking the urns that enclosed the hearts of several kings and queens of France, dashed them to pieces upon the marble pavements. The public gardens and the Palais Royal rang with applause whenever an impassioned orator declared that the safety of the Republic depended upon the death of the king.

In the view of a celebrated French historian: "Neither Robespierre, Danton, Marat, nor the Girondins thirsted for the blood of Louis XVI or believed in the political utility of his sentence. Had they been isolated each of these parties and these men would have saved the king; but face to face, and each struggling to display the most patriotism to the Republic, these parties and men accepted the challenge mutually given. It was no faction, no opinion that immolated the king. It was the antagonism of all these opinions and factions." In other words, fearing that an opposite faction might gain an ascendancy in popular favor, they juggled with the head of a king for their own party's advancement. It was better, each thought, that Louis should perish than that political prestige and power should be lost or imperiled, and thus the desire for party safety and supremacy induced to the commission of a crime.

Danton at first had decided to take no part in the prosecution, but public sentiment was so strong and the people so wrought up by the enemies of royalty that he was swept along with the tide.

Madame Roland urged the Girondins to save the life of Louis; she declared that his death would be political murder and that it would be suicidal for the Girondins to vote for it. "Defend him," she exclaimed, " in a brave and manly way, openly and in the sight of the people." It was easy to give this advice in her parlors, but on the streets such a declaration would perhaps have been followed by death or mutilation.

The Jacobins favored the execution of the king because it would secure for them the support of the masses, and further because it would destroy the popularity of the Girondins in case the latter declined to vote for a death sentence, for it was well known that there were dissensions in their ranks in relation to this matter. The Girondins, as usual, were broken into factions, whereas their enemies, the Jacobins, far better organized politically, were united and presented a solid front; therein lay the power and greater influence of the latter party.

CHAPTER XXVI

TRIAL OF LOUIS XVI

The trial of Louis began on December 26, 1792. It was a farce, as were nearly all the State trials at that period. A member of the Convention, a lawyer, observed: "I expected to find here an Assembly of judges and I find an Assembly of accusers." The three questions submitted to the vote of the delegates were: First, "Is Louis guilty of conspiracy against the nation?" Second, "Shall the judgment be subject to the sanction of the people?" and third, "What shall be the penalty?"

The voting began on the 15th of January, 1793. Out of 739 members, 683 voted guilty on the first question, none for acquittal. On the same day a vote was taken on the second question. There were 717 members present; 424 voted against the appeal, and 283 in its favor; 10 refused to vote.

On the 16th day of the month the voting on the final and all important question began. It lasted from Wednesday to Sunday morning, the continuous sitting being about seventy-two hours. It was a slow and tedious process because each member took time to explain his position or to give reasons for his vote.

THE FRENCH REVOLUTION

During this time it might be supposed that an appearance of solemnity and restraint would have been present; instead of which everything bore an air of gayety, even lively dissipation. The lobby was crowded with ruffians drinking wine as in a tavern. Men and women in the galleries chatted and laughed as if they were at an entertainment. Waiters went here, there, and everywhere with ices, oranges, and sweetmeats which they served on order. Boxes had been arranged in the rear of the hall, and set apart for the lady friends of the delegates, many of whom wore costumes more appropriate for a ball than a court-room. Special quarters with reserved seats were provided for the mistresses of the duke of Orleans; these ladies, while indulging in ices and dainty wines, entertained and held animated conversation with visiting delegates. Bets were made on the result as at a horse race, and women kept tally of the votes by pricking cards with pins. Men in everyday working attire sat on the steps of the amphitheatre and noisily expressed their opinions. Occasionally a shout of disapproval, mingled with threats, would go up when a delegate disappointed and displeased the audience by a vote for acquittal and an appeal for clemency. The Jacobin *menads* from the slums, drunk and disorderly, would bandy words with such delegates or quarrel among themselves.

Crowds were gathered at the doors of the Convention to threaten and intimidate the wavering deputies. "His death or thine," was the cry of

DANTON

the mob, and these words rang in the ears of the delegates every hour of the session. No such scheme of intimidation was ever so successfully worked to effect a judicial result. The inflexible radical members were applauded; the timid were brow-beaten and denounced. The Marquis de Villette, advanced in years, but withal a bold, an intrepid man, was seized as he was about entering the hall and twenty poniards were pointed at his heart while he was asked to make oath that he would vote for the death of the king. Releasing himself from the grasp of his assailants, he exclaimed: " No, I will not vote for his death and you will not kill me." They drew back, awed by such courage, and he passed unharmed to his seat.

During the night sessions, the hall was dimly lighted, deputies lounged in their seats, or sprawled out at full length on the benches, some of them sound asleep but having made arrangements to be aroused in time to vote. Out of this gloom and confusion came in monotonous succession and in sepulchral tones the simple words, " death," " exile," as the various members gave their votes. When Vergniaud's name was called, the first to be reached among the Girondins, a hush fell upon the assemblage. He slowly mounted the tribune, stood facing the audience, his head bent as if collecting his thoughts, and then, as if dreading to hear the word he had promised not to utter, he voted " death." It was only the night before, while supping with a lady who begged him to be merciful to the captive,

THE FRENCH REVOLUTION

that he had sworn by his life to save the king. "I vote for death!" he had exclaimed with indignation in answer to a question by De Séze; "it is an insult to me to suppose me capable of an act so disgraceful." Yet the next day he did that very thing. As his vote was given Robespierre smiled with contempt; Marat muttered the word "imbecile"; Hébert and Billaud-Varennes laughed outright; Danton sneered, and, turning to Brissot, said in a whisper: "These are your orators; sublime language and base conduct! What is to be done with such men? Don't talk of them to me. Your party is destroyed." "I do not like Vergniaud," said Madame Roland, "his speeches are strong in logic, burning with passion, sparkling with beauties, sustained by a noble elocution; what a pity genius like his is not animated by love of the Commonwealth and by tenacity of purpose!" In sealing the doom of Louis, he sealed as well that of his own party, and dragged his friends down to destruction.

The deputies from Paris, among them Danton, Marat, Billaud-Varennes and Collot d'Herbois voted death, as did Siéyès and Buzot the lover of Madame Roland. A deputy named Duchatel was brought into the Convention on a cot; close to his own end he sympathized with the king and voted against death. The galleries jeered and mocked him. The last deputy called was the duke of Orleans, Egalité. He walked from his seat to the tribune with a steady step, but his face was as pale as death. All noise and clamor ceased; the Assembly watched with breathless interest, for there had been many conflicting rumors as to his intention. A shudder ran through the house when he, a prince of the royal line, voted for his cousin's death. Even the Mountain looked with contempt upon the creature who, to win the favor of the rabble, abandoned every sentiment, every principle of humanity. Even among the most brutal, nature revolted against an act so inhuman and men stood aghast at so cruel a deed. In explanation of his motive he muttered something about the spirit of a Brutus. Alas! how many assassins have covered themselves with the mantle of this old Roman. But Brutuses are not often needed; usually they are born Pharisees and their deeds are made to fit their ambitions.

When Louis heard of the duke's conduct he exclaimed: "It hurts me more than all else." He should not have been surprised, however; he knew the character of the man and he had provoked his enduring hatred when, to show his utter contempt, he appointed him colonel of dragoons at a time when the duke was a candidate for admiral of the navy.

While the voting was in progress, the arrival of an intercession from the king of Spain was announced. The Assembly was thrown into a state of the wildest excitement. Delegates marveled that any foreign king would have the impertinence to dictate at such a time what should be the action of the Convention or the policy of France. Danton in his eagerness to be heard,

THE FRENCH REVOLUTION

without even asking permission of the chair, fairly leaped into the tribune and, with a voice of thunder, in his most impassioned manner exclaimed: "I am astonished at the insolence of a power which does not fear to assume an influence over our deliberations. If everybody were of my opinion, the Assembly would instantly declare war against Spain on that ground alone. What! they will not recognize the Republic and yet desire to dictate laws to us! Yet hear this ambassador if you wish to do so. But let the president make a reply worthy of the people whose mouth-piece he is. Let him tell the vain and impudent Castilian that the conquerors of Jemappes will not belie the glory they have acquired and will again exert their strength in order to exterminate all kings who have conspired against us! No dealings with tyranny! The people will pass sentence on their representatives if their representatives attempt to deceive them!"

There were many influences at this time, both inside and outside of France, working in behalf of the king. It is said that the exiled Theodore Lameth came to Paris in disguise a few days before the trial and sought at once the house of Danton. He found the great tribune in his bath and explained the reason for his unexpected and perilous visit. "To save the king I am quite willing," said Danton, "but I must have a million to buy certain votes and I must have it in eight days. I warn you, however, that I myself will vote for death; I am quite willing to save the king's life, but not willing to lose my own." Lameth failed, so the story goes, to send the money, and the plan fell through.

At the time of the taking of the final vote on the king's sentence, the Convention comprised 721 delegates; 334 voted for exile or imprisonment, 387 voted for death. Of the latter many favored delay. There was a majority of 53 votes for death; 43 of which were for death on condition of suspension of execution, so that there was a majority of only 10 votes for death without condition or restriction. Manuel tried to falsify the count and so exasperated the radical delegates that he nearly lost his life.

It was the Girondins who murdered the king; for while they really wished to save him and could probably have done so had they stood firm, they feared the imputation of royalism and so voted for his death. The Jacobins absolutely favored death, and under the popular tumult had made their political enemies their accomplices, it may be said their tools. The Jacobins voted death for, as they thought, the security of the Republic; the Girondins for the safety of their party; which was the nobler of the two motives? It will be a very difficult task for the most ardent admirer of the men from the Gironde to defend them against the charge of trimming. They favored the appeal to the people, an act of clemency in itself, for it gave Louis a chance for his life; but, when it came to the final and all-important question, they voted outright for his death.

THE FRENCH REVOLUTION

Such conduct, if it is not classified as cowardly, is at least inconsistent.

On the evening of the final vote a life guardsman named Paris, wrapped in a great cloak, strolled into the Palais Royal determined to avenge the death of the king. Lepelletier St. Fargeau, a royalist who had enthusiastically espoused the popular cause, was sitting at a table in the restaurant of one named Fevrier. He had been marked for vengeance by the royalists because of his apostacy and for having argued and voted for the king's death. Paris stepped up to him and asked: " Are you the villain who voted for the death of the king? " " Yes," he answered, " I so voted; but I am not a villain. I voted according to my conscience." " If that be so," said the life guardsman, " take that for your reward," and he plunged his sword into his side. Lepelletier expired almost immediately, his last words being " I am cold." This assassination gave rise to all sorts of rumors as to the conspiracies and uprising of the royalists.

It was decided immediately after the final vote was recorded that the execution of Louis should take place within twenty-four hours. Malesherbes pleaded, with tears streaming down his cheeks, for delay, but the Convention would listen to no appeal. It was contended that if the Republic required the sacrifice there was no reason for respite or clemency. The execution was appointed to take place on Monday, January 21st.

DANTON

The Mountain rejoiced over the result, but it is certain that the great body of the better class people were shocked. " Paris," says Thiers, " was in a profound stupor; the audacity of the new government had produced the ordinary effect of force on the masses; it had paralysed and reduced to silence the greater number and had excited to outspoken indignation only those who were of most resolute spirit. The blow was so sudden that peaceful citizens and royal sympathizers with the king were stunned; there was no intermission in the work from the beginning to the end of the prosecution so that amidst the public clamor there was no opportunity for remonstrance."

CHAPTER XXVII

EXECUTION OF LOUIS XVI

On Sunday the king was officially notified of the action of the Convention. He asked for a respite of three days, but his request was refused and there was nothing left for him to do but to prepare for death. He selected the Abbé Edgeworth as his confessor.

Henry Essex Edgeworth de Firmont was born in Ireland in 1745. His father was a clergyman in the Church of England, who embraced the Roman Catholic faith and went with his family to France. The abbé was a man of the purest and simplest piety. After the execution of Louis, he escaped from France; William Pitt offered him a pension which he refused. In his last hours the Duchess d'Angouléme watched over him; the royal family followed him to his grave; and Louis XVIII wrote his epitaph.

Louis was given permission to see his family without the presence of strangers. There was but one meeting; it was too sad to be described in detail, but the interview was most affecting and the demeanor of Louis throughout was heroic.

After he tore himself from the arms of his wife, his children, and his sister, he straightway sought his confessor, to whom he said: " We

DANTON

are done with time, let us now occupy ourselves with eternity." At midnight he retired, giving instructions to his valet, Cléry, to call him at five o'clock. Worn out with the excitement and anxiety of the day, he slept soundly.

Cléry, following closely the instructions of his master, aroused him at the appointed hour. "Has it struck five?" asked the king. "Not yet," answered Cléry, "by the clock of the tower, but several of the clocks of the city have already struck." Louis carefully made his toilet; he wore a purple coat, a white waistcoat and gray silk knee breeches. The priest performed mass and Louis took communion. Then turning to Cléry he said: "After my death you will give this seal to my son, this ring to the queen; this small parcel contains locks of hair of all my family, this you will also give to her. Tell the queen, my sister and my children that I promised to see them again this morning, but the parting would be too bitter and might unnerve me for the ordeal through which I have to pass and further I desire to save them from the agony of another separation. Tell them too that they know not how much it has cost me to depart without receiving their last embraces."

It was a cold, bleak morning, cloudy and sleety, and the dawn came on slowly. Cléry had made a fire in the stove and the king, immersed in deep thought, sat close to it warming his hands. In the streets below were heard the trampling of armed men, the galloping of horses, and the rumbling of artillery. The king, suddenly

THE FRENCH REVOLUTION

aroused from his revery, remarked: "Here they come." On the staircase were heard approaching the Committee of Municipals, with Santerre at their head, and the *gens d'armes* appointed to escort the king to the scaffold. When the door was opened Louis said: "You are come for me. I will be with you in an instant; await me there," pointing to the threshold of the chamber. He then retired and once more knelt at the altar with the priest. Finishing his devotions he stepped forward and addressing Jacques Roux, one of the committee, said: "This is my will; may I ask you to give it to the president of the Council Générale of the Commune." "We did not come here to do your errands but to escort you to the scaffold," was the brutal reply. "Very true, very true," said Louis, and looking for a kindlier face he turned to Baudrais, who without hesitation accepted the trust.

Roux had been a priest before the Revolution, but throwing his frock aside he plunged into politics and became one of the most rabid and rampant of the radicals. Fearing his loyalty to the Revolution might be suspected, because of his former calling, he thought it necessary in order to remove all suspicion to become specially furious. He simply evinced the temper of the apostate and his contemptible spirit was shown in his treatment of Louis at this time, when he insolently refused the last request of a man about to die.

"Let us go," said Louis. As he passed down

the staircase he spoke to one of the jailers, whom a few days before he had rather sharply reprimanded for some misconduct. "Forgive me, Mathey," he said, "I spoke too harshly the other day;" but the jailer, not generous enough to accept the courteous apology of a man going to his death, turned away and made no reply. The system of compelling fear and terror had made men cravens, wretched cowards. Seeing that Santerre kept his hat on, Louis remarked: "I remember the last time you accompanied me, you had lost your hat and were involuntarily bareheaded. I see, to-day, that you intend to have no recurrence of such an accident and so you keep it securely on your head."

The king entered the carriage awaiting him, accompanied by his confessor and two *gens d'armes*. It took two hours to go from the Temple to the place of execution. The beating of drums prevented the king's conversing with the abbé and so he spent his time in reading his prayer book, paying but little attention to the crowds upon the streets. The carriage was halted but once and that was when a quartette of enthusiastic royalists flashed their swords and called upon the people to rescue the king. Their effort was futile, and receiving no support they ran for their lives. Two were overtaken and killed; the other two, Baron de Batz and his secretary, Davaux, effected their escape. Along the entire route all windows were closed and there were no signs of gayety. Great crowds were gathered on the sidewalks, but a universal silence

THE FRENCH REVOLUTION

prevailed, only occasionally broken by the cry of " Long live the nation."

Around the guillotine a large space was kept vacant. One hundred thousand men under arms were drawn up to the limits of this space. Cannon were in position and cannoneers stood close at hand with lighted matches. The guillotine loomed up in the centre of the square and seemed to be a thing instinct with life, waiting to taste the blood of a king. Samson, who was but a part of the machine, stood ready for his task.

To this public executioner, the horrible work now allotted him was but a portion of the day's routine. The heads of the mighty had rolled at his feet. Patrician and plebeian, prince and prelate; all heads to him were the same. He chopped them off with an utter indifference; he asked no questions; he literally dabbled in bood; his trade was death. Yet this gory headsman was not a ghoul, but a man with human affections and desires. When the day's work was over he would go home and at supper, surrounded by his family, would recite, no doubt, time and again the thrilling events of the day. For recreation he often went to the theatre and, it is said, laughed heartily, for no one had a keener zest for a joke. He enjoyed good health, ate and slept well, and apparently was easy in his conscience. He sent into eternity a host of men and women without evincing the slightest tremor or sensibility. He was a dweller on the banks of the river Styx, the companion and assistant of the grim old ferryman, with hundreds of the wandering spirits as his victims. No one man in all history ever kept old Charon busier. In his quiet moments in later life, if such a man ever did reflect, the past must have been a hideous nightmare.

The day of the king's execution was out of the ordinary, however, and while awaiting his arrival Samson, standing on the platform—the stage upon which was to be enacted one of the greatest tragedies of history—was in the view of tens of thousands of people, the principal figure in the scene. He appreciated the distinction that his position gave him. Everything was spick and span, the platform had been swept and washed, the knife scraped and cleaned, and the executioner had put on fresh linen and dressed himself with some care in honor of the event.

At about ten o'clock the carriage reached the scaffold. Louis alighted, and three assistants to the executioner came forward to aid in removing his coat. He waved them aside, however, and made his own preparations, unfastening his neckcloth, opening his shirt, and turning back the collar. The assistants then began to bind his arms, but at this he displayed some indignation and was about to resist when his confessor reminded him of the indignities that had been heaped upon his Lord. At this Louis submitted and then, leaning on M. Edgeworth, ascended the steps of the scaffold, which were covered with sleet. When he reached the platform he came forward to address the people. "Frenchmen," he said, "I die innocent of the crimes imputed

THE FRENCH REVOLUTION

to me. I forgive the authors of my death and I pray that my blood may not fall upon France." He was about to proceed when the drums were ordered to beat and the noise drowned his words. M. Edgeworth, extending his hands in a final blessing, said: " Son of St. Louis, ascend to heaven." The king was violently seized, placed upon the plank, and his head at one blow was severed from his body. This was twenty minutes past ten by the clock. One of the executioners held the head aloft and the people shouted: " Long live the nation."

The body was immediately removed to the cemetery of the Madeleine. It was not placed in a coffin, but was thrown into a deep ditch and covered with great quantities of quicklime, the head being placed between the legs.

The spot where Louis was sacrificed in expiation of the crimes of his ancestors is marked to-day with a red-granite obelisk brought from Egypt by the French government in 1831. This monument, whose sides are chiseled with the hieroglyphics of an ancient and a long since departed people, has witnessed the rise and fall of dynasties, the development and decadence of past civilizations; yet perhaps never did it see a people so athirst for blood as were the French for the blood of their king.

After the execution, when the barriers were removed, the crowds that had been confined within limits soon swept over every inch of vacant space, like an incoming surf. Men and women fought with desperation over the king's hat and coat until these articles were torn to shreds. Many dipped their pikes and handkerchiefs in the blood and one creature, taking some upon his finger, actually tasted it and declared to a jeering crowd that it was atrociously bitter. One heartless wretch showered a handful of clots over the heads of the people.

Almost immediately after the execution, shops were opened and business was at once resumed, newsboys cried the latest editions, and street venders sold their usual wares. The cafés and gardens were crowded, and the taverns were filled with drinkers toasting the health of the nation and riotously singing a song whose wild refrain was, "With the guts of the last of the priests, we will strangle the last of the kings."

In the evening the theatres were thronged and Paris seemed to be even gayer than usual. The clubs were noisy with the declamations of the orators, and above them all could be heard Danton's voice ringing out in clear and emphatic defiance, challenging the enemies of France. Long before midnight it was time for all honest people to be within doors, for the night was made hideous with the howling imprecations of drunken men and women, who reeled like bacchanals through the streets till morning dawned. "O! the monsters," cried the queen when she heard their shrieks under her windows; "they rejoice over the death of their king!" The following article, which appeared in the "Gazette de France," a Parisian journal, doubtless fairly reflected the prevailing sentiment with regard to

THE FRENCH REVOLUTION

the execution: " The tyrant is no more. A terrible example has been given to the despots of the world. The axe of justice has struck down him who already was condemned by the conscience of the French people. This memorable judgment rests solely on the responsibility of the nation itself which takes this responsibility on its shoulders. The nation knows its enemies—the kings of the earth; and if they demand an account of the Republic for a judgment which by the death of a king has placed all humanity on an equal footing, every French citizen will present himself as the responsible party."

There is only one ground upon which to base a justification for the death of Louis, and that is its political necessity. The charges preferred against him did not warrant his execution, but the argument was that a sacrifice had to be made to secure the safety and the stability of the Republic, even though it resulted in the death of an innocent man. It was not the only state trial in the world in which political considerations were of greater weight in effecting a judgment than proof of actual guilt. When Charles Stuart, king of England, was brought before the Court of High Commission in Westminster Hall, he was found guilty and sentenced to death upon charges that were less grave than those that induced the conviction of Louis Capet, king of France.

Louis XVI would have been an amiable monarch with good intentions and tendencies in a time of rest and contentment, but in a revolution

DANTON

his weakness was one of the causes of its violence. The period in which he reigned called for a king who had the qualities of a reformer or of a despot, but he was without the attributes of either. When he ascended the throne the people were tired of arbitrary rule and he was willing to renounce it, but he did not know how to grant concessions or to restrain violence. Overtaken and overwhelmed by the Revolution he was made the scapegoat for the sins of his ancestors and paid the penalty for their tyranny and crimes.

CHAPTER XXVIII

DANTON OPPOSES FACTIONAL STRIFE—THE TREASON OF DUMOURIEZ—LASOURCE ATTACKS DANTON—THE REPLY OF DANTON

Now was resumed the struggle for supremacy between the two dominant factions. It was a war to the death, to the bitter end. The trial and execution of Louis had so absorbed public attention that the parties had ceased their bitter recriminations and had only been watching each other for points. Royalty, aristocracy, the hierarchy, and a king's life had been swept away. What was next to be done? If it was to be a republic of the masses then the party that stood for the middle classes was in turn to be destroyed.

Girondins, do you not read the handwriting on the wall? Do you not know that it will require the clearest-headed statesmanship to avoid the perils that beset you? In the natural sequence of events you are the next to fall. Can you not see that the Revolution is working down to the rabble?

At this time Danton came to the front and put forth every effort to allay the prevailing dissensions and to unite all factions in the interest of the Republic. "Citizens," he said, "now that the tyrant is dead let us turn our energies to the valiant prosecution of the war. We must fight

DANTON

Europe; let us now reorganize the Committee of General Security and remove Roland from the ministry because he abuses all that do not share his opinions. Let us banish this habit of mutual recrimination, for France will soon not know to whom to accord her confidence. As for me, I am a stranger to the passion for revenge, but if we must drink blood let it be the blood of the enemies of humanity. What have I not done to maintain the spirit of peace in the executive council? I have only one desire and that is for my country's welfare, and to secure this I would willingly sacrifice even my life."

At first Danton had done everything in his power to avoid the war. Especially did he warn the Convention against provoking the enmity of England, but now that the conflict was on he devoted his best efforts to its energetic and successful prosecution. He believed it had been favored by the Girondins from a selfish and an ulterior motive, not so much for the glory of France as for the strengthening of their popularity as a party; but Danton was a Frenchman before all else and he allowed nothing, not even the selfish purposes of an opposite faction, to weaken his sentiments of loyalty and patriotism. He had been in Belgium and was well informed on the condition of affairs at the seat of war, and he believed that a defeat of the French armies was not only possible but highly probable. He knew full well what such a repulse would mean if the government at home was not strong enough to counteract its effects.

THE FRENCH REVOLUTION

After the death of the king the allies pressed with their armies on the borders of France and threatened an overwhelming invasion. The answer to this threat was a decree by the Convention authorizing a levy of 300,000 men. Roland resigned from the ministry on the 22d, and Garat was named to fill the place temporarily.

The commander of the army, Dumouriez, was in an ugly mood. He complained that he received no home support, that he was covered with reproaches and continually suspected of conspiring to establish a military government. "Though I be called Cæsar, Cromwell, or Monk," he declared, "I will save my country in spite of the Jacobins and the Constitutional regicides who protect them, and I will re-establish the Constitution of 1791." Danton and Lacroix were dispatched as commissioners to the army. Danton, seeing the way things were going, hastened back to Paris and made his report to the Convention.

"When the invader," he exclaimed, "is at the gates of Paris, I know no enemy but the foreign foe. Your quarrels are contemptible. They do not kill a single Prussian. You fatigue me with your feuds; let us beat back the enemies of France, let us conquer our freedom. Let us conquer Holland; let us reanimate the republican party in England. Let us roll France forward to meet her foes. Fulfil your great destiny. No more quarrels, no more factional strife and the country is saved. I have been personally assailed but I care not for that if only France be free."

DANTON

Dumouriez had invaded Holland and had won a succession of victories. He was now in a position of power; beloved by his army and enjoying by reason of his triumphs great prestige in the capital, he thought the road to his ambition was open. Thereupon he made preparations to organize an army in Belgium and Holland, march to Paris, overthrow the revolutionary government, and establish a constitutional monarchy with the Duke of Orleans on the throne; but

> " The best laid schemes o' mice and men
> Gang aft a-gley."

The Austrians under Archduke Charles attacked Miranda, one of the generals who commanded a division of the grand army of Dumouriez, and disastrously defeated him. Quickly following up his victory the duke drove the French out of Belgium. This disconcerted the plans of Dumouriez and shattered his hopes. He put forth, however, stupendous efforts to unite his scattered forces, and made a stand at Neerwinden, but was severely beaten and compelled to retreat into France.

His designs being by this time pretty well understood and his loyalty suspected, the Convention sent three commissioners to question him as to his purpose. The soldier with his characteristic boldness frankly admitted that he favored a counter-revolution. Upon the return of the commissioners to Paris, the Convention, on the strength of their report, sent agents to arrest him; he surrendered them at once to the Aus-

THE FRENCH REVOLUTION

trians, who threw them into prison, where they were detained for three years.

When the soldiers were informed of the real facts and convinced of their commander's disloyalty they turned upon him, and to save his life he galloped in hot haste across the borders. He was shot at but escaped unhurt. The next day he had the effrontery to return and make an earnest appeal to the troops to desert their colors; his argument was so persuasive that he actually succeeded in carrying off 800 officers and men. He joined the Austrians but lost heart in fighting against France in the ranks of her enemies, and shortly afterwards retired to Amsterdam. He subsequently took up his residence in England, where he died in 1823.

The defection of Dumouriez reflected upon Danton, for it was owing mainly to his influence that the general had been given his command; further than this, Danton, during his visits to Belgium, had been in communication so close and so frequent with him that he was suspected of being a party to the scheme to overthrow the Republic. A few days after the desertion of Dumouriez, Lasource attacked Danton in the Convention, and intimated that he had participated in the treason of the general. "I move," he said, "that a committee of investigation be named that the facts may be inquired into and the truth ascertained. The people have seen the throne and the Capitol; let them now behold the Tarpeian rock and the scaffold. Let us declare that we will never make terms with a tyrant and let us swear the death of him who shall attempt to make himself king or dictator." The whole Assembly rose and repeated the oath.

As he sat writhing under the attack of his assailant, Danton revealed in his face the emotions that were struggling within him. When on his way to the tribune he stopped in front of the benches of the Mountain and, leaning over to the friends of Robespierre, said in an undertone while pointing with his hand toward the Girondins: "The wretches, they would cast their crimes upon us." His reply from the tribune was furious and crushing, his enemies recoiling under the attack. "No peace," he cried, "no truce, no further negotiations with them." These words sounded the death knell of the Girondins.

At the conclusion of the speech the Mountaineers welcomed the new convert to their ranks with open arms and with every manifestation of joy. They knew full well what his accession meant to their cause. The Girondins on the other hand, with their usual political blindness or obliquity of vision, failed to see that they had stricken down the one man above all others whose prowess and friendship they could have depended upon in the final struggle with their enemies. Nor were they right in their conclusions in so far as their suspicions of his loyalty were concerned. They not only assailed a friend, but misjudged him.

At the time of his victories the popularity of Dumouriez was unbounded, and Danton was at the summit, in the very plentitude of his power.

THE FRENCH REVOLUTION

One was the commander-in-chief of the army, the other was the leading representative of the people; that is to say one was the arm and the other was the head of the nation. If these two men had formed a combination, they might have divided the raiment of France between them, but there is not the slightest proof that Danton ever thought of such a thing. Dumouriez was an arch-conspirator, he loved intrigue, his ambition for political power was all but boundless—it was measured only by the limit of its possibilities. For personal advancement he would willingly have betrayed his country by overturning the Republic and declaring himself military dictator. When his plots were discovered he deserted his colors, abandoned the army, and fled from his native land. The Revolution to him was only a game in which ambition played for the stakes. So far as its real purposes and principles were concerned, it had to him no meaning; it was merely an opportunity.

Danton, be it said to his honor, was not given to conspiracies of this character, nor to treasonable designs. He loved France and her people; his patriotism was circumscribed alone by the borders of his country; her welfare was his sole consideration, and he never gave the slightest intimation, even when his influence was dominant, of centring in himself the exercise of absolute power or the setting up of a dictatorship. In truth, when he thought that France had been sufficiently purged by the Revolution, he announced that it was time for a reaction, for the establishment of a stable and righteous government. He had not the temperament of a usurper; he was not worried by a teasing ambition that urged him to usurp the sovereignty of the people; he was constantly loyal to the principles of the Revolution and to the Republic.

It was Madame Roland that instilled into the minds of the Girondins her dislike, her hatred for this man. No matter how earnestly he declared his friendship, she always suspected his purpose. It made no difference how much he proved his fealty, his conduct was misinterpreted. Controlled alone by her prejudices she at last succeeded in separating her party entirely from his influence, and thus was lost the only safeguard between them and destruction. It is not hard to believe that the attack made by Lasource upon Danton was instigated by her. In alluding to Madame Roland, Danton upon one occasion asked, "Why do these Girondins not take a man for their leader? This woman will destroy them. She is the Circe of the Republic."

Although the Girondins had ignored the advice of Danton, had humbled his pride, and had openly assailed him, he always had a secret admiration for his rivals, and even when he assisted in their downfall he sought only their humiliation, not their destruction.

The struggle between the Jacobins and the Girondins did not abate as time wore on. The Republic was not big enough to contain both parties and it was but a question which would survive. The Girondins had lost in a great meas-

THE FRENCH REVOLUTION

ure their popularity among the Parisians. They had made a grave mistake in showing a loyalty to the provinces rather than to the capital. In fact some of their orators in their hot and vehement speeches intimated that the time was not far distant when the provinces would be arrayed against the capital. These indiscreet expressions greatly incensed the Parisians, and the Girondins, contemptuously designated as "mere provincials," were most bitterly denounced in every quarter of the city. The newspapers were especially denunciatory in charging them with attempting to create antagonism between the town and the country districts.

How different was the patriotic sentiment of Danton, who exclaimed: "As for me, I am not a child of Paris. I was born in a department toward which I always turn an affectionate and a longing eye. But no one of us belongs to this or that department; we all belong to the whole of France. It is said there are men among us who wish to cut France into pieces. France must remain an undivided whole with an undivided representation. The citizens of Marseilles want to clasp the hands of their fellow citizens of Dunkirk."

CHAPTER XXIX

DANTON—MARAT'S ARREST AND TRIUMPH—GIRONDINS—CHARLOTTE CORDAY—ASSASSINATION OF MARAT—EXECUTION OF CHARLOTTE CORDAY—MARRIAGE OF DANTON—TRIAL AND EXECUTION OF MARIE ANTOINETTE

Danton at this time was the first man in the Republic. His reputation had been seriously affected by the defection of Dumouriez, but by reason of his energetic measures to recover lost ground and to repair the damage done by the general's treason he had re-instated himself in public favor and had removed every vestige of suspicion.

His appeals to the patriotic ardor of the people rang through the Republic like a trumpet blast. There was no hesitation, no despondency about him; the gloomier the hour the more courageous his soul. He kept alive the war spirit; at the stamp of his foot armies rose out of the earth and France was surrounded by a barrier of freemen. " Let us fulfil our grand destiny," he cried. " No more dissensions, no more internal quarrels, and the fatherland is saved." He saw that a grave mistake had been made by the enactment of the decree of November 18, 1792, in which the Republic had declared war against all kings. It but provoked opposition. It was simply a reckless

THE FRENCH REVOLUTION

defiance that arrayed all Europe against France, and to counteract the effect of legislation so foolish and bombastic, the decree at his instance was repealed on April 13, 1793.

Marat was like a famished wolf on a trail of blood in his pursuit of the Girondins. They never were radical enough for him and they had always been subjected to his scurrilous attacks, but now in view of their unpopularity he was more than ever fierce and vindictive. Next to an aristocrat he despised one of these perfumed and silken republicans. "The death of tyrants," he cried, "is the last right of slaves. Cæsar was assassinated in the public Senate, let us treat the traitorous representatives of the country in the same manner—let us slay them upon their benches, the theatre of their crimes." Of course the enmity of the Girondins was aroused and they but waited for an opportunity to entrap their foe.

In his rantings Marat had advised the mob that when hungry they should help themselves; the consequence was that bread and meat shops were plundered in every direction. The Girondins, believing that the time had come to retaliate upon their enemy, publicly condemned the preaching of such doctrines, and upon their motion Marat was brought for trial before the Revolutionary Tribunal, April 22, 1793. He came with an army of hoodlums at his back, for this king of the slums had retainers as loyal as any that ever followed a prince of the blood royal to court or to battle.

After a short trial he was unanimously acquitted, as was to be expected under the circumstances, when the *personnel* of the court and the persuasive presence of the mob are taken into consideration. Marat was carried by his enthusiastic followers in triumph through the streets. He was seated on a chair, which was fastened to a plank, " the buckler of sedition on which the *prolétaires* inaugurated the king of indigence." Four stalwart men bore him aloft above the heads of the crowd. This squalid creature with his patched coat, soiled linen, and long hair falling over his shoulders presented a woeful appearance, but his very poverty was picturesque and appealed to the sympathies of the people. To them it was his badge of honor, the distinguishing sign of his loyalty. He was proud of his exaltation and the homage paid him and he manifested in his look and manner every expression of joy. The women from the markets crowned him and covered him with flowers, working men abandoned their toil to greet him, the windows in the houses were filled with applauding admirers. The streets were crowded with multitudes of people that enthusiastically joined in the ovation. He was carried to the Convention, which was invaded by the mob and the sitting interrupted. Here he made a short address in which he declared that the Girondins too would have their day of triumph but it would be on the way to the scaffold. As usual he was arrogant, presumptuous, ferocious. His acquittal had made him, if possible, even more insolent and had whetted his appetite for blood. His apostrophes were so

THE FRENCH REVOLUTION

wild that he provoked the sneers of Robespierre, who in sheer disgust of declarations so anarchistic shrugged his shoulders and exhibited every sign of impatience. Marat observing this threw a glance of defiance at Robespierre and called him "*lâche scélérat,*" but the latter deigned no reply—every feature of his face, however, revealed his scorn and the contempt he felt.

After leaving the Convention the crowd carried their idol to the Club of the Cordeliers. Here Marat harangued the people without restraint or reserve; he breathed out fire and blood, every sentence was inflammatory and sanguinary and punctuated by the cries of the people: "*Mort aux Girondins.*" Night had fallen when Marat started to return to his lodgings, the crowd escorting him with torches. The houses in his neighborhood were illuminated.

"Behold my palace," he exclaimed, as he ascended the rickety staircase of his humble home, and "behold my sceptre," as he pointed to his pen; "it is with this that I have effected the transfer of the sovereignty of the Tuileries unto this den."

The mob lingered around as all mobs do, even after there is no further reason for their presence, but later in the night dispersed after shrieking in chorus, "*Vive l'ami du peuple.*" Such was the triumph of Marat. He had been crowned and enthroned by the rabble and in him now, more than ever, was personified the multitude.

Danton had advised several of the members of the Girondins with whom he was still friendly, to act with caution and not to arouse needlessly the passions of the people. He urged them to withdraw the prosecution, warned them against the danger of what he called "mutilating the Convention," and declared that they made a mistake in establishing a precedent by the arrest of a deputy and that this act would come home in time to plague and distress them. Not only did the Girondins refuse to take his advice, but they turned upon him and denounced him most bitterly as a defender of anarchists and anarchy. They did not seem to know it, but it was his hostility they had to fear more than that of a dozen Marats.

So bitter had the public feeling grown against the Girondins that a motion was made to expel them from the Assembly. The Commune made a formal demand on the Convention to deliver up twelve of the members of that party to the Revolutionary Tribunal for trial. Isnard, the president of the body, being provoked almost to desperation by these motions and threats against his party, greatly increased the public anger by exclaiming in a speech from the tribune: "If by any of the insurrections that have grown so frequent since the 10th of March, a hostile hand be raised against the national representatives, I declare to you in the name of all France that Paris will be destroyed.—Yes, France would rise against such a crime and it soon would be a matter of doubt on which side of the Seine Paris had stood." Danton, fairly bristling with rage, denounced Isnard for his insolence and declared that his words were tumultuous and insurrectionary. After this violent scene, the Convention adjourned, but the combat was renewed the following day.

The mob gathered outside the hall and loudly clamored for the accusation and arrest of twenty-two Girondins specially objectionable to the people. A warrant had been issued for Roland, but he fled before it could be served. His wife came to the hall of the Convention hoping to gain admission and make one of her appeals, but the crowd was so dense and the disorder so great that she could not secure access. It was also deemed prudent by her friends, because of the mob's temper, that she should at once withdraw. It is very doubtful if, at this time, her beauty and eloquence could have calmed the tumult. It had gone far beyond the stage when it could be controlled by the honeyed words of a fascinating woman.

Under the stress of public opinion a decree of accusation was passed against the Girondins on June 2, 1793. Notwithstanding this fact they were generally allowed to go and come as they pleased, but their presence was not tolerated in the Convention. It was the purpose of their enemies at this point to terrorize and not to punish them further.

After they were expelled from the Convention they naturally chafed, as proud and independent men, under the humiliation and appealed to their constituents for assistance; for, as their popularity had waned in the capital, it had in a

DANTON

greater ratio increased in the provinces. Many of the departments unfurled the banner of revolt and denounced the unjust and arbitrary action of the Assembly, that deprived them of the representation they were entitled to in the National Congress under the law of the land. It looked as if a spirit of insurrection would possess the Republic from one end to the other. Two-thirds of the departments already threatened rebellion.

Danton rose equal to the occasion and his voice rang out above all the alarm and confusion. "We are in the midst of storms; the thunder rolls. It is in the midst of these clashings that the work will be done that will immortalize the French nation. They claim that it is the insurrection of Paris that causes these movements in the departments. I declare in the face of the universe that the events of May 31st and June 2d constitute the glory of this superb city. I proclaim in the face of France that without the cannon and the insurrection the conspirators would have triumphed. We are willing then to face the whole responsibility resulting therefrom. I myself incited to the rising of the people by saying that if there were in the Convention a hundred men like me we should overcome the conspiracy and found liberty on immovable foundations. Do not mind the addresses, full of calumnies against Paris, which the conspirators have sent to the departments; they are no new things. Paris remains the centre where everything must concentrate. Paris is the focus that will gather all rays of French patriotism which

THE FRENCH REVOLUTION

will consume our enemies." He declared that to oppose the Assembly was to surrender France to the emigrant princes and to foreign kings.

Upon his motion Commissioners of the Convention, representing, like the envoys of ancient Rome, the integrity of the Republic, were sent at once into the disaffected districts. In their hats they wore three plumes of the national colors, red, white and blue; around their waists were tri-color scarfs and at their sides in black leather belts hung naked swords, the scabbards having been thrown away. There was no use, it was thought, to sheathe that which the Republic straightway might have to use. The envoys were resolute men and they soon made it known that rebellion against the Convention was treason to the Republic, and France was pacified in three days. "The seventy-two departments which had declared for us," cried a disheartened Girondin, "turned round and abandoned us in twenty-four hours."

The Girondins as a party formed one of the most interesting groups of men in the Revolution. Their ranks contained some of the greatest orators of that period and their weakness as a party was that they depended more upon their eloquence than upon political organization. They were poorly directed in their policies and conduct. None of their measures succeeded, as they were imprudently proposed and badly sustained. Their threats were ill-timed and their attacks were only half fought out. "They assailed the Mountaineers without weakening them, the Commune without subduing it, the faubourgs without suppressing them, and irritated Paris by invoking the aid of the departments without procuring it." They assailed Robespierre without destroying him, accused Marat without convicting him, and denounced Danton without sustaining their charge. They thus imprudently arrayed against themselves the strongest forces and individuals in the Revolution. Although somewhat too provincial in their views they were nevertheless thoroughly patriotic and loved every inch of the soil of France. Many of them were dreamers, visionaries, but the majority were practical enough to establish a stable popular government if they had been given a fair chance. Had they been allowed to fashion the Republic, it would have been eminently respectable and the rabble would have had but little to do with the manipulation of its machinery.

As the Revolution plunged along on its course, however, their hopes and illusions vanished. Outwitted and overthrown by their unscrupulous adversaries, they saw the government fall into the hands of corrupt and reckless men. They endeavored to stem the current, but it was too strong for them to direct or control. The riotings, the massacres, and the executions sickened them and they pleaded for moderation and favored a counter-revolution. Their method to bring this about was abstract speculation and their action consisted only in declamation. It was a combat between eloquence and force, and the result was a foregone conclusion; it reminds

THE FRENCH REVOLUTION

one of the contest between Demosthenes and Philip. The Olynthiacs and the Philippics, whose eloquence has thrilled the hearts of all succeeding generations, and ought to have saved Athenian liberty, could not prevail against the gold and the phalanxes of the sturdy conqueror from Macedon. Metaphysical statesmen, a fascinating woman, parlor politics, and drawing-room caucuses were of no avail in this controversy; they went for naught in the desperate game that was being played for supremacy, a game that had for its stakes an empire and its political control. " Les Girondins," said Danton, " sont de beaux diseurs et gens de procédés. Mais ils n'ont jamais porté que la plume et la baton d' huissier."

In the midst of these exciting scenes and times, Danton, notwithstanding his engrossing cares and duties in the political field, was being plagued by Cupid, and on the 17th day of June, 1793, married Mademoiselle Gély, a girl but sixteen years of age. Her parents were respectable, royalistic and religious. Her father, through the influence of Danton, had secured a lucrative government position, and the family in consequence felt themselves under obligations to the great politician; but it was a long while before the mother could be induced to give her consent to the marriage. She instinctively drew back from Danton; she looked upon him with feelings akin to horror because of the part he had taken in the events of the 10th of August, and in the September massacres, and it required much persuasion to remove her prejudices and objections. But he was so ardent and so vehement a lover that he broke down all opposition between him and the object of his desire, and argued away even the scruples of a pious mother. The ceremony was performed by an orthodox priest and Lamartine states that just before the marriage Danton retired to an inner room and made confession. Belloc asserts that the union was not a happy one, but we know that when Danton was upon the platform of the guillotine the only thought that unnerved him was the recollection of his " dear, beloved wife." Danton had no children by this marriage, but he had two sons by his first wife, and after his death they were cared for by their step-mother and her family. In after years they were engaged in business at Arcis sur Aube and lived on the family farm near that town. They sought a life of seclusion to avoid hearing the execrations heaped upon the memory of their father, for during the days of the reaction and the restoration his enemies then no longer spared him.

At this time Marat was demanding a strong executive, intimating a dictatorship, that the powers and functions of government might be more efficiently exercised and that the enemies of the country might be more summarily dispatched. In the meantime, in place of the despotism of kings, the Revolution had established the despotism of the mob. The rabble was supreme. The agitation had brought the dregs to the top.

Marat was still pursuing the Girondins with

THE FRENCH REVOLUTION

a hatred made more bitter because of his recent prosecution and in the columns of his paper he denounced them with all the venom and malignity of his nature. He was not satisfied with their expulsion from the Convention, but demanded that they be brought before the Revolutionary Tribunal. He was no apprentice in the use of his pen, in his style he was a writer of no mean ability and his attacks were not only irritating but exasperating. He was the father of yellow journalism, and knew how to build a structure of apparent truth upon a mere rumor. Personal reputations were nothing to him if by ridicule and defamation he could weaken or destroy the power and influence of an enemy.

Men in public life may appear to disregard the attacks of newspapers, but that man is coarse and insensate who does not feel the sting of abuse. "I am destined," said Napoleon, "to be a fine morsel for the pamphleteers, but I have no fear of becoming their victim, they will gnaw on granite." He thought he was a law unto himself, and yet no autocrat ever so resented adverse criticism and so arbitrarily censored the press. No man should object to just censure or even the denunciation of his views, but by abuse is meant the impugning of his motives or a reflection upon his honor and his conduct. "Censure is the tax a man pays to the public for being eminent," but no one likes to be held up to the scorn, contempt, or ridicule of his fellow men.

At nothing did Marat hesitate in his attacks upon the Girondins; they were stigmatized as

DANTON

traitors, aristocrats, conspirators, provincials, who sought the destruction of the capital and the restoration of the monarchy. They were charged with being inimical to the Constitution and the Republic and with having favored even the secession of the Gironde from France. The constant repetition of these allegations induced the public to believe they were true, for the people are impressed by what they see in print. Hébert joined in the hue and cry and poured a torrent of abuse through the columns of his filthy paper.

The Girondins had acted imprudently in attacking Robespierre, in assailing Danton unjustly, in pressing the prosecution against Marat, and in threatening the destruction of Paris, and they were paying a heavy penalty for their indiscretions. Because of their unfair treatment of Danton they had provoked the resentment of his friend, Camille Desmoulins, whose anger was something to be feared and whose pen touched the quick.

Although as a party the Girondins were not popular in the capital, they still had many friends in the provinces and their supporters believed that Marat was chiefly responsible for all the ills and defeats that had befallen them.

In a diligence that ran from Caen to Paris, on a bright, clear morning in July, 1793, a young woman took passage booked for one seat for the whole distance. Glowing with beauty and intelligence she attracted at once the attention of her fellow passengers. Modest in demeanor, but with a carriage that denoted refinement, she had safe-

CHARLOTTE CORDAY
From an engraving in the collection of
William J. Latta, Esq.

THE FRENCH REVOLUTION

guard enough, though traveling alone, to protect her from insult and from any undue familiarity.

After a long journey, over dusty roads in the heat of mid-summer weather, she reached Paris, sought the *pension* that had been recommended to her by a friend in Caen, and when night fell, retired early. In the morning she wrote a letter to Marat, and then strolled to the Palais Royal, where she purchased in a cutler's shop a sheath knife. Concealing it under her shawl she went to Marat's lodgings, and after a spirited altercation with the housekeeper, who insisted upon closing the door in her face, she was, at the command of Marat, who overheard the controversy, admitted into his presence. While the doctor was seated in his bath she allayed his suspicions, if he had any, by engaging him in conversation, and giving him a list of the prominent traitors in Normandy. Gloating over the information, chuckling with glee, and impatient to hear more, he exclaimed: " Go on! my child, go on!" Quickly drawing the knife from beneath her shawl and summoning all her strength, she plunged the weapon into the heart of the wretch all the way to the hilt. The water of the bath was soon crimsoned with his gore and it looked as if the monster had, at last, met his just doom, —drowned in a tub of blood. A cry of agony from the dying man soon brought assistance and the assassin was arrested.

It was Charlotte Corday who committed this crime to avenge the wrongs inflicted upon the Girondins. She saw in Marat their arch-enemy and from among all the radicals she selected him as the one who was chiefly responsible for the ills her friends had suffered. Brooding over these matters and anxious to serve her country, she made up her mind—a mind inflamed by the excitement of the times and the rumors and stories that were in circulation—to save the Girondins from further abuse and injustice by the assassination of their enemy. Nothing could have been worse for the cause she espoused, for she opened the way to the scaffold for her friends and transformed Marat from a monster into a martyr.

At her trial counsel was assigned her in the person of a brave young lawyer named Chaveau Lagarde, who afterwards attained distinction in his profession. It was an honor fraught with danger to be chosen to represent the accused, for it must be borne in mind that an attorney in those days shared the peril with his client. There was not much need for counsel, however, for the trial was of short duration. When the prosecuting officer called a witness to prove that the knife had been purchased from a cutler in the Palais Royal the prisoner arose and frankly declared that there was no use to go to the trouble of questioning witnesses. "It is I that killed Marat," she said. "What tempted you?" she was asked. "His crimes," she replied; "I killed one man to save one hundred thousand." She declined the services of a priest on the ground that she needed no shriving.

She was carried to the guillotine in the midst

THE FRENCH REVOLUTION

of a terrific storm, the lightning flashed and the rain came down in torrents. She was robed in scarlet, the garb of a murderess, and her wet garments clinging to her form revealed the beauty of its contour. With a courageous, but not defiant mien, she sat erect, with her arms pinioned behind her back, and looked into the faces of the cold and unsympathetic crowd. Danton and Robespierre stood together in the recess of a window watching the procession. Only one person in all that vast multitude of people gave her a look of sympathy. It was Adam Lux, a young deputy to the Convention from Mayence. After her death he spoke in admiration of her deed and in denunciation of her murder, but he paid the penalty for his treason by carrying his head to the scaffold. He gloried in his death, yet he sacrificed his life for a mere sentiment. "She has ruined us," said Vergniaud, "but she has taught us how to die."

By rotation Danton became president of the Convention on July 25, 1793. France was disturbed by internal dissensions and threatened with invasion. Trade was languishing, commerce was dead, every port was blockaded, the assignats were daily depreciating in value. The soldiers had neither bread nor shoes and the supply of powder was almost exhausted.

The British and the Austrians had united their forces and were overrunning the northern frontier. The Prussians were in Alsace. The English flag was flying over Toulon, and Mayence had surrendered. The allies were so confident of

DANTON

the outcome that they already were beginning to consider the question of the dismemberment of France. Austria had her eye on Flanders, Lorraine, and Alsace; England was looking askance at Dunkirk; Prussia was willing to take as her share of the booty some territory that lay close to her borders; and Spain thought Rossignal would about satisfy her cupidity. But the real energy of France had not yet been tested. Apparently overwhelmed, she rose in all her strength and hurled back from her gates the insolent invaders who already in their imagination had divided her raiment.

The spirit of Danton was undaunted even in the face of impending disaster; at no period of his career did he display greater ability and courage. On the 2nd of August he ascended the tribune and urged the creation of a revolutionary government, to be vested with absolute power under the control of the Committee of Public Safety. "The peril is imminent," he said, "but our people are determined. Since it is to be war let us be terrible; let us make war like lions; let us boldly establish a revolutionary government that can utilize the whole national energy for gigantic measures. I declare it is my firm intention not to be a member of that government; I want to be always free to spur on those who carry on the government. I demand that fifty million francs be placed at its disposal, for which funds it shall render account when its mission is at an end, but with power of spending the sum in one single day if thought expedient. Let us be

THE FRENCH REVOLUTION

extravagantly prodigal for the cause of liberty and it will be returned to us a hundred fold. It would be shameful for us if the haughty minister of a despot should have superior resources and a larger purse than those charged with the regeneration of the world." The haughty minister referred to was William Pitt.

The Committee of Public Safety had originally been created on January 21, 1793, and was composed of nine members. Danton was president during the summer of that year and he knew by experience the terrific power that was wielded by such a body, but he believed the conditions of the country were such as to require an enlargement of the scope of its authority.

The new Committee of Public Safety was organized and vested with dictatorial power, the fortunes and even the lives of citizens were at its disposal—a body with the power of a despot and the heart of a patriot. It was soon known as the Great Committee. At first it was composed of twenty-five members, which number was afterwards reduced to twelve, and these were Robespierre, Carnot, St. Just, Billaud-Varennes, Collot d'Herbois, Couthon, Robert Lindet, Hérault de Séchelles, Barère, Jean Bon, Prieur of the Marne and Prieur of the Cote d'Or.

This body controlled the whole machinery of government, its power was absolute, its sessions were held in secret, it nominated and dismissed envoys, ministers, generals, judges, magistrates and juries of the Revolutionary Tribunal. It suggested measures to the Convention and dominated legislation, controlled all the departments, supervised the army, and made requisitions of men and money. It pursued inexorably the violators of the law of the Maximum and counterfeiters of assignats. To prevent speculation it summarily closed the Stock Exchange, and even attempted to expel all notoriously lewd women from France because " the Republic needed vigorous bodies and Spartan souls."

It was the despotism that France submitted to as the price of her liberty. " We despots!" exclaimed Jean Bon; " Ah, no doubt we are, if despotism is to secure the triumph of freedom. Such a despotism is political regeneration."

Danton made a great mistake from both personal and political considerations when he refused to become a member of this committee. Less than a year from its creation it sacrificed its creator. After the decree was passed directing the organization of the Committee of Public Safety, Danton came forward with another measure to meet conditions; it was heroic in character and provided for a *levée en masse*. " All unmarried citizens and childless widowers between eighteen and twenty-five years of age shall go forth," was the language of the decree. " So long as the fatherland is in danger all Frenchmen shall be liable to military service. Let the young men go to battle, the married men forge arms and transport subsistence; let the women make tents and clothes and serve in the hospitals; let the children make old linen into lint; let the old men gather in the public places, encourage the soldiers and preach the hatred of kings and the unity of the Republic." Four hundred thousand men under the act of conscription went forth to battle.

On the 14th of October, 1793, Marie Antoinette was brought before the Revolutionary Tribunal. There was nothing of the queen about her but her stately bearing and dignified composure. All her beauty was gone; gray, emaciated, and wrinkled, she revealed in every feature of her face the agony through which her soul had passed. The indictment against her contained any number of charges, many of them offenses she had never committed; among them was one alleging that she had debauched her son.

To this she deigned no reply, and upon a juror's asking her if she had anything to say on that point, she calmly answered: "I appeal to every mother in this room whether such a crime be possible." Even the rough women from the slums who came to mock and jeer her were silenced into pity. The matter was pushed no further, for the galleries began to murmur their disapproval. So foul an accusation found its conception only in the putrid mind of Hébert, the infamous editor of "Pére Duchesne." "Madman!" exclaimed Robespierre, "was it not enough for him to have asserted that she was a Messalina without making an Agrippina of her!"

She was found guilty, among other things, of having corresponded with the leaders of the coalition, and this without anything else was enough to seal her doom. As she left the court-room and was descending the staircase she complained of not being able to see. A guard more polite than discreet offered her his arm and for this gallantry he was subsequently dismissed from his position by the Commune. Surely the age of chivalry had departed. She was no longer queen, but a woman in distress; not the royal Marie Antoinette, but the sorrowing widow Capet, yet she aroused no sympathy in the hearts of men, and woe to him who dared to offer her even the common civilities of life. The heart of charity as well as the spirit of gallantry was out of France. This hatred was not engendered in a fortnight; it took centuries of insolence and tyranny to develop such a feeling. It long antedated the reign of Marie Antoinette; she was but the victim who paid the penalty for the despotism of past ages.

On the day of execution as she came out of the prison, a shade of horror passed over her features when she saw the tumbril awaiting her. She had expected to be conducted to the guillotine in a closed carriage as was the king. For a moment she recoiled and hesitated as if about to retrace her steps, but bowing in submission to this last indignity, she ascended the car. She bore her trials with fortitude, with a spirit of resignation. "In prosperity she had been frivolous, in misfortune she was sublime." She no longer complained. "I am," she said, "beyond the limit of suffering."

While on the way to the scaffold the crowd

THE FRENCH REVOLUTION

mockingly cried, "*Place à la veuve Capet!*" Once when the cart almost jolted her off the seat some lusty viragoes on the sidewalk shouted in derision: "Would Madame like a soft cushion from Trianon?" Upon reaching the platform she stumbled and stepped on the foot of Samson who uttered a cry of pain. "Oh, I beg your pardon, Monsieur," she said in her most gracious tones. As she stood upon the platform she cast one longing, lingering look towards the palace of the Tuileries. Oh, what a flood of recollections must have swept over her as she recalled the happy days long gone!

> "*Nessun maggior dolore*
> *Che ricordarsi del tempo felice*
> *Nella miseria.*"

When her head fell into the basket the crowd shouted, "Long live the Republic." Then the multitude melted slowly away, wondering who would be the next victim to call them to the Place de la Revolution.

There is no woman in all history whose story is so pathetic as Marie Antoinette's. Born to the purple, the daughter of an empress, she became the wife of a king. Attractive, vivacious, and with a beauty that was resplendent, it seemed as if Fortune had showered upon her every favor; but Nemesis must have stood at her cradle, for she was pursued and overtaken by a fate that was relentless and merciless. The contrasts in her life give her woes a darker shade. She danced at Trianon and languished in a prison.

DANTON

The nation that welcomed her to the throne, jeered her on the scaffold. She quaffed the waters of "the well-spring of pleasure," but at last she drank the cup of sorrow to its dregs. Deprived of her children, her boy placed in the care of a brutal master, she felt the agony that only a mother's heart can know. The indignities, the humiliations she suffered were more than human nature could bear; her hair grew white in a night and her eyes were smitten with blindness.

"It is now sixteen or seventeen years," wrote Burke, "since I saw the queen of France, then the Dauphiness, at Versailles—glittering like the morning star, full of life and splendor and joy. Little did I dream that I should have lived to see such disasters fallen upon her in a nation of gallant men, in a nation of men of honor and of cavaliers. I thought ten thousand swords must have leaped from their scabbards to avenge even a look that threatened her with insult. But the age of chivalry is gone."

CHAPTER XXX

TRIAL AND EXECUTION OF GIRONDINS—EXECUTION OF MADAME ROLAND, PHILIPPE D'ORLEANS, BARNAVE, BAILLY—DETHRONEMENT OF RELIGION—DANTON FAVORS REACTION

The Girondins soon followed in the wake of the queen. When they appeared at the bar for trial the court-room was crowded, for it was expected that a group of lawyers and orators with talents so magnificent would revive the days of Demosthenes and Cicero; but, like all others before that inexorable tribunal, they lost their presence of mind. They well knew that an arraignment at that bar meant the sealing of their doom, and men do not make a grand effort in the face of the inevitable, nor set up a strong defense and eloquently plead in a case where there is not a ray of hope.

The trial lasted for a week amidst much confusion. The bitterest enemies of the defendants were called to the stand and the most irrelevant testimony was submitted, for Fouquier was determined they should not escape from the meshes of the indictment in which like a net he had entangled them. At last, the judges and the jury complained of weariness and it was decided to bring the case summarily to a close; besides it was thought and feared that a further continuance of the trial would increase the public sentiment for clemency, for there had been a slight reaction in favor of the prisoners.

When the verdict was rendered there was the greatest uproar. Several of the accused had expected an acquittal and they cried out in bitter disappointment. Boileau loudly protested against the finding, flung his hat in the air, and declared that he was a Jacobin, a Montagnard, and that it was unjust to confound him with the Girondins. The only answer to his outcry was a look of contempt from the spectators. Sillery threw away his crutch exclaiming: "It is the most glorious day of my life." Many embraced and the weak-hearted were encouraged. In a far corner of the room a young man suddenly forced his way through the crowd, trying to reach the open air, and in desperation called out: "It is I that killed them, their blood is upon my head." This was Camille Desmoulins, and he was right in a measure; for it was an article he had written in his journal entitled "The Unveiling of Brissot" that had been taken as the foundation of the accusation. The counts in the indictment were virtually the charges contained in the denunciation of Camille, and Fouquier had woven them very skillfully into his bill. Gladly would Camille have obliterated every word he had written in condemnation of these men, but it was too late. Spoken words may be forgotten, they pass into thin air; but written words live.

It was after the first excitement was over that

THE FRENCH REVOLUTION

the prisoners displayed their real heroism; then their courage returned and they faced death with composure. " We die innocent. *Vive la République,*" they exclaimed almost in one voice. Valazé suddenly slipped from the bench upon which he was sitting and fell to the floor. Brissot, leaning over him, said: " Are you afraid? " " No," was the answer, " I am dying." He had thrust a dagger into his breast and expired almost immediately while holding the hilt in his hand. It was eleven o'clock at night when sentence was imposed, and this included even the suicide who was to be carried back to prison, conveyed in the same cart with his accomplices to the scaffold and then interred with them. This is perhaps the only instance on record where a court punished the dead.

When the condemned returned to the prison they made the arches and corridors ring with the singing of the Marseillaise. One of their friends outside had conveyed to them wines and viands for a last supper and shortly after midnight the table was spread in the great hall of the dungeon. Vergniaud's eloquence was never more brilliant. The conversation was spirited but thoughtful; the wit was lively but not coarse. Their conduct was in no sense frivolous, nor did they display a foolish bravado in the nearness of death. It was a symposium of philosophers. They discussed the future of the Republic and then turned to the question of an eternal life. It was almost dawn before they separated, each to go to his cell to sleep if possible.

DANTON

It was a beautiful morning in the autumn of 1793 when five carts drove out of the prison yard into the street. "Here they come," shouted the crowd; necks were craned and men and women stood on tip-toe to get a last glimpse of "the immortals." The condemned were bareheaded and in their shirt sleeves, their coats loosely thrown over their shoulders. They stood upright and met the gaze of the multitude with intrepidity, but not with disdain, for in their hearts they loved the people. In unison their voices rang out in the chorus of the Marseillaise:

"*Allons enfans de la patrie
La jour de gloire est arrivé.*"

They went to their death singing a song triumphant. They died like men, giving all they had to France, even their blood; that they would willingly have sacrificed, had they been sure it was for the welfare of their country, but they departed this life, fearing that the Republic was doomed. "We have killed the tree by pruning it," said Vergniaud; "it was too aged. The soil is too weak to nourish the roots of civic liberty; this people is too childish to wield its laws without hurting itself. It will return to its kings as babes return to their toys. We were deceived as to the age in which we were born and in which we die for the freedom of the world. We deemed ourselves at Rome and we were at Paris." They had hoped to give an ideal republic to France, but the Revolution would not have it, and in return for all their noble efforts they were carted like cattle to the shambles. They were not criminals, but martyrs in the holy cause of human liberty and death upon the scaffold, under such circumstances, is not a disgrace, but an honor. *" Le crime fait la honte et non pas l'echafaud."*

After the execution of the living, the corpse of Valazé was beheaded. There was no satisfying the voracious appetite of the guillotine for blood, even the dead were devoured. One cart bore away all the bodies and one grave received them. The entire cost of their burial was 210 francs, less than 10 francs each.

Of the Girondins who were not at this time executed, Guadet and Salles had fled, but were captured later and executed at Bordeaux. Barbaroux, Pétion, and Buzot escaped arrest and wandered as fugitives, suffering untold agonies, until the midsummer of 1794, when Barbaroux, worn out by anguish and suspense, blew out his brains with a pistol. A few days after Pétion and Buzot were found in a cornfield, their bodies half eaten by dogs. Louvet, after untold hardships, returned to Paris, had a meeting with his sweetheart and afterwards reached Switzerland in safety. His sufferings would have been unendurable to any man with a spirit less indomitable than his.

"That party," said Napoleon, "might have destroyed the Mountain and governed France if they had pursued a manly and straightforward course. It was the refinements of metaphysicians that occasioned their fall." Dumouriez in his

DANTON

Memoirs writes, "One man alone could have saved the Girondins, but they completely alienated him, although I had counseled them to keep fair with him. This man was Danton. . . . If the Girondins had possessed good sense enough to have coalesced with him, he would have humbled the atrocious faction of Marat, either tamed or annihilated the Jacobins, and perhaps Louis would have been indebted to him for his life; but the Girondins provoked him and he sacrificed everything in his vengeance." This imputation of vengeance is entirely false.

Danton was in Arcis at the time the Girondins were executed, and when the information reached the town a neighbor asked Danton if he had heard the good news. "Good news," said Danton, "that is a terrible misfortune and menaces all of us; it imperils the future of France." He had tried hard to save them, for he clearly saw the dangerous path they were treading. He even had a secret conference with them at midnight, but they would not hearken to his advice. "These orators whom he would have defended and whose genius he loved" would not trust him. "I did my best," he said, "to save them; I wish to God I could have saved them."

Garat, the minister of the interior, entreated Robespierre to come to their assistance. "Do not speak of it again," said Robespierre impatiently. "I cannot save them; there are periods in revolutions when to live is a crime and when men must know how to surrender their heads when demanded."

THE FRENCH REVOLUTION

Emerging from the prison and stepping gaily to the scaffold, "clad in white, with her long black hair hanging down to her girdle," came Madame Roland, the plebeian queen, she whose radiant beauty and brilliant conversation had so often enlivened the *salons* of the Girondins. All her dreams and illusions, all her hopes and ambitions, were dissipated. The ideal republic that she had reared in her imagination was in ruins and France had fallen into the hands of vulgar despots.

Lamarche, one of her companions in execution, trembled with fear and to show him how easy it was to die she requested Samson to allow her to go first. "It is against the order," replied Samson. "Pshaw!" she said, "you cannot refuse the last request of a lady." The grim executioner shrugged his shoulders and yielded. She went to her death without a tremor, exclaiming as she ascended the steps of the platform: "O Liberty, what crimes are committed in thy name!" She died with an aphorism upon her lips, but not a word of supplication nor a prayer. Her husband, who some time before had fled into exile, upon hearing of her death committed suicide.

In the early days of the Revolution Foulon declared, "France needs to be mowed." As a royalist he thought it high time to set the reaper at work. Those days had gone by, yet the mowing was being done with a vengeance, but the scythe was in other hands. Such a chopping off of heads the world has never witnessed. "*Sainte Guillotin,*" said a well-known revolutionist, "*est dans la plus brillante activité! Quel maitre*

DANTON

boucher que ce garcon là!" A long procession marched daily to the scaffold, and it looked as if the executions would never end. France was bleeding at every pore. *"Guillotin va toujours."* It was drenched with blood. Only when the darkness of night fell upon the city was this implement of death at rest, and then Samson to relieve the monotony of his life work would hie him to the playhouse.

In this march of death came statesmen, politicians, ex-ministers, unsuccessful generals and even a prince of the blood royal. Philippe d'Orleans, Egalité, " Jacobin Prince of the Blood," was summoned before the Revolutionary Tribunal and condemned. He confronted his accusers calmly. Cool and polite he displayed a remarkable nerve. When sentence was pronounced not a muscle quivered. He was a man of infamous character and had devoted his life to high-living and debauchery. He early espoused the principles of the Revolution for no other reason than his personal dislike of the king and consequently he was despised by royalty and the noblesse. Not possessing that high type of character that would have been the guarantee of his sincerity in adopting a course that apparently was so diametrically opposed to that which he should have taken, his conduct naturally induced to an impugning of his motives.

As a prince of the blood royal he had turned his back upon his class by an open espousal of the popular cause, and his purposes of course were suspected. He was charged by the royalists

THE FRENCH REVOLUTION

with conspiring to overthrow and supplant the king, but he really seems to have been actuated and controlled in his conduct more by hatred than ambition. The queen despised him and the mere mention of his name in her presence would make her face turn white with rage. The rabble soon found this out and when they desired specially to offend or insult her they would shout long life to the duke. Though a cousin of Louis, after voting for his death, he was brutal enough to attend the execution and then drove away to one of his retreats to celebrate the event with revelry and debauch. He had faith in neither God nor man and his only regret in dying was that he left so much behind and in comparatively so early a period of his life, when his zest for its pleasures was still keen—he was forty-six years of age.

On the morning of his execution he ate a hearty breakfast of oysters and steak, drank a bottle of claret, and was even particular about having the wine of a certain vintage. He arranged his toilet with more than usual care, he was shaved, powdered and perfumed as if going to a ball. He wore a green frock coat, a waistcoat of white piqué, yellow buckskins, and high boots.

On his way to the scaffold he was driven past the old Palais Royal, at that time called the Palais Egalité, the property no longer of his princely house but of the nation. The crowd purposely delayed the cart at this point, in cruel mockery; they jeered and hooted and showered their imprecations upon him who had once been their idol

DANTON

and whose bust they had once carried through the city in triumph. He appreciated the truth that popularity is but a passing echo when he exclaimed: "Those people used to applaud me." Upon reaching the guillotine Samson insisted upon drawing off the duke's boots. "Tush," said Philippe, "they will come better off after. Let us make haste."

> "Nothing in his life
> Became him like the leaving it; he died
> As one that had been studied in his death,
> To throw away the dearest thing he owned
> As 'twere a careless trifle."

In this train of death came Madame Du Barry, " ex-harlot of a whilom majesty," she at whose feet the mighty had begged for favors and in whose *boudoirs* Louis XV had met and advised with his ministers of state. Death had its terrors for her and on her way to execution she shrieked and begged for mercy. Adam Lux, a deputy from Mayence, also went to the scaffold for the pamphlet he had written in affectionate commemoration of Charlotte Corday. Another who bravely met his doom was Barnave—the elegant Barnave, patriot, lawyer, orator, adviser of the queen, whose heart's sympathy for a suffering woman had weakened his ardor for the Revolution.

The gentle, kindly Bailly, philosopher and astronomer, suffered a cruel fate. It would have been better for him had he kept on watching the stars instead of meddling in the affairs of men.

THE FRENCH REVOLUTION

It was a cold and cheerless day when they carted him to execution, and the mob compelled him to stand in " a sleety drizzle " while they took down and removed the guillotine from the Champ-de-Mars, where he had ordered the troops to fire upon the people on the memorable 17th of June, to set it up in another place,—on a dung hill at the riverside. " You are trembling," said a bystander. " Yes," said Bailly, " but it is from the cold, not fear." They prolonged his sufferings and mocked him in his agony, but the valiant soul of the good man sustained him to the last.

Olympe de Gouges, Rouget de Lisle, the author of the Marseillaise, the priest Lamourette, he of the kiss episode, took their places in the column; and General Custine, who had fought so bravely under the standard of the Republic, marched with the air of a soldier to his death. When his troubles came, he wittily said: " Fortune is a woman and my hair is growing gray." On rolled this mighty torrent into eternity. The Revolution in its desire for victims was insatiable. It was an orgy of death. Rich and poor, high and low, sage and fool, priest and layman, dame and harlot, locked step in this dark line leading to the guillotine that seemed to stretch out to doomsday. In this eventful month of November, 1793, occurred scenes unparalleled in the world's history.

Next after the monarchy had been destroyed came the dethronement of religion. A spirit of infidelity spread suddenly throughout the nation like an epidemic. A curate wrote to the Convention that he had been preaching a lie all his life, was tired of the occupation, and requested that he be assigned to employment more useful. The archbishop of Paris, Gobel by name, publicly renounced his faith. Influenced by this example and the prevailing spirit of the day, curates threw off their frocks, and monks and nuns their habits, and in sheer mockery of their vows many entered into civil contracts of marriage. Marriage was no longer a sacrament but an agreement, its duration in many instances measured only by the convenience and desires of the parties. Bells were taken from the steeples and melted into cannon; the silver vessels of the church were sent to the mint to be coined, and the pewter was molded into bullets.

In Paris mobs broke into the churches, drank the wine out of the chalices, and in contempt put fish on the patenas. A procession passed through the streets chanting in a serio-comic strain the music of the Te Deum set to profane and vulgar words. Men dressed in sacerdotal vestments rode on asses which were "housed with priests' cloaks and reined with priests' stoles." The riders, drunk with the wine they found in the churches, mockingly carried the communion cup and sacred wafer. "They stopped at the doors of dramshops, held out *ciboriums,* and the landlord, stoup in hand, had to fill them thrice." Crosses were borne aloft and holy water was sprinkled over the heads of a laughing, jeering crowd that thronged the sidewalks. This grotesque procession wended its way to the Conven-

THE FRENCH REVOLUTION

tion, was admitted to the hall, and before it retired danced the Carmagnole, several deputies joining in the orgy. Danton, it is said, sat in his place watching gloomily the frenzy.

This spirit was not confined to Paris, but spread like wildfire throughout all France. Bonfires were made of church paraphernalia, priests' vestments, and prayer books, while crowds danced the Carmagnole and in ecstasy sang the wild strains of the *Ça ira*.

Poor France, what will she do next? Of course she had to have a religion of some sort or form and so she set up a demoiselle of the opera, "a woman fair to look upon when well rouged," as the Goddess of Reason. There were no church vestments left so they clothed her in the habit of the Republic—on her head a Phygian cap garlanded with oak, over her shoulders a mantle of blue, and on her feet a pair of Roman sandals. In this attire, borne aloft upon a palanquin, she was carried to the cathedral of Notre Dame, amidst music and flowers, where a pompous ceremony enthroned the new divinity. The monarchy, the king, the queen, the hierarchy, the aristocracy, the Girondins, and the church itself had been destroyed; it was time to restore order, to establish peace, and to build up and strengthen the Republic; but the appetite for blood was not yet satisfied and the Revolution began to gnaw at its own vitals.

There were but two parties left to battle for supremacy, the Dantonists and the Jacobins, and the final struggle at once began. The Revolution devoted itself to political assassination. Danton favored a reaction; he thought the time had arrived when the results of the Revolution should be secured, he seemed to face about and turn his back upon the guillotine. To him the assassination of rivals was murder; the encompassing of the death of men merely to open the way for personal ambition, a heinous crime.

After the execution of the Girondins he became supine, indifferent, his old-time vigor departed. He had gone to Arcis on October 12th to enjoy a short vacation, "to loaf and invite his soul." He wandered in the autumn woods, culled wild flowers, and listened to the song of birds. He delighted to visit those places that revived pleasant memories and he loved in his talks with the neighbors to become reminiscent and to recall the days gone by and the companions of his youth, many of them alas! long since departed. He was out of the turmoil enjoying the association of his friends and renewing "the old glad life" of his early years. Besides he was still indulging in the pleasures of a honeymoon. During his vacation he was given ample time and opportunity to meditate. The past in some aspects was like a nightmare and he was anxious that the results of the Revolution should, at the earliest possible moment, be secured and enjoyed that they might justify the necessity for many of the deeds that otherwise would appear only as crimes.

His friends in Paris appealed to him to come out of his lethargy and to return forthwith to the capital; they informed him that his enemies were

THE FRENCH REVOLUTION

taking advantage of his absence to undermine his power and that he was putting in peril his party, the lives of his friends, and the cause he loved so well. But, conscious of his strength, he dallied with his dangers and laughed at their fears. He was evidently tired of the Revolution —that is, its massacres and executions. The death of the Girondins deeply affected him, for he believed they had been sacrificed to party clamor. He now favored a reaction, longed for peace, for the destruction of government by committee, and for the establishment of a republic resting upon a strong constitution.

During the spring and summer of 1793 he had been the most powerful man in France; he was the spirit of the Revolution, its leader, its incarnation, but now he seemed to lose all ambition and energy and allowed the power he had so tenaciously held and so potentially wielded to slip from his grasp and pass into the hands of weaker men. It was not until December, 1793, that he returned to Paris from Arcis; by that time his enemies had woven a net about him, and the more he struggled to be free the more he became entangled in its meshes. Hercules, at last, was in the shirt of Nessus and the giant could do nothing but writhe.

CHAPTER XXXI

TRIAL OF THE DANTONISTS

"I am not a drinker of blood; I am tired of this slaughter," exclaimed Danton. "Is it never to end? Is France to bleed to death?" While taking an evening stroll with Camille on the banks of the Seine he suddenly cried out: "The river is running blood."

He longed for peace. He believed France had been sufficiently purged and was now ready for a new order of things under a stable government. He was never sanguinary in disposition; the mere shedding of blood to him was an abomination. He had accepted "the fury of popular passion as an inevitable incident in the work of deliverance" from tyranny, but the day for violence had passed. His yearning for peace was taken by his enemies as a sign of weakness, or as they pretended to believe, the betrayal of the popular cause; in other words treason to the Revolution. "It is necessary," they said, "to wrest this false god from the multitude. This Pericles of corrupted Athens does not belong to Sparta." He was not the Danton of old and it seemed impossible for him to throw off his lethargy. He was like a wounded wolf and the hungry pack now turned to rend and tear him to pieces.

THE FRENCH REVOLUTION

He was quoted as having said that he wished the French people were not quite so ready to find men guilty. "Who informed him," exclaimed Robespierre sneeringly, "that any innocent men had been convicted?" He was induced at this time by the Jacobins, against his inclination, to aid in the conviction of the Hébertists, and on March 24, 1794, they were guillotined. A fouler group of men the Revoution did not produce. As we look through the din and smoke of that murky period we can see the leer on the face of Hébert as he scoffs at everything sacred in religion and pure in social and domestic life. As atheist and anarchist and as the author of the filthy publication entitled "Pére Duchesne," he exerted a most pernicious influence in every direction. His execution was a blessing to France, but his death weakened Danton in that it strengthened his enemies, especially Billaud-Varennes, the most influential member of the Great Committee and one of Danton's most bitter and relentless foes. Napoleon in referring to Billaud declared that he was the most sanguinary of all the monsters that ruled in the "Reign of Terror."

The destruction of the Hébertists was of great political advantage to Robespierre and was a move in the game well played by that wily politician who was gradually hewing his way to the front. Danton knew the qualities of Robespierre and he was the only man in the Revolution whom he feared. In character and disposition they were so diametrically opposed that they never

DANTON

could form a firm personal friendship. One was cold, calculating, and reserved; the other was ardent, bold, and free.

Danton had come to the assistance of Robespierre time and again and Robespierre had returned the favor more than once. In fact when the Jacobin Club was purged in the winter of 1793, Danton would have been expelled as a moderate had he not been defended by Robespierre.

Billaud-Varennes, who with all the venom of his nature hated Danton, was determined to effect if possible his overthrow, and he at last persuaded Robespierre to join in his plans. Robespierre was without the sentiment of gratitude; service rendered to him was forgotten if its remembrance interfered with his ambitions, and he was induced from selfish motives to surrender Danton to his enemies. It was one of the greatest blunders of his political career, for it only opened the way to his own destruction.

Danton dreaded the envy of Robespierre. He at one time declared: "All will go well so long as men say Robespierre and Danton, but woe to me if ever they should say Danton and Robespierre." This expression shows, or at least intimates, that Danton was willing ostensibly to hold second place if Robespierre were thereby placated. It further shows that he knew the danger that lurked under the consuming ambition of the man. It is the only phrase on record emanating from Danton that evinces the slightest tremor of fear or dread of any man's power.

THE FRENCH REVOLUTION

There had been a time when he held a mean opinion of Robespierre as a revolutionary leader. Expressing himself in one of his characteristic references he said: "*Cet homme là ne saurait pas cuire des œufs durs.*"—" That man is incapable of boiling eggs hard." But as time ran on he changed his mind concerning this persistent, indefatigable, crafty fanatic.

Robespierre had often expressed the wish to have the Revolution end in himself. This wish could not be consummated so long as Danton was alive, for the great tribune far overshadowed the little, scheming politician; so his death was decided upon. It was not a political necessity, which was the argument that had so often been made in the past to excuse the commission of crimes; it was only to effect the carrying to a successful conclusion of the plans of Robespierre. It was simply the removal of a political rival; it was not to insure the safety of the Republic, but to secure the ambitions of the man from Arras. Danton's execution was sheer murder.

If at this period Danton had possessed his old-time vigor and Robespierre had assailed him, he would have strangled the viper; but at the critical moment he weakened. His friends, who clearly saw the menacing danger, could not induce him to " dare." In the same way, later on, Robespierre lost heart when he saw his approaching downfall, and yielded submissively to the attacks of his foes. During this period Robespierre evinced no open hostility to Danton; indeed he allayed suspicion by appearing more friendly than ever, like the serpent he was licking his victim before swallowing him. It was only the day prior to the arrest of the Dantonists that he fondled with affection Camille Desmoulins' little boy.

When Danton was informed that Robespierre was scheming to overthrow him, he replied, " If I thought that were so, I would eat his bowels out." In a controversy he had with some of the political friends of Robespierre, he threatened to show on the floor of the Convention that the Great Committee was guilty of malversation and tyranny in the conduct of the war in La Vendée. This, of course, was carried to Robespierre in a greatly exaggerated form, and not only aroused his anger but put him on his guard, for he understood to the full what a threat meant coming from such a source. To threaten without striking in politics is to expose one's defense.

As if smitten with blindness Danton seemed to be groping his way. This Ajax who had defied the thunderbolts of Jove became almost as weak, as powerless as a child. Here in the crisis of his life his nerve failed him. He who had " saved France from Brunswick," he who in the past had assured the faint-hearted and by his example had encouraged even the strongest, was unable to strike a blow in his own defense. He weakened at the wrong time. He had enlisted for the Revolution. A soldier has no right to rest upon his arms until the combat be over.

THE FRENCH REVOLUTION

"To arrest me," he cried, "they will not dare;" then in the same breath he added, "Let them kill me if they will; I would rather be guillotined than guillotine." When some one suggested that he should depart, he answered: "If France drives me out where shall I go? I would be an outcast in any other land. One does not carry his country on the sole of his boot. I could enjoy no liberty abroad; because of the part I have taken in the Revolution prisons and dungeons yawn for me in foreign lands!"

For some time past Camille had been writing in the columns of the "Vieux Cordelier" with more than his usual vigor and with the incisiveness of Tacitus,—for "French under his pen was as concise and as monumental as the Latin" —those "fervent articles so full of earnest passion and genius, those satirical, eloquent pages inspired by the fleeting events of the day and yet stamped with immortality." He had become the apostle of peace and was preaching the gospel of clemency. He eloquently appealed to the nation for the establishment of order. His articles were beginning to soften the hearts of the people and were creating a reaction in the public mind. He, too, appealed personally to Robespierre, "his old school companion," to exert his influence in effecting a change in public sentiment. He flattered his vanity, touched with a master hand his weak points, and almost reached his heart; but the Committee of Public Safety saw in these articles only an attempt to weaken

DANTON

their powers and they determined to aid in accomplishing the overthrow and destruction of the Dantonists.

The following is a characteristic article from his pen and it is not hard to imagine that, at the time it was written, it was too caustic to meet the approval of those who were responsible for the prevailing system of suspicion and terror. It was one of the articles that provoked the resentment of the Great Committee.

"At the present epoch words become state crimes; and from this the transition is easy to simple looks, which, with sadness, compassion, sighs, nay, even absolute silence itself, are made the ground-work of suspicion. Is a citizen popular? He is a rival of the dictator; and might excite commotions. Does he on the other hand avoid society and live retired, in the bosom of his family? This secluded life makes him remarked, and excites the suspicion that he is meditating sinister designs. Are you rich? There is imminent peril that the people may be corrupted by your largesses. Are you poor? You must be the more closely watched, because there is none so enterprising as those who have nothing to lose. Are you of a thoughtful and melancholy character with a neglected exterior? You are afflicted because in your opinion public affairs are not well conducted. Does a citizen indulge in dissipation and bring on indigestion? He is concealing ambition under the mask of pleasure. Is he virtuous and austere in his morals? He has constituted himself censor of the government. Is he a philosopher, an orator, a poet? He will soon acquire more consideration than the rulers of the State. Has he acquired reputation in war? His talents only make him the more dangerous and render it indispensable to remove him from the army, perhaps to send him to the scaffold. The natural death of a distinguished person, particularly if in place, has become so rare that historians transmit it as an event worthy of record to future ages. Even the death of so many innocent and estimable citizens seems a less calamity than the insolence and scandalous fortunes of those who have denounced, and murdered them. Every day the accuser makes his triumphal entry into the palace of death, to reap the harvest of some rich succession, and the tribunals which were once the protectors of life and property have become mere slaughter houses, where that which bears the name of confiscation and punishment is nothing but robbery and murder."

The graphic pen of Camille had described too realistically the conditions to suit the views of the committee, and he was marked in their minutes as one whose loyalty to the Revolution was doubted and whose temerity was treason. Accusation soon followed suspicion.

When Danton was informed that the authorities had decided upon the arrest of the Dantonists he muttered, " They will not dare—they will not dare." " You must resist," his friends said. " That means the shedding of more blood," he cried, " and I am sick of it."

The warrant for Danton's arrest was issued on the 29th of March, 1794, and at midnight the armed police came to his house to serve it. They woke the echoes of the street by grounding their arms and then knocking loudly at the door. Danton offered no resistance, but there was no tremor in his voice nor terror in his heart. His wife tremblingly embraced him, but he quieted her fears with an assurance that he would return in the morning at sunrise. " It is only *au revoir,*" he said, " not adieu."

Camille, who occupied the room above Danton's in the same house, on hearing the noise in the street below turned to his wife and exclaimed: " They have come to arrest me." Lucile fainted. Poor Lucile! how our hearts go out to her in sympathy. She soon followed her husband to the scaffold. Death came to her as a boon; her only offense was that she had been the wife of Camille. What purpose could the Revolution have had in the execution of so gentle a creature?

The arrest of Danton created, of course, the greatest excitement; people spoke in whispers as if afraid to complain aloud. The very audacity of the act terrorized the hearts of men. In the Assembly the anxiety was expressed in looks, not words. At last Legendre had the courage to say, " Citizens, four members of this body have been arrested during the night; Danton is one of them. I believe him to be as pure, as patriotic as myself; yet he is in a dungeon. The committee feared, no doubt, that his replies would overturn the accusations brought against him. I move, therefore, that before you listen to any report, you send for the prisoners and hear them." The motion was received with

THE FRENCH REVOLUTION

favor, but Robespierre mounting the tribune soon turned the current by saying: "It is easy to see by the agitation that pervades this chamber that a question of great interest is before us, a question whether two or three individuals shall be preferred to the country. We shall see to-day whether the Convention can crush to atoms a mock idol, long since decayed, or whether its fall shall overthrow both the Convention and the French people." This was enough to restore silence and even make Legendre apologetically explain and excuse his temerity. Everyone hastened to make peace with tyranny.

In the prison Danton railed at death; he alternately ranted and jested, laughed and swore. His conduct was that of a man incensed, but defiant even in the face of the inevitable. "I shall leave things in a frightful welter," he exclaimed, "but if I could leave my legs to Couthon [who was paralyzed] and my vitality to Robespierre, things might still go on." "It is better," he cried again, "to be a poor fisherman than to meddle in the affairs of men." Turning to Hérault de Séchelles he declared: "When men do foolish things they must know how to laugh at them. The cowardice of my enemies quieted my fears, I was deceived by their base policy." Addressing Camille, who was weeping, he said: "Of what use are those tears? Should they send us to the scaffold let us walk there gayly." Mignet says of Danton: "Revolution in his opinion was a game at which the conqueror, if he required it, won the life of the conquered." Danton had lost and was about to pay forfeit.

In the adjoining cell to Danton was Westermann; he quietly accepted his doom, an illustration of the difference between the emotional Gaul and the phlegmatic Teuton.

On April 2, 1794, the prisoners were arraigned before the Revolutionary Tribunal, a tribunal that had been created by Danton himself. After its institution he asked pardon of God and man for having established it; "I did not think," he declared, "that it would become the scourge of humanity."

The prisoners at the bar included Danton, Desmoulins, Westermann, Hérault de Séchelles, Fabre d'Eglantine, Lacroix, and Philippeaux. Their attitude was haughty and resolute; their speech was audacious in substance and in manner and they treated their judges with an air of disdain and contempt that if not wise nor prudent was, at least, courageous.

Hermann was president of the trial and Fouquier Tinville the prosecuting officer. It was mainly through the influence of Camille that Fouquier had originally secured the appointment. His ugly, forbidding countenance but revealed the black perfidy and the cruel wickedness of his heart. Of all the faces that look at us out of the Revolution his seems to be the most hideous. He exhibited a most remarkable combination of qualities, and was truly one of the enigmas of those extraordinary times. He apparently had no idea that as prosecuting officer he owed a duty to the prisoner at the bar, while at the same time guarding the pleas and the interests of the State. In his desire to secure a conviction he would ignore every rule of evidence, introduce testimony neither true nor relevant, personally abuse the defendant, and browbeat the jurors as well as the witnesses. He outraged every principle of justice, ignored every form of law, and made the court a charnel house. An acquittal put him in a condition of vexation and despondency, while a conviction would lighten up and animate his gloomy features. A death sentence was agreeable and consoling and the only recreation he indulged in was a visit to the scaffold to see his victims perish. He was as inflexible as a rod of steel; money, women, the pleasures of the table or the theatre had no attraction for him, nothing could seduce him from the pursuit of the accused. He might have amassed an immense fortune but he remained to the last poor; it is said his wife died of starvation. His lodgings were mean and cheerless, destitute of every comfort and the furniture after his death sold for less than five hundred francs. The tribunal that he so long dominated sentenced him to the guillotine in 1795. At the time of his accusation Fréron demanded that "the earth be freed from this monster and that, drunk with the blood of his victims, he be sent to hell to sleep himself sober."

Such was the creature who, by his cold-blooded methods, drove the prisoners almost to exasperation.

DANTON

On being questioned Danton replied: "My name is not unknown in the Revolution, my residence will soon be nowhere—I shall live in the Pantheon of history." Desmoulins replied in dramatic style: "I am thirty-three, the age of the Sans-Culotte Jesus—an age fatal to reformers." Westermann, in answer to the questions of the public prosecutor, said: "I am a general. I was a soldier at sixteen. I have seven wounds in front and I was never stabbed in the back until now." The charges preferred against Danton were absolutely without any foundation upon which to base a conviction. He was indicted *inter alia* for having served the king, for having drawn the people to the Champ de Mars, where they were slaughtered in July, 1791, for having failed to do his duty on the memorable 10th of August, for having enriched himself at the public expense, and for having conspired to overthrow the Republic. When he heard the counts in the indictment read, he flew into a rage and became so incensed that he did not even attempt to set up a defense in detail. It would, however, have made no difference, in so far as the final result was concerned, before that tribunal of inexorable men. He was adjudged guilty before his trial began. In those days men did not strike and then relent.

When he heard the report read by St. Just he raved like a wild beast. He designated the accusations "a list of lies." As he thundered forth his denunciation of the charges, the methods of trial, and his accusers, his great

THE FRENCH REVOLUTION

voice was heard beyond the walls of the courtroom, even to the other side of the Seine.

"Come now," he said, turning to Cambon, a witness, "do you really think we are conspirators? Look, he is laughing, he believes nothing of the sort." Addressing the jury he smilingly said: "Put down in your notes, make a record of the fact that he laughed." Continuing Danton said: "We only ask an opportunity to be heard. If we are allowed to speak and the French people is what it should be, it will be my business later to ask pardon for my accusers."

In his defense he made a speech that was characteristic, revealing his old-time vigor and ringing with an eloquence that was thrilling. "You say that I have been paid," he cried, "that I sold myself to Mirabeau, Orleans, and Dumouriez; but I tell you that men like me cannot be paid nor bought nor sold. I have served long enough and my life is a burden to me, but I will defend myself by telling you what I have done. It was I that from the Jacobins kept Mirabeau at Paris. It was I that made the pikes rise suddenly on the 20th of June and prevented the king's visit to St. Cloud. The day after the massacre at the Champ de Mars a warrant was out for my arrest. Men were sent to kill me at Arcis, but my people came and defended me. I had to fly to London, but I came back the moment Garran was elected. Do you not remember how at the Jacobins' I asked for the Republic? It was I that prepared the 10th of

DANTON

August. You say that I went to Arcis. Yes, I did go there, and I am proud of it. Danton is a good son and I went to bid my mother good-by and to arrange my affairs because my life was about to be in peril. It was I that had Mandat killed because he had given an order to fire upon the people. I have served the Revolution in my own fashion and I would embrace my worst enemy for the sake of my country and I will give her my body if she needs the sacrifice."

In this strain Danton swept on. When he grew too impassioned and impressive, Hermann would try to drown his voice by ringing the bell, which only increased the noise and confusion. "A man speaking for his honor and his life," cried Danton, "cares nothing for your bell."

The crowd outside, swayed by the passion and eloquence of the orator, responded at times to his appeals and muttered their disapproval of the methods of the court. Even the jurors were beginning to show signs of weakening. The judges saw the danger of continuing the trial and an adjournment was taken.

The next day was given over to the examination of Camille and Hérault. Poor Camille's defense was weak and disjointed. He was in no sense an orator; it was with the pen, not with the tongue that he expressed his thoughts. Camille was the most brilliant journalist of his times, indeed France has not in any period produced one that surpassed him, but when it came to making an extended speech in his own defense he was at a sad disadvantage. In the first place he was not accustomed to forensic speaking, and athough when upon his feet he did not lose the power of utterance, he thought and spoke so fast that his sentences became involved and did not convey the sense he intended. He was of a most nervous temperament and under the irritation of the proceedings he grew excited and incoherent; besides he had an impediment in his speech which at times made him halt and stammer. In consequence his whole address was a mere jumble of words.

He had carefully prepared a written defense, but when the court paid no attention to its reading he tore it up and in desperation threw the pieces broadcast. This was the incident that gave rise to the story that the prisoners, to show their contempt for the proceedings, threw pellets of bread at the judges. They did not indulge in conduct so silly; they knew to the full the danger that confronted them and appreciated the gravity of the situation. They were at all times bold, often defiant, but never frivolous.

Every moment the trial continued made it more difficult to secure the conviction of the accused, and the managers of the prosecution decided to adopt heroic measures to bring it to a termination at the earliest possible moment. Accordingly St. Just appeared before the Convention and stated that the prisoners were in revolt, that their conduct was tumultuous, and that an end should be put to this public scandal by a decree directing the trial to close. Could there be anything more contemptuous of justice than such legislation?

The court met on the 5th of April at half past eight instead of ten o'clock, the usual hour. It was at the close of this day's session that a copy of the decree of the Convention was handed to the prosecuting officer, who exclaimed. "It has not come a whit too soon, we hold them now." The decree was at once read and the jury were asked to deliberate. The law gave juries the right to decide after three days' trial whether or not they were satisfied with the evidence submitted. If in their opinion enough testimony had been produced to enable them to pass intelligently upon the facts, the trial rested and a verdict was rendered. This decree was as vile a piece of legislation as was ever enacted. It gave a partisan jury, in a political trial, the power summarily to dispose of the accused. In fact at the time of its passage, its supporters had no hesitation in declaring that such was its real purpose. From beginning to end, in every phase of its proceedings, the case was a farce. The trial was a travesty of justice; it was but the means to effect the commission of a crime. The death sentence imposed upon the prisoners was but a decree of assassination. Some of the jurors protested against rendering a verdict of guilty upon testimony so weak, but they were browbeaten and soon driven into line. "Which do you prefer," they were asked, "the death of Danton or Robespierre?" "Of course," they stammered, feeling their necks to see if their heads were still on their bodies, " we would rather sacrifice Danton than jeopard the life of the gentle and virtuous Robespierre."

Thus Danton and his friends were convicted, but not in accordance with the rules of evidence, nor the forms of law. The charges were not in any item or particular sufficient to warrant a conviction, and even such as they were, they were not made out. The defendants were not permitted to call a witness, nor were they given a fair opportunity to present a defense. But no matter what might have been done, no matter how strong the testimony might have been, the result would have been the same. The prisoners were prejudged and nothing could have changed the purpose of their relentless accusers.

CHAPTER XXXII

EXECUTION OF THE DANTONISTS

On the 5th day of April, 1794, between half past four and five o'clock in the afternoon, the carts carrying the condemned drove out of the prison yard into the public highway. It was a lovely, cloudless spring day and as the afternoon wore on the air grew cool and refreshing. Crowds were in waiting and lined the streets from the prison gate to the scaffold. A mob of hags and harridans, paid for their services, followed the carts, shouting their wild and hellish imprecations.

As the people watched the passing tumbrils, it must have occurred to many of them that the Revolution was undergoing a great change. To be sure revolutionists had heretofore gone to the guillotine, but they had become moderates, or had fallen out of public favor; but these men, passing, were the children of the Revolution, born of its spirit, its very bone and fibre. What had they done that the Revolution should seek their blood? Saturn truly was now devouring his own offspring, his first-born.

Camille, that creature of emotion, was not wanting in moral courage, but he was so incensed and indignant at what he deemed the injustice of his fate that he raved and fumed like a madman. Between his paroxysms he tried to press his pinioned hands to his lips to kiss a lock of Lucile's hair. Leaning over the side of the tumbril and appealing to the multitude he cried: "Do you not know me? I am Camille, Camille Desmoulins. I was the first apostle of Liberty; it was I that called the people to arms at the beginning of the Revolution in the gardens of the Palais Royal." But the crowd, which never acts without a leader, gave him in return a stolid stare, or else brutal derision. It was for them he had striven and was now to shed his blood, a martyr in the holy cause of freedom, one of those heroes who die upon the scaffold in the world's everlasting struggle for man's liberty and redemption.

Danton, like an elder brother, tried to calm and comfort him. "Do not," he said, "appeal to that vile rabble; they are deaf to your eloquence. Leave them alone." By the time the guillotine was reached Camille had ceased to rave. Philippeaux and Lacroix were quiet, but disconsolate. Fabre sat in a corner of the cart with his head resting on his breast, muttering to himself and complaining because they had not given him time to finish a play he had in the course of composition. "*Tais toi!*" said Danton, "*Dans une semaine tu feras assez de vers.*" Hérault de Séchelles, brave, noble, of gentle birth, who early espoused the principles of the Revolution because he loved the people and hated injustice, bore himself with a quiet dignity and went to his death like a gentleman and a hero. While passing the *Garde Meuble* he looked up at one of the high windows and saw a fair white hand wave him a last farewell.

Westermann, the soldier, who had lived in camps and had faced the terrors of the battle-field from boyhood, composed, resigned, without a murmur on his lips, accepted his fate and met his doom with a nerve of iron. As a gamester who had played and lost, he paid the forfeit like a man.

Danton laughed and sang. "I have gloried in the Revolution," he exclaimed; "I have worked much, enjoyed much. Many a revel have I had in my day. Now I will go to sleep." One saying of his worthy of remembrance is: "I have the consolation of believing that posterity will pardon the man who dies as chief of the faction of clemency."

The condemned passed the house of Duplay, the carpenter, where Robespierre lived. The shutters were closed and there was no sign of life about the premises. Suddenly Danton rose to his feet and, turning in its direction, shrieked at the top of his voice: "You will follow us soon; your house shall be beaten down and salt sown in the place where it stood." Perhaps behind the shutters, peering through the slats, was Robespierre watching the passing carts that held his victims, and wondering after all whether or not the Revolution would end in himself. He could rejoice, at least, in that he had overthrown the giant.

THE FRENCH REVOLUTION

In a doorway, sketching the occupants of the tumbril, stood David, the artist, who had been one of Danton's most implacable foes and who openly rejoiced over his downfall. Danton seeing him cried out: "You are there, are you, varlet?"

On they went, down the road at the end of which loomed up a great bare thing, as gaunt and as cheerless as a tree without leaves. In the crimson rays of the declining sun it seemed to be blood-red—dripping blood. The lengthening shadows of the afternoon made it look as if its long arms were stretched out to take into their embrace the victims in the approaching carts. "May I sing?" asked Danton when he reached the guillotine. "I know no reason why you should not if you so desire," answered Samson, and the great tribune sang a song which describes him and his friends as reaching the banks of the river Phlegethon and paying to Charon, "*citoyen redoutable,*" more than the amount required for ferriage across the black stream; when the old man is about to give the change he is told to keep it to help pay for the passage of Robespierre and his companions who will soon be along.

"*Garde, lui dit Danton, la somme tout entiere,*
Ce sera pour Couthon, Saint Just et Robespierre."

One by one the prisoners ascended the steps to the platform, each stopping a moment to say farewell to Danton. As Hérault turned to kiss his friend and leader on the cheek, the executioners tore them violently apart. "Fools," cried Danton, "do you not know that our heads will in a moment meet in the basket?" At last Danton was left alone, having witnessed with heroic fortitude the death of his friends—an ordeal through which to pass without flinching, required the greatest nerve.

At times he was overheard by the executioners saying: "My poor dear wife, am I never to see you again?" but instantly recovering himself he would mutter, "Courage, Danton! no weakness!" Addressing Samson he said: "You must show my head to the people, they will like to see it." This sounds like a reverberating echo from the egoism of Mirabeau.

For a few moments he stood on the platform, erect, with his head thrown back, his great figure outlined against a cloudless sky. A hush fell upon the people as he without trepidation looked over the multitude of upturned faces. His gaze fell upon a priest, whom he recognized by a prearranged signal, and he was given the sign of absolution. Then his great soul went out into eternity.

CHAPTER XXXIII

DANTON—HIS APPEARANCE—HIS STYLE OF DRESS—HIS CHARACTER—HIS RELIGIOUS BELIEF—WAS HE VENAL?—POLITICIAN—STATESMAN—ORATOR—HIS SHORT POLITICAL CAREER—RESULTS OF THE FRENCH REVOLUTION

With the exception of Mirabeau, Danton was the strongest character the Revolution produced. "He bore," says Mignet, "a physical resemblance to that tribune of the higher classes. He had irregular features, a powerful voice, impetuous gesticulation, a daring eloquence, a lordly brow. Their vices too were the same, only Mirabeau's were those of a patrician, Danton's those of a democrat. That which there was of daring in the conceptions of Mirabeau was to be found in Danton, but in another way, because in the Revolution he belonged to another class and another epoch." So much, in many ways, did they resemble each other that Danton was frequently alluded to as the "Mirabeau of the Sans Culottes."

In appearance Danton was impressive, picturesque. His massive, herculean frame towered above his fellows; his head was surmounted by a heavy shock of black hair that resembled the mane of a lion; his shirt, open at the front, re-

DANTON

vealed the sinewy neck of a bull; his eyes were small, deeply set but piercing; his nose was crushed; his face scarred, and his features were pitted with the smallpox. His very homeliness seemed to add force, even dignity, to his presence, and when he arose to address the Assembly he displayed a vigor and exerted a power that not only riveted the attention of men but made his adversaries quail. As homely and as scarred in feature as Mirabeau, he followed the example of his great compeer by frequently in his public speeches alluding to his ugliness. Upon one occasion he cried out: "My Medusa head that makes the aristocrats to tremble." At the Jacobins' he declared that he had the harsh expression of freedom. *"La nature m'a donné en partage les forces athletiques et la physiognome âpre de la Liberté."*

"His rugged face reminds us," said one of his contemporaries, "of a caricature of Socrates." "He was marked," says a French author, "with the smallpox like Robespierre, but had a masculine countenance, broad nostrils, forward lips, and a bold air wholly unlike his." "The broad, rude features speak withal of wild human sympathies," says another. Carlyle, in his vividly descriptive style, pictures him as: "The huge, brawny figure; through whose black brows and rude, flattened face there looks a waste of energy as of Hercules not yet furibund." To appreciate the force of such a countenance one must study every detail, every feature, and then combine them. "Paint me as I am," cried Cromwell, "warts and all."

When animated in discussion Danton's face revealed every emotion of his soul. A distinguished French historian describing him says: "What a frightful visage has this Danton! Is this a cyclop or some goblin? That large face, so awfully scarred by the smallpox, with its small, dull eyes, looks like a brooding volcano. No, that is not a man, but the very element of confusion swayed by madness, fury, and fatality! Awful genius, thou frightenest me! Art thou to save or ruin France?" Further on the same writer continues: "What frightens me the most is that he has no eyes; at least they are scarcely perceptible. What! is this terrible blind man to be the guide of nations? . . . And yet this monster is sublime. This face almost without eyes seems like a volcano without a crater—a volcano of horrors or of fire—which in its pent-up furnace is brooding over the struggles of nature. . . . How awful will be the eruption. . . . That face is like a nightmare from which one cannot escape, a horrible oppressive dream. . . . We become mechanically attracted towards this visible struggle of opposite principles. . . . It is a devoted Œdipus who, possessed with his own enigma, carries within his breast a terrible sphinx that will devour him."

It is always interesting to picture a man whose character we are studying as he appeared to his

DANTON

contemporaries in the everyday walks of life. During his attendance upon the sessions of the Assembly, he wore a dark blue coat with full skirts cut in the fashion of the period, broad flaps at the pockets, and two rows of brass buttons; a colored vest or waistcoat, usually buff or yellow; *culottes* and top boots. If he had ever worn silk stockings and buckled shoes, he had long since discarded them. A stock and an expansive scarf or tie encircled his neck. He carried a watch and wore a fob. In the matter of attire it is certain he was not so particular or fastidious as Robespierre, but there is sufficient proof that he was neither slouchy nor untidy, and that he did not affect that carelessness in dress that was the homage the demagogues paid to the rabble.

He was a whole-souled man of the world, fond of its pleasures; he often gave offense to many of his colleagues because of his aristocratic taste and extravagance, which they thought were not consistent in one who professed the austere virtues of republicanism.

"There have been few stronger men than this Danton," says Watson. His natural endowments were great. They would have been great in any period, but in stirring times, that is in a revolution, they were of the highest order. His courage and daring were superb; when others quailed in the face of disaster, when the armies of allied Europe threatened France, and the provinces were in revolt, he never wavered. It may be said of him, as Livy said of a celebrated

THE FRENCH REVOLUTION

Roman: "He never despaired of the Republic."

Carlyle asserts that the French Revolution did produce some original men among the twenty-five millions, at least one or two units. Some reckon, he says, as many as three and then names them in the following order: Napoleon, Danton, and Mirabeau. Whether more will come to light he cannot say, but in the meanwhile he advises the world to be thankful for these three, well knowing how rare such men are. That indeed is a great group, and it may be said that without Danton, Napoleon, perhaps, would have had no theatre for his genius. So deeply did Danton impress himself upon the Revolution that it is difficult to imagine what its history would have been without him. No crisis daunted, no defeat disheartened, no danger nor disaster appalled him.

"It is not the alarm-cannon that you hear," he cried when the Prussians were at Verdun and Paris was stricken with terror, "but the *pas de charge* against our enemies." "Retire behind the Loire? No!" he exclaimed, "rather than retreat and abandon the capital we will burn it to ashes." His was the ruling influence that effected the dethronement of the king, the destruction of the monarchy, and the establishment of the Republic.

There were periods in the Revolution when he made its events, when he stamped his personality upon its character. He stood for its purposes, its principles. In him were concentrated its vigor, its force, its energy; he was the em-

DANTON

bodiment of its violence. When it wavered he gave it an impetus; when its advance column halted or recoiled, he seized the standard and led the way. He had the superb qualities of leadership—those qualities that are not acquired by time, labor nor even experience, but are innate. Lord Brougham, who knew personally many of the patriarchs that survived the Revolution, said that they were all of one mind in declaring that Danton was unquestionably its principal leader. There was not one of his contemporaries, in the later period of the Revolution, that was his equal. It can almost be said that during a portion of 1793 he *was* the Revolution.

Such men as Danton make revolutions and reach results that weaklings could not encompass. They are made to fit conditions and they become instruments in the hands of Providence to effect those changes that are for the betterment of the human race in the eternal struggle for the ideal. They fill up large spaces in the exciting and transforming periods of the world's history. Without fear themselves, audacious and defiant, they inspire the confidence and the courage of other men by their conduct and example. Their bravery is contagious and infectious.

Danton was the man for his times. He was possessed of the spirit of the Revolution, he loved to breathe its atmosphere. He delighted to brave its dangers, to bridge over its perils. The din and turmoil of controversy and contention were music to his ears. "Bold, ardent, greedy of excitement, he had thrown himself eagerly into

THE FRENCH REVOLUTION

the career of disturbance and he was more especially qualified to shine in the days of terror." He was seldom if ever disconcerted; in an emergency, he had the presence of mind that comes from courage and possessed that quickness and accuracy of perception that enabled him to act with judgment and wisdom on the moment. He could perceive instantly the mistake of an adversary and had a fertility of resources upon which to draw to take advantage of the error.

This man in his passion was as savage as a tiger, and yet naturally in disposition he was as affectionate as a child and as tender as a woman. "One sees those fire-eyes . . . fill with the water of tears." He presented a mixture of the most opposite qualities. "He had impulses of humanity as he had of fury; he had low vices but generous passions—in a word he had a heart."

"They say best men are molded out of faults."

Lord Macaulay in describing him says: "He was brave and resolute, fond of pleasures, of power, and of distinction, with vehement passions, with lax principles, but with some kind and manly feelings, capable of great crimes, but capable also of friendship and of compassion."

In the opinion of Morley, "He was one of the men who strike deep notes. He had that largeness of motive, fullness of nature, and capaciousness of mind which will always redeem a multitude of infirmities."

He was ardently fond of his mother; he was

DANTON

a faithful husband, a devoted father, and a loyal friend. " No man was truer to his friends or more dangerous to his foes." The love he had for his first wife was ideal and the affection he had for Camille was that of Jonathan for David. By nature he was a man of sentiment and deep emotions; he had fine taste and was passionately fond of books, music, and flowers. He was open-hearted, generous, of a most forgiving disposition, too big to harbor a grudge, and no one would accept an apology more quickly, if sincere and offered in a proper spirit.

In those days of slaughter, when life was so cheap, he would not encompass the death of a rival for the sake of advancing his own ambitions. " He was," says Stephens, " above petty feuds and laughed at the idea of vengeance on his personal enemies." At the time of the September massacres he sacrificed none to personal animosity, as it was said Robespierre did, but, at his own instance and risk, saved enemies as well as friends from slaughter by having them released from prison. Appeals to his heart were seldom made in vain. He was not plagued by envy nor jealousy; those mean and little qualities were foreign to his nature. He was absolutely free from cant; bold, outspoken, natural, with no affectation in manner or language, he was without the pretension to sincerity that so characterized Robespierre.

His religious faith was not well defined; it is very evident he was not hampered in his conduct by the influence of any creed; even the

THE FRENCH REVOLUTION

principles of Christianity did not restrain him. Religion was not fashionable nor popular during the Revolution. The Church itself, for a century or more, had been honeycombed with scepticism and because of the corruption and extravagance of the upper clergy it had fallen into disfavor. There may, however, have been lingering in the heart of Danton, as there is in the heart of almost every man, the sweet influence of that early religious training at the mother's knee.

When Danton was married the second time, which was in July, 1793, at the very height of the Revolution, the ceremony was performed by an orthodox or non-juring priest. This may have been at the suggestion of the bride, for her mother was a very religious woman, and a man like Danton, who was not in any sense of the word a bigot, would be likely to treat such matters with an utter disregard. So far as he personally was concerned, it would not have made much difference to him who officiated, provided the ceremony was legal; yet Lamartine says that he retired to an inner room and made confession just before he was married. As already stated, it is said that when he was upon the platform of the scaffold, a priest in the crowd, whom he recognized, gave him absolution.

There were several instances when he spoke as if he believed in a living God. A notable occasion was when La Fayette entered the Club of the Jacobins after the flight of the king. Danton, who was on his feet and speaking at the time, turned suddenly upon the general and exclaimed: "I am going to talk as though I were at the bar of God's justice and I must say before you, Monsieur de La Fayette, what I would say in the presence of Him who reads all hearts." This is thoroughly orthodox in tone. It may have been, however, the mere fustian of the orator, or for the sake of emphasis, but it surely is the language that would come from the lips of a true believer.

In opposing a motion of Cambon to separate the Church from the State he said: "It is treason against the nation to take away its dreams. For my part I admit I have known but one God. The God of all the world and of justice."

At the time of the accusation of the Hébertists, a godless faction, he cried out against them: "We have not destroyed superstition to establish the reign of atheism."

It may be safely asserted, that is if a man's language can be taken as proof of his religious faith, that Danton did believe in the existence of a God, of an overruling Providence.

At his trial, when interrogated he answered: "I call myself Danton; my sojourn will soon be in annihilation."—"*Ma demeure sera biéntôt dans le néant.*" This language does not make it appear that he had much hope in an after life; and this was the moment, when he was facing death, to test his real faith, for he knew when arraigned that he was doomed. His conduct at this time does not show that he was very much concerned about the question of religion or a

THE FRENCH REVOLUTION

future existence. He surely did not, from a Christian's point of view, make much preparation for the world to come.

He has been charged with venality, but a careful examination of the testimony fails to make out a case that would support a conviction in any tribunal of justice. After the discovery of Mirabeau's bargain with the court, charges of bribery against public men in those days of acute suspicion became very common. In extenuation of Mirabeau's corruption some one has said: "He may have sold himself, but he surely never delivered himself." So far as Danton was concerned there is not a scintilla of evidence that he even without delivery, ever sold himself.

At his trial he said in answer to one of the charges: "You say that I have been paid, but I tell you that men made as I am cannot be paid, and I put against your accusation, of which you cannot furnish a proof, nor the shadow, nor the beginning of a witness—the whole of my revolutionary career." This is a bold denial and does not sound like the language of a guilty man. The testimony upon which the charge is based is as follows: Bertrand de Molleville stated that he discovered, in an examination of the papers of Montmorin, proof that Danton had been paid out of the civil list, and that he wrote to Danton in December, 1792, about the time of the trial of the king, that he had his receipt for 50,000 francs paid to him by Montmorin. De Molleville admits that he lied when he wrote that he had the receipt in his possession, but says that

DANTON

he had seen it and knew that it was in existence, for it had been shown to him a year before personally by Montmorin. He threatened to expose Danton in the Assembly if he did not moderate his rage against the king.

It does not seem reasonable to believe that Danton, a trained lawyer, would have given a receipt for money paid under such circumstances. Moreover, he voted for the death of the king, and yet de Molleville did not publish him as he threatened. La Fayette, in his Memoirs, says that Danton's receipt was in the hands of Montmorin for 100,000 francs, but La Fayette's enmity against Danton was so bitter that he was willing to believe any story that reflected upon his honor. It is evidently based on the merest hearsay and it will be seen that the amount has risen from 50,000 to 100,000 francs.

Brissot declared that he had seen a receipt for 500,000 francs in the hands of Montmorin; still the amount is growing and the increase shows that somebody is wrong. This is the flimsiest kind of testimony to support such a charge. The original paper is not produced, the amounts named are various, and the witnesses have no personal knowledge of the matter. It must also be taken into consideration in judging the accused that he was neither sordid nor avaricious, nor was he ever in circumstances so strained as would have induced him to yield to temptation.

Perhaps the whole story rose from the fact that in 1791, at the time of the abolition of the

THE FRENCH REVOLUTION

"*Avocats aux Conseils du Roi,*" Danton was paid 70,000 livres as compensation for the suppression of his office. It is well known that this matter passed through the hands of Montmorin in whose department the negotiations in relation to the settlement were had.

Lamartine, who at times is very unfair in his criticisms of Danton, says: " The court well knew the tariff of his conscience, he threatened it in order to make it desirous of buying him, he only opened his mouth to have it stuffed with gold. . . . He was bought daily and next morning was again for sale. Mirabeau, La Fayette, Montmorin, M. de Laporte, the duc d'Orleans, the king himself, all knew his price. . . Any other individual would have felt shame before men who had the secret of his dishonor, but he only was not ashamed and looked them in the face without a blush. His was the quietude of vice."

Madame Roland, who disliked Danton, charged him with having gone to Belgium to enrich himself, stating that he dared to admit a fortune of 1,400,000 francs. That statement goes for what it is worth. If Danton made such an admission he must have been a greater fool than he would have been had he signed the receipt. Lamartine, in commenting upon this matter, says: " The stories of the immense fortune he possessed, said to be the result of his speculations in Belgium, were apparently refuted by the scanty dower he settled on his wife, consisting of three thousand francs in assignats, which soon after were worth only twelve hundred."

On December 3, 1793, when attacked by the Hébertists, he uttered the following emphatic denial: "You will be astonished, when I lay bare to you my private affairs, to see the colossal fortune which my enemies and yours have charged me with, reduced to the little amount of property which I have always had. I defy my opponents to furnish the proof of any crime whatever to me." He demanded that a committee be appointed to examine into the charges, but after a speech by Robespierre it was considered not at all necessary.

At Danton's death his estate was sequestered, and he left just about what he could honestly have made and saved in his professional and public career. These matters have been most carefully investigated and considered by M. Bougeart and Dr. Robinet, and they acquit Danton of every charge of venality.

One of the greatest lawyers England ever produced, Lord Brougham, in commenting upon this question, writes: "A charge of corruption has been brought against Danton, but upon very inadequate grounds. The assertion of royalist partisans that he had stipulated for money and the statement of one that he knew of its payment and had seen the receipt (as if a receipt could have passed) can signify nothing when put in contrast with the known facts of his living

THE FRENCH REVOLUTION

throughout his short public career in narrow circumstances."

Stephens and Aulard both favor this view of the case. The former author says in his French Revolution: "Mirabeau declares openly in a letter to La Marck that the triumvirate and Orleanists had intrigued with Danton and had bribed him with a large sum, but all such stories have been proved to be false by the careful examination of his monetary affairs during the Revolution."

As a politician Danton was original, ingenious, resourceful, and possessed to a high degree the arts of the demagogue—we mean by this a demagogue in the best sense of that word, a leader of the people. He was not of the type of John Wilkes. Danton was denominated "the Alcibiades of the Rabble," but this designation was not altogether apposite; he was of the people and loved their cause and never flattered or cajoled simply to mislead them. His patriotism was unquestioned; he was devoted to France and every inch of her soil was dear to him. He was a partisan or a party man in the full meaning of the term. Mignet goes so far as to say: "The welfare of his party was in his eyes superior to the law and even to humanity."

His ambition was not personal; he would willingly have sacrificed himself for the Republic or his party. "*Que mon nom soit flétri*"—"Let my name be blighted if but the cause succeed," he cried out in one of his heated harangues. At

DANTON

times he was not particular in the choice of the methods he employed to attain an object; he believed in the dangerous doctrine, "the end justifies the means," and so was not always governed by high moral principles.

Revolutionists cannot be saints nor be expected, perhaps, to practise a fine code of ethics in so fierce a conflict as was being waged in France. "He deemed," says Mignet, "no means censurable so they were useful." Thiers writes of him: "Prompt and decisive, not to be staggered either by the difficulty or by the novelty of an extraordinary situation, he was capable of judging of the necessary means and had neither fear nor scruple about any." Citing from Lamartine, "Danton's revolutionary principles were well known. To abstain from a crime necessary or barely useful he considered a weakness." The same author on another page says: "He was devoid of honor, principles, or morality; he only loved democracy because it was exciting." Quoting further from the same writer: "He had everything to make him great but virtue." But he will stand a fair comparison in these particulars, that is in so far as his methods and principles are concerned, with the other public men of his day. He no doubt in a desperate game did not scruple about the means to reach an end, but it must be said to his credit that he would rather play fair than false. There was an underlying foundation of honor and truth in his character.

Every man with a virtuous strain, who in

4.166.13.42.   7bre 1792.

Messieurs les Commissaires de la trésorerie
nationale voudront bien faire payer à
M. Fabre d'Eglantine secrétaire general
du département de la justice le Cicondvoir
de mon traitement

Le Ministre de la justice

Danton

Paris 28 7bre 1792
1er de la république

FAC-SIMILE OF A LETTER WRITTEN BY DANTON
The original is in the possession of William J. Latta, Esq.

THE FRENCH REVOLUTION

order to win when in a contest ignores or offends moral considerations, always tries to satisfy his conscience by making a promise to reform after the conflict. That cold, crafty politician, Louis XI, worked the two ends of the line, for he fumbled his relics and mumbled his prayers both before and after the commission of his political crimes. Even Marat was wont to say that if he lived long enough to witness the triumph of the Republic he would take refuge in the sphere of his scientific and literary studies. Danton persistently contended that everything he did was for the welfare of his country and the restoration of order; he always had a reason for his action and even excused his conduct in reference to the September Massacres (which by many is considered the greatest blot upon his character) by declaring that the slaughter of the aristocrats was to insure peace and the safety of the Republic and that the security and perpetuity of the nation were paramount to all other considerations. It is the same argument advanced as an excuse for war when both sides are praying to the one God for victory, but what may be justified as a necessity in a nation is denounced as a crime in an individual.

Whatever else may be said of Danton, he was not mean nor contemptible in his methods. " His vices," declares a distinguished French historian, " partook of the heroic." He was a Colossus of tremendous force, whom nothing could affright, nothing dismay. He would combat man or devil and defy single-handed the allied armies of

DANTON

Europe. It is the inborn courage of the man that commands our admiration. We have no time to criticise his faults or the means he adopted to reach his ends, we are so impressed with his superb boldness and audacity. In judging men of that period, and considering them from a moral standpoint we are apt to apply the rules that obtain to-day. This is wrong; it is not fair to them. It was an exceptional era, everything was topsy turvy—religion, society, politics, government. "All men were under the influence of a temporary delirium, a delirium which rendered them alike insensible to their own sufferings, blind to their own perils, neglectful of their duties, and regardless of other men's rights." All these matters must be taken into consideration when we judge the actors of those days, if we desire to do them justice.

Danton was a good reader of human nature, he could "see quite through the thoughts of men," but he was at times too confiding and trustful and placed faith and reliance in those whom he ought to have known would betray him. Like a man who always fights in the open, he often expressed himself too freely.

As a politician he was not cunning, in a low sense, and he therefore in this particular was no match for his wily adversary, Robespierre; so at last this great leader of almost superhuman power, this giant, was like Samson shorn of his strength and bound with thongs, falling an easy prey to his crafty and relentless foe.

In diplomacy Danton was clever and keen;

THE FRENCH REVOLUTION

he was shrewd in negotiation and well equipped to further and protect the interest committed to his care. Dumouriez was an intriguer and a diplomat of the first order, but Danton saw through his plans with an unerring eye and measured exactly the purposes of his ambition.

As a statesman Danton had a constructive intellect, but he left to smaller men the carrying out of his plans; he had no special aptitude for details. "He was the most constructive mind of all the public men of the Revolution, as constructive as it was possible to be at the threshold of a transition period." A distinguished French author goes so far as to say: "He was even a greater statesman than Mirabeau, if by that appellation we mean the man who understands the mechanism of government independently of its ideal. He had political instinct."

It was he that, in the spring of 1793, proposed and had carried a measure abolishing imprisonment for debt. It was he that favored the abolition of slavery in all the French possessions. "By sowing liberty in the new world," he said, "we shall cause it to bear abundant fruit and shoot profound roots there." This was at a time when slavery was an established institution in the American Republic. He advocated the pensioning of maimed soldiers. "Would it not be well," he urged, "to grant land in the suburbs of Paris to those worthy citizens who have been mutilated in the defense of the Republic, and also give them beasts and thus start, under the

DANTON

very eyes of the Convention, a colony of patriots who have suffered for the fatherland?" This suggestion led to the appropriation of large sums of money for the pensioning of veterans. A decree providing that the husband should not dispose of the common property without the consent of the wife received his warm approval. He believed children belonged to the State rather than to their parents, and as we have already seen strongly favored compulsory education, especially did he endorse a system of manual training.

"When you sow the vast field of the Republic," he said, "do not, I beg you, count the cost of the seed. Next after bread, education is the first necessity of the life of the people. . . . After giving France liberty and conquering her enemies, nothing will be more glorious than to secure to coming generations an education worthy of our liberty."

It was on Danton's motion that the Convention decreed, on April 2, 1793, that "in every section of the Republic, when the price of corn is not in a just proportion to wages paid, the treasury shall levy a contribution on the rich, out of which shall be defrayed the difference between such price of corn and the wages of the needy." This smacks of Socialism, but under an orderly condition and outside of a revolutionary period Danton would probably not have favored such a plan. He believed the law of the Maximum, which fixed a price above which the necessaries of life could not

THE FRENCH REVOLUTION

be sold, was a proper and beneficial regulation under prevailing conditions.

The law of Forty Sous, proposed by him in September, 1793, provided that "the sections of Paris shall assemble in regular sessions every Sunday and Thursday, and every citizen so attending shall be paid forty sous for each and every session." This was a sop to the multitude.

One of the most remarkable features of the French Revolution was the eloquence that suddenly burst forth from every quarter; it seemed as if the thoughts of men, so long imprisoned, when freed, broke out into triumphant song. It was the renaissance of liberty; the minds of men were aflame and their tongues but expressed their joy in the liberation. No period in history ever produced a greater number of orators. Vergniaud stands in the very front rank; he would have stood high in any age. He had the soul, the emotion, the imagination of the born orator. His flights were into the empyrean, his imagery was beautiful, his figures strong, his allusions apt, his logic clear, and his argument cogent and convincing. Mirabeau's eloquence was in many respects unsurpassed. He stood in a class by himself. Isnard's impassioned utterances thrilled the heart of France. "He was the most ardent of them all." Barnave, who coped even with Mirabeau, was an orator of marvelous power; and so we could go on through a long list of names.

Many of the orators of the Convention, unless

DANTON

they spoke extemporaneously, revealed in their finished orations the care taken in their preparation; their speeches had the smell of the lamp about them. Not so with Danton; in his " eloquence there appears no preparation, no study, nothing got up for mere effect." His speeches were harangues; they were nearly all short. They came red-hot from his soul and carried the truth home to the hearts of men; in their vehemence they bore down all opposition. He had the faculty of expressing a thought in a flash. In a few living words he could weave a vivid epigram. He was always a master of commanding phrase and on the spur of the moment would utter those fiery sentences that became party shibboleths and aroused courage even in the faint-hearted.

His argument was a succession of blows dealt quickly upon vital spots. Some one has said: " Eloquence with Danton was an explosion of the soul." A well-known French author calls him " the Pluto of Eloquence." Another says: " His eloquence was like the loud clamor of the mob." His oratory had a simplicity, a beauty, a rugged strength all its own. What can be finer than his defiant challenge, after the death of Louis, to the allied kings of Europe, at whose feet he threw down " as gage of battle the head of a king."

Sometimes, from a rhetorician's point of view, his figures were unrefined, coarse, exaggerated, and defective in taste. For example, in a speech of remarkable power in answer to an attack made

THE FRENCH REVOLUTION

upon him in the Assembly, he closed with the following metaphor: "I have entrenched myself in the citadel of reason. I shall sally forth with the artillery of truth and I shall crumble to dust the villains who have presumed to accuse me." Such metaphors may be unpardonable in the opinion of a schoolman, but the action of Danton was so strong, his expression so energetic that under the spell of his eloquence his auditors did not stop to criticise his figures of speech. Language so bombastic, had it come from a little man, or a speaker with a weak voice, or one without strong emotions, would have set the Assembly in a roar. A most distinguished British orator in commenting on this speech says: "Such violent metaphors, of a vulgar class, Danton could venture upon from his thundering voice and overpowering action. In another they would have excited the ridicule from which those physical attributes rescued them in him." In pure declamation Danton must have been magnificent.

Were we to look for a specimen of his manner, perhaps none more characteristic could be found than his reply to an attack made upon him by Lasource, who charged him with his known partiality for Dumouriez (whose treason at this time was laid bare), and with playing with that ambitious soldier the part of Cromwell. Stung and incensed by so foul an accusation, the great tribune retorted with all the strength he could summon and in conclusion said: "If then it be the profound sense of duty which dictated the condemnation of the king—if you conceived that

DANTON

you thereby saved the people and thus performed the service which the country had a right to expect from its representatives—rally, you who pronounced the tyrant's doom, rally around me against the cowards who would have spared him; close your ranks; call the people to assemble in arms against the enemy without and to crush the enemy within; confound by the vigor and steadfastness of your character all the wretches, all the aristocrats, all the moderates, all those who have slandered you in the provinces. No more compromise with them! Proclaim this, you who have never made your political position available to you as it ought to be, and let justice at last be done you! You perceive by the situation in which I at this moment stand, how necessary it is that you should be firm and declare war on all your enemies be they who they may. You must form an indomitable phalanx. It is not you who love the clubs and the people that desire a king. It is your part to root out such an idea from such as have contrived to save the former tyrant. For me, I march onward to a republic; let us all join in the advance; we shall soon see which gains his object—we or our slanderers!"

Another fine example of his style, perhaps even more characteristic than the foregoing, is the speech he made in reply to Gensonné, the Girondin, who had as usual been theorizing and at the same time reflecting upon the political supremacy assumed by Paris: "What are your laws and theories to us, when the only law is to triumph and the sole theory for the nation is the theory of existence? Let us first save ourselves; we can discuss matters afterwards. France at this moment is neither at Lille nor Marseilles, nor at Lyons, nor at Bordeaux, but is everywhere where men think or act or fight for her. We have no longer departments nor separate interests, lines are obliterated between the provinces, all is France. Geography is at an end; there is but one people—there should be but one republic! Was it at Lyons they took the Bastile? Did Marseilles effect the 20th of June? Do we owe to Bordeaux the 10th of August? Everywhere, wherever she has been saved, wherever her flag floats, wherever her cause is waged, or her principles are triumphant, there is France—there the one entire indivisible nation. What mean you by the tyranny of Paris? It is the tyranny of the head over the limbs—the tyranny of life over death. You seek to parcel out liberty so as to make it weak and vulnerable in all its members; we would declare liberty as indivisible as the nation, so that it may be unassailable in its head."

Danton's voice was of immense scope and volume; he could tone it down to the soft and tender notes of a cooing dove, or could bellow like a Stentor. When angry or emphatic he could be heard an incredible distance. Michelet describes him as shaking the windows while addressing the Club of the Cordeliers. At his trial he was distinctly heard by a vast multitude of people that had gathered outside of the court house.

The energy of Danton in the days of his activity was prodigious; his labors were titanic, no

DANTON

task was impossible, and yet we marvel that in the time allotted to him he accomplished so much.

His entire political career extended over a comparatively short period, three years at the most; but in that brief space he made his reputation. It was not a slow ascent to fame by years of preparation and service under a settled government, but an immediate, a sudden rise to power, to be cut short in the heyday of his manhood, for he went to the scaffold in the thirty-fifth year of his age, even before he had reached the real prime and vigor of his life.

He was handicapped, as we have seen, at the opening of the Revolution because of the affair of Marat, and it was not until the death of Mirabeau that he took a prominent part in the politics of the nation. Before that his reputation was local, virtually confined to the section of the Cordeliers, so that his political career covered a period of perhaps less than three years; but it was a most strenuous period, for in those three years history was made faster than it is in a decade under a settled government in time of peace.

A superficial glance at the French Revolution is apt to give the impression that it was but a saturnalia of crime. A closer inspection, however, will prove that this was not the case. It had a meaning and a purpose; it was a dreadful reckoning with the past; it was a heroic effort for the liberation of mankind from tyranny. "When oppression renders a revolution necessary," said La Fayette, "insurrection is the most sacred of duties."

THE FRENCH REVOLUTION

" The nation was worn out with long wars and exhausted by supplying the extravagance of its rulers, who gave themselves up alternately to a fondness for pleasure and for arms." The leaders of the Revolution saw in man, irrespective of his position in social and political life, a human being entitled to the sympathies of his fellows and the protection of government, not a creature to be oppressed but to be elevated, not to be deprived of his rights but to be secure in their enjoyment.

The energies of the Revolution may have been misdirected by vicious and ambitious men, in its excesses it may have disgraced and dishonored humanity, it may not have accomplished all that it should have attained, but it must be admitted that it did moderate the power of the tyrant and if it did nothing more than effect the abolition of feudalism that was worth all the blood that was shed. It was a tremendous burst of energy, agitating all France and every state in Europe. It was like a seething volcano that had been accumulating its force for centuries, and when it broke forth it overwhelmed and submerged everything in its pathway and shook the earth with its vibrations. Paris was the crater of this volcanic eruption.

The French Revolution was a war of ideas, and, although the ideas at times were confused, out of all this chaos were at last evolved the principles of law, justice, equality, and humanity. Judge it not alone by its excesses but also by its results; for notwithstanding its terrors, its horrors, its crimes, it was a blessing to mankind, overthrowing many vile institutions and reforming many others which it did not destroy. In the life of the civilized world to-day are to be traced its principles, its purposes, its philosophy.

INDEX

A

Aboukir, 302
Achilles, 21
Addison, his works in Danton's library, 49
Administration of Law, 28
Agriculture in the middle of the eighteenth century, 26
Agrippina, 381
Alcibiades, 167
Alva in the Netherlands, 299
Andu Renée, 292
Ankarstrom assassinates Gustavus III of Sweden, 193
Antonini Itinerarium, 22
Antony, 134
Antwerp, 317
Arcis sur Aube, birthplace of Danton, 22
Arcola, 302
Ariosto, his works in Danton's library, 49
Artois, Count d', his opinion of La Fayette, 215
Assembly declares the country in danger, 225
Augustus, 22
Avocats aux Conseils du Roi, 47

B

Bailly attacked by Marat, 83, 102; proclaims martial law, 157; withdraws from the club of the Jacobins, 161; his execution, 394, 395
Barbaroux, instigates presentation of petition to the Assembly, 197, 198; welcomes the Marseillais, 234; commits suicide, 389
Barentin, de, 47

INDEX

Barère, 150, 313, 328, 329; member of the Committee of Public Safety, 379
Barnave, 21; appointed commissioner by the Assembly to escort the King to Paris, 137; withdraws from the club of the Jacobins, 161; his execution, 394; his oratory, 443
Barras on Marat, 81
Batz, Baron de, attempts to rescue King, 346
Baudrais, 345
Belloc, Hilaire, on Marat, 95
Bérardier, Abbé, saved at the time of the September massacres by Danton, 296
Billaud-Varennes, 150; votes for death of the King, 337; member of the Committee of Public Safety, 379; encompasses the overthrow of Danton, 402
Black Breeches, Day of the, 200
Boccaccio, his works in Danton's library, 49
Boileau, 386
Bon, Jean, member of the Committee of Public Safety, 379
Bonju, Marie Louise, 292
Bougeart, 436
Bouillé, General, in conspiracy to aid King in his flight, 107, 115, 116
Bourbons, 169
Bourdier, Dr., prescribes for Marat, 95
Bourrienne, 202,
Bozé, 328
Brienne, Lomenie de, minister of Louis XVI, 58
Brissot, 337, 434
Brougham, Lord, 428; on the question of Danton's venality, 436
Brune, a friend of Danton, 50
Brunswick, Duke of, his proclamation, 227, 228, 229, 230, 231, 232; besieges Verdun, 259
Brutus, 134
Buckle, 194
Burke, Edmund, 295, 319, 321; description of Marie Antoinette, 384
Buzot, 185, 389
Byron, Lord, 287

INDEX

C

Cæsar, Julius, 22, 134
Cafés, 278
Ça ira, 397
Calonne, minister of Louis XVI, 57, 72
Cambon, witness at trial of Dantonists, 413
Campan, Madame, 63, 64, 109
Carlyle, description of Danton, 424, 427
Carmagnole, 397
Carnot, on execution of King, 327; member of the Committee of Public Safety, 379
Carra, 241
Cassius, 134
Catharine II of Russia, 168, 194
Cazotte, his daughter saves his life at the time of the September Massacres, 273
Chalons, 116
Champ de Mars, 155; Fusillade of, 157
Champfort on revolutions, 252
Champs Elysées, 236
Charenton, 234
Charles, Archduke, defeats Miranda, 356
Charles VII, 42
Charles IX, 299
Charles, Professor, controversy with Marat, 80
Charolais, Count de, 29
Charpentier, Antoinette Gabrielle, 47
Chartres, Duke de, advised by Danton, 304
Chaumette, 281
Choiseul, 124
Cicero, 385
Clavières, 197
Clermont, 119
Cléry, King's valet, 344
Clootz, Anacharsis, 281
Clovis, 41
Coffinhal, 281
Commissioners of the Convention sent out to quiet spirit of insubordination in the provinces, 369

INDEX

Committee of Public Safety, 379; its members, its power, 379, 380
Condé, 188, 193
Condorcet, 92; comments on Madame Roland, 183; approves appointment of Danton as minister of justice, 257
Condorcet, Madame, 292
Constitution of 1791 adopted, 162
Corday, Charlotte, 293; comes to Paris from Caen, 374; murders Marat, 375; her arrest and trial, 376; her execution, 377
Cordeliers, Club of the, issues public address, 152, 177
Couthon, member Committee of Public Safety, 379
Crawford, Quentin, aids in flight of the King, 108
Cromwell, 315
Custine, General, his victory, 303; his execution, 395

D

D'Acloque, Marshal Mouchy, guards Louis on the "Day of the Black Breeches," 203
D'Alembert, 92
D'Allonville, 193
Damiens, his punishment for attempting to assassinate Louis XV, 30
Dampiere, M. de, killed while attempting to pay respect to the King, 140
D'Andoins, Captain, 118
D'Angouléme, Duchess, 171, 343
Dandies, their attire, 279
Dante, 49
Danton, gave to the Revolution a fresh impulse, 18, 19; at first he was loyal to the monarchy, 20; his birth, 22; his father, 35; his mother, 35; his character as a boy, 36; attends school at Arcis, 38; enters seminary at Troyes, 38; witnesses coronation of Louis XVI at Rheims, 40; studies law, 45; comes to the bar, 45; becomes an "Avocat aux Conseils du Roi," 46; marries Antoinette Gabrielle Charpentier, 47; his income, 47; his studies, 48, 74; not a delegate to the States-General, 77; arrests

INDEX

Soulés, 77; President of the Club of the Cordeliers, 78; undertakes defense of Marat, 99, 102; elected administrator of the department of Paris, 103; opposes King's visit to St. Cloud, 104; attacks La Fayette at the Jacobins', 133; leader of the ultra-revolutionists, 148; favors a republic, 149; reads petition on July 17th at the Champ de Mars, 156; compelled to leave Paris, 159; returns to Paris, 175; at first opposes war, 186; subsequently gives it his loyal support, 187; his admiration for Dumouriez, 192; meets the Marseillais, 234; his part in the events of the Tenth of August, 256; made minister of justice, 257; defies the allies, 260, 261; proposes domiciliary visits, 261; held responsible for the September massacres, 295; father of the Republic, 297; his energy, 303; advises duke de Chartres, 304; inveighs against the foreign policy of the Girondins, 318; goes to Belgium as commissioner, 323; fathoms the designs of Dumouriez, 323; the death of his wife, 324; votes for the death of Louis, 337; denounces the insolence of the King of Spain, 339; visited by Theodore Lameth who negotiates to save the life of the King, 339, 340; denounces factional strife, 353; sent with Lacroix as commissioner to the army, 355; attacked by Lasource in the Convention, 357; his reply, 358; defends Paris against the threats and imputations of the Girondins, 361; the first man of the Republic, 362; appeals to the patriotism of the people, 362; replies to Isnard's threat to destroy Paris, 366; marries Mademoiselle Gély, 371; becomes by rotation president of the Convention, 377; urges reorganization of the revolutionary government and the vesting of absolute power in the Committee of Public Safety, 378; proposes decree providing for *levée en masse,* 380; regrets execution of Girondins, 390; becomes supine, 398; longs for peace, 400; aids in the accusation and conviction of the Hébertists, 401; his early opinion of Robespierre, 403; warrant for his arrest issued, 407; arrested jointly with Camille, 408; his trial, 412; his conviction, 417; his execution, 421, 422; his appearance, 423; his dress, 426; his power, 428; his character, 429; his

INDEX

religious faith, 430; the question of his venality, 433, 434, 435; his qualities as a politician, 437; as a diplomat, 440; as a statesman, 441; his eloquence, 444; his voice, 447; his energy, 447, 448; duration of his political career, 448

D'Aumont, Duke, saved by La Fayette, 131

Davaux attempts to rescue the King, 346

David arranges obsequies of Marat, 95; sketches Danton and his friends while they are on their way to the scaffold, 421

Davoust, 227

Day of Federation, 225

Declaration of Rights, 103

Declaration of War, 196

Diderot, 33

Demosthenes, 371, 385

De Séze defends the King at his trial, 331, 337

Deslon comes to King's assistance, 125

Diana of Poitiers, 22

Desmoulins, Camille, 23; the friend of Danton, 50; his character, 51; calls the people to arms in the Palais Royal, 52; designated the Attorney General of the Lamp-post, 52, 78, 110, 134, 160; his estimate of La Fayette, 215; welcomes the Marseillais, 234; his comments on the death of Danton's wife, 325; his outcry at the trial of the Girondins, 386; urges reaction and clemency, 402; his arrest, 408; his trial, 410; his execution, 421

Desmoulins, Lucile, 51, 408

D'Herbois, Collot, 307; votes for death of King, 337; member of the Committee of Public Safety, 379

D'Hervilly, Captain, 250

Dillon, Theobald, murdered by his troops, 197

Domiciliary visits, 261, 262

Dormans, 137

Drouet, 117; identifies and intercepts the King at Varennes, 122; accompanies the King to Paris, 141; his character, 141

DuBarry, Madame, her designation of Louis XVI when dauphin, 59; her execution, 393

Dumont on Louis XVI, 66; on Burke, 320

INDEX

Dumouriez, warns the queen, 71; attacked in Marat's journal, 83; snubs Marat, 88; enters the ministry, 191; his character, 191; named successor of La Fayette, 300; visits the capital, 306; endeavors to retain the neutrality of England, 319; complains of the treatment by the home government and shows signs of disaffection, 355; conspires to overthrow the revolutionary government, 356; his army defeated at Neerwinden, 356; deserts his colors, 357, 362

Duport, 21; withdraws from the Club of the Jacobins, 161; saved at the time of the September massacres by Danton, 296

Durler, Captain, in command of the Swiss at the palace of the Tuileries on the Tenth of August, 249

E

Elizabeth, Madame, 137, 205
Eloquence of the Revolution, 443
Emigrant princes threaten the destruction of Paris, 219
Encyclopedia, 34
England declares war, 321
Eperney, the commissioners of the Convention meet the royal fugitives on their return from Varennes at, 137

F

Fabre d' Eglantine, 310; his trial, 410; his execution, 419, 420, 421
Favras, Marquis de, 101
Ferron, 131
Fersen, Count, friend of the queen, aids in the flight to Varennes, 107; inquires as to whether the queen has accepted the Constitution, 163
Feudalism, 24
Feuillants, 176
Filles St. Thomas, attacked by Marseillais, 236, 237
Firmont, Henry Essex Edgeworth de, Confessor to the King at the time of his execution, 343, 348

INDEX

Flahaut, Madame, comments on Louis XVI, 60
Fleury, Mademoiselle, shelters Marat, 99
Fox, 321
Foulon, 391
Fournier, 241
Francesca da Rimini, 51
Francis I, 22
Francis II, his proclamation, 194
Franklin, Benjamin, 80
Fréron, his parting salutation to Fouquier Tinville, 411
Frogs of the Marsh, 286
Fusillade of the Champ de Mars, 157, 158, 159

G

Gamain, the locksmith, reveals the secret of the iron chest, 327
Garat named as minister to succeed Roland, 355; appeals to Robespierre to save the Girondins, 390
Gély, Mademoiselle, 371
Gensonné, 328
Girondins, 178; favor war, 185, 186; denounce the King, 223; boast of the part they took in the events of the Tenth of August, 258; strongest party in the Convention, 307; their views, 309; vote the King's death, 340, 353; popular feeling against them, 366; decree of accusation against them, 367; expelled from the Convention, 367; their trial, 385; their execution, 388, 389
Gobel, archbishop of Paris, renounces his faith, 396
Goddess of Reason, 397
Goguelat, 124
Gouges, Olympe de, 294; her execution, 395
Gregoire, Abbé, 307
Guadet, 328
Guicciardini, his works in Danton's library, 49
Guilhermy, 140
Guillotine, the, 288
Guillotin, Dr., his character, 288, 289
Guise, Duke de, 132
Gustavus III, assassination of, 193

INDEX

H

Hazlitt, 321
Hébert, votes for King's death, 337; accuses Marie Antoinette of foul crime, 381; his execution, 401
Helvetius, 32
Henry of Navarre, 146
Henry II, 22
Henry III, 132
Hermann, president of the Revolutionary Tribunal at the time of the trial of the Dantonists, 410

I

Inviolability of the King decreed, 152
Iron chest, 327
Isnard, threatens destruction to Paris, 366; his oratory, 443

J

Jacobins, 174; their attire, 278, 279; as a party, 310
James II, 106
Jemappes, victory of, 315
Joan of Arc, 41
Johnson, Dr., his works in Danton's library, 49
Jourdan, 227

K

Korf, Baroness de, 110

L

Lacombe, Rose, 292
Lacretelle on Danton, 297
Lacroix named with Danton commissioner to army, 355; his trial, 410; his execution, 421
La Fayette, Marquis de, attacked by Marat, 83, 102, 130; fires upon the people on the Champ de Mars, 157, 158; withdraws from the club of the Jacobins, 161; leaves his command and comes to Paris, 209; scorned by the King and the queen, 209, 210; his life and character, 211, 212, 213, 214, 215, 216, 217; abandons his command and flees from France, 300

INDEX

Lagache, 119

Lagarde, Chaveau, represents Charlotte Corday at her trial, 376

Lalande, 92

Lamarche, 391

Lamartine on Danton as a boy, 36, 37; describes Marat, 87, 135, 168; describes the Marseillais, 222; on Danton, 435, 438

Lamballe, Princess de, 273; her massacre, 273, 274

Lameth, Charles, saved by Danton at the time of the September massacres, 296

Lameths, The, 21

Lamourette Kiss, 224

Laplace, 92

Lasource attacks Danton, 357

Lavoisier, 92

Leaders of the Girondins, 178

Legendre, 204, 408

Leipsic, 302

Leopold, emperor of Austria, 189; his death, 193

Lepidus, 134

Lettre de cachet, 28

Lichtenau, Princess, 302

Lindet, Robert, member of the Committee of Public Safety, 379

Lisle, Rouget de, composer of the Marseillaise hymn, 220; his execution, 395

Longwy, fall of, 259

Louis XI, 439

Louis XIV, glory of his reign, 24; length of his reign, 24, 67, 68

Louis XV, 23; length of reign, 24; his extravagance, 53; predicts the deluge, 71

Louis XVI, 23; his coronation at Rheims, 42; his ministers, 56, 57, 58; his character, 59; his personal appearance, 59, 60; his habits, 61; attempts to go to St. Cloud, 104; his flight to Varennes, 107, 108, 109, 110, 111, 112, 113, 114, 115, 116, 117, 118, 119, 120, 121, 122, 123, 124, 125, 126; returns to Paris, 137; issues manifesto, 144;

INDEX

vetoes decree for enlistments, 197; before the attack upon the palace of the Tuileries, August the tenth, he takes refuge in the Assembly, 247; witnesses the vote on his deposition, 254; summoned to the bar of the Convention, 328; his trial, 334; condemned to death, 340; his execution, 348, 349

Louis XVIII writes epitaph of Abbé Edgeworth, 343

Lower classes, social and political conditions, 25

Lux, Adam, 377; his execution, 393

Lytton, Lord, on Diderot, 34

M

Macaulay, Lord, describes Danton, 429

Maillard, his character, 265; in charge of the September massacres, 265

Malesherbes, minister of Louis XVI, 59; defends the King, 330, 331; pleads for delay, 341; his appeal refused, 341

Mandat, General, commands the royal troops at the Tuileries on the Tenth of August, 239; summoned to appear before the Commune, 244; shot by Rossignol, 244

Manuel, 307

Marat, Jean Paul, 79; quarrels with professor Charles, 80; gains friendship of Benjamin Franklin, 80; practices medicine in London, 80; receives honorary degree of M. D. from university of St. Andrew, 80; publishes "Chains of Slavery," 80; appointed physician to bodyguards of Count d' Artois, 80; becomes journalist, 82; attacks in his newspaper Mirabeau, Necker, Bailly, La Fayette, and Dumouriez, 82; his ferocity, 84; his dwelling, 86; his library, 86; his attire, 87; interrupts functions at Roland's and Talma's, 88; his persecutions, 89; describes himself, 91; his teachings, 94; his obsequies, 95; attacks in his paper Necker, Bailly, and La Fayette, 97; prosecuted for libel, 97; fails to appear, 98; La Fayette attempts to serve warrant, 98; Marat hides, 98; Danton undertakes his defense, 99; clamors for death of Bailly and La Fayette, 132, 160, 241; his dislike of the Girondins, 258; requests Roland to lend him printing

INDEX

presses, 259; supports Robespierre, 313; votes for death of Louis, 337; pursues the Girondins, 363; urges the mob if hungry to help themselves, 363; brought before the Revolutionary Tribunal, 363; acquitted by the court, 363, 364; his triumph, 364; persistently assails the Girondins, 373; assassinated by Charlotte Corday, 375

Marbourg, Latour, appointed by the Assembly a commissioner to escort King to Paris, 137, 138

Marc Antony, 167

Marie Antoinette, 23, 71, 145, 173, 193, 205, 291; brought before Revolutionary Tribunal, 381; her appearance, 381; her trial, 381; found guilty, 381; her execution, 382; sketch of her life, 383

Marseillais, The, march to Paris, 220; enter the capital, 235, 236; brush with a battalion of the regiment known as the Filles St. Thomas, 236

Marseillaise Hymn, 221, 315

Masaubré, his massacre, 272

Mathey, Louis apologizes on the way to execution, 346

Maurepas, minister of Louis XVI, 56

Maximum, Law of the, 309, 380

Massena, 227

McCarthy, Justin, on Marat, 95

Mericourt, Théroigne de, arouses the mob on August the Tenth, 248, 292

Messalina, 381

Metastasio, his works in Danton's library, 49

Michelet on Danton, 20; on Voltaire and Rousseau, 32, 67

Mignet on Danton, 297, 409, 423, 437

Milton, 49

Mirabeau, his death gave new phase to the Revolution, 18, 23; attacked by Marat, 83; his death, 102; his opinion of La Fayette, 215; his oratory, 443

Miranda, his defeat, 356

Molleville, Bertrand de, 433, 434

Monge, 92

Montesquieu, Spirit of the Laws, 32, 80

Montgaillard, 290

Montmirail, 114

INDEX

Montmorin, 110, 433
Mont St. Michel, 30
Moore, Dr., on Marat, 85, 86
Moreau, 227
Morris, Gouverneur, 60
Mountain, The, 285, 286; rejoices over the conviction of the King, 342, 389
Mountaineers, 286, 309

N

Napoleon, 23, 29, 147, 202; his estimate of La Fayette, 215, 302, 389; on Collot d'Herbois, 401
Necker, 57; attacked by Marat, 83, 102;
Nile, The, 302

O

Oratorians, 38
Orleans, Duke d', votes for death of Louis, 337; his trial, 392; his execution, 393
Olynthiacs, 371

P

Paine, Thomas, announces advent of the Republic, 151
Paris, 54; drought, 54; suffering of the poor, 54; early riots, 55; rejoices over the adoption of the Constitution, 164; manners and customs, etc., during the Revolution, 277, 278
Peasant, The, his condition, 26
Penelope, 185
Pétion, friend of Danton, 50; commissioner to escort King to Paris, 137; his conduct on the "Day of the Black Breeches," 206; his death, 389
Petit Carrousel, 111
Philip, 371
Philippeaux, his trial, 410; his execution, 421
Philippics, 371
Pichegru, 227
Pitou, 281

INDEX

Pitt, averse to war, 318, 319, 321; offered pension to Abbé Edgeworth, 343
Pompadour, Madame de, 71
Pont-Sommeville, 116
Pope, his works in Danton's library, 49
Prieur of the Cote d'Or, member of the Committee of Public Safety, 379
Prieur of the Marne, member of the Committee of Public Safety, 379
Proclamation of the Duke of Brunswick, 227
Prudhomme, as to Danton's responsibility for the September massacres, 295

Q

Queen Coco, 185

R

Rambouillet, 57
Red Book, 73
Repaire, Bernard de, 64
Reveillon, 54; destruction of his factory, 55
Revolution, French, 448, 449, 450
Revolutions begin at the top, 74
Rheims, 41; coronation of Louis XVI in the cathedral of Notre Dame at, 42
Ricordain, M., marries Danton's mother, 36
Rivarol calls the guillotine La Mirabelle in ridicule of Mirabeau, 289
Robespierre, 23, 52, 90; assails La Fayette, 134, 174; on the Girondins, 310; assailed by the Girondins, 311; accused by Louvet, 312, 318; favors execution of King, 327, 365; conspires to overthrow Danton, 402
Robinet, Dr., on the charges of venality made against Danton, 436
Roederer advises King to withdraw from palace on the morning of the Tenth of August, 245
Rohan, Cardinal de, 28
Roland, M., inspector general of Lyons, 180; marries, 181; enters the ministry, 191; dismissed, 197; comments on events of September the second, 297; resigns from ministry, 355; his suicide, 391

INDEX

Roland, Madame, comments on Danton, 48, 50; on reign of Louis XVI, 56, 161, 179; her life and character, 180, 181; her marriage, 181; comes to Paris, 183; her affection for Buzot, 185, 219, 291; on Danton, 297; her opinion of Vergniaud, 337; inspires hatred for Danton among the Girondins, 360; her execution, 391; charges Danton with venality, 435
Roman literature, its influence on the French mind, 39
Romilly, 321
Roscommon, 167
Rosny sur Bois, 159
Rousseau, his "Contrat Social," 33
Roux, Jacques, brutally declines last request of Louis XVI, 345

S

Saint-Amaranthe, Madame, 294
Sainte-Marie, Miomandre de, 64
Sainte-Menehould, 117, 118, 119
Saint Huruge, 200
Samson the headsman, 347
Santerre, his part in the events of the Tenth of August, 245; accompanies Louis to the scaffold, 345; rebuked by Louis, 346
Sausse, Mayor of Varennes, 122
Scheldt, opening of the, 316
Scott, Sir Walter, on Marat, 85, 95; on Burke, 320
Seasons under the new calendar, 285
Séchelles, Hérault de, present at the taking of the Bastile, 75; member of the Committee of Public Safety, 379; his trial, 410; his execution, 421
Seine frozen over from Paris to Havre, 54
September massacres, 264, 265, 266, 267, 268, 276
Servan dismissed from the ministry, 197
Sicard, Abbé, 266
Shakespeare, his works found in Danton's library, 49
Sheridan, 321
Sillery, 386
Sombreuil, his massacre, 272

INDEX

Soulés arrested by Danton, 77
Soult, 227
Staël, Madame de, comments on Napoleon, 29; comments on new Assembly, 165, 171, 292, 329
States-General, 77
St. Cloud, 57, 103, 107
St. Fargeau Lepelletier, assassinated by Paris for having voted for death of the King, 341
St. Just, 52; on Louis XVI, 65; member of the Committee of Public Safety, 379, 412
St. Mart, Count, his massacre, 271
Stock Exchange closed by order of the Committee of Public Safety, 380
Sullivan, Mrs., 108
Swiss guards at the Tuileries on the Tenth of August, 250, 251

T

Tacitus, 39
Taille, 24
Talma, 88
Target refuses to act as counsel for Louis at his trial, 330
Tenth of August, 238, 239, 240
Thiébault, Baron, 62; his Memoirs, 127; his description of the Marseillais, 236, 248
Thierry, his massacre, 271
Thouret announces completion of the Constitution, 161
Tinville, Fouquier, conducts trial of the Dantonists, 410; his character, 411
Tourzel, Madame, governess of the King's children, 111, 137, 152
Treaty between Austria and Prussia, 189
Trianon, 57
Tricoteuses, Les, 293
Tronchet, one of the counsel for the King at his trial, 331
Turgot, minister of Louis XVI, 56

INDEX

V

Valazé commits suicide after trial, 387; his corpse beheaded, 389
Valmy, engagement at, 301; Prussians retreat from, 301
Varennes, 120, 125
Vaublanc, 189
Venuti, his works in Danton's library, 49
Verdun, Brunswick besieges, 259
Vergniaud, 39; receives King in the Assembly on the Tenth of August, 247; attacks Marat, 313, 328; votes for death of Louis, 336, 337; his trial, 386; his oratory, 443
"Vieux Cordelier," 405
Villette, Marquis de, 336
Voltaire, 32

W

Waterloo, 302
Westermann, 234, 241; leads the assault on the Tuileries, on the Tenth of August, 245; his arrest and trial, 410; his execution, 421
Women, their influence in the Revolution, 292

www.ingramcontent.com/pod-product-compliance
Lightning Source LLC
Chambersburg PA
CBHW032028150426
43194CB00006B/188